Mehinaku

The University of Chicago Press
Chicago and London

Thomas Gregor

Mehinaku
The Drama of
Daily Life in a Brazilian
Indian Village

The University of Chicago Press, Chicago 60637
The University of Chicago Press, Ltd., London

Published 1977
Phoenix edition 1980
Printed in the United States of America
86 85 84 83 82 81 80   98765432

Library of Congress Cataloging in Publication Data

Gregor, Thomas.
  Mehinaku: the drama of daily life in a
Brazilian Indian village.

  Bibliography: p.
  Includes index.
  1. Mehinaku Indians—Social life and customs.
I. Title.
F2520.1.M44G73   301.45′19′8081   76-54659
ISBN 0-226-30744-1
ISBN 0-226-30746-8 (paper)

THOMAS GREGOR is associate professor of
anthropology at Vanderbilt University.

For Arthur

Contents

The Script for Social Life

Figures

ix

Tables

xi

Acknowledgments

Mehinaku *is a dramaturgical description of social relationships among the Mehinaku Indians of the Upper Xingu River in Central Brazil. The theoretical perspective of the book derives, however loosely, from the work of Erving Goffman. His contributions will be frequently cited. Of equal importance, however, has been Robert F. Murphy, who guided my graduate education in anthropology at Columbia University. His original approach to ethnology has always informed my own work.*

My field work in Brazil was made possible by many individuals and institutions. Major financial backing came from the National Science Foundation, who generously funded most of my research. Additional support was provided by the National Institute of Mental Health of the U.S. Public Health Service, the Latin American Studies Program and the Center for International Studies at Cornell University, and Vanderbilt University's Research Council. Within Brazil my work was sponsored by the Museu Nacional in Rio de Janeiro, the Museu Paraense (Emilio Goeldi) in Belém, and the Brazilian Indian Foundation (Fundação Nacional do Índio).

Roberto Cardoso de Oliveira and Rocque de Barrios Laraia of the Universidade de

Brasília, Roberto da Matta of the Museu
Nacional, and George Zarur, Mario Pompeu
and Ney Lande of the Brazilian Indian Foundation greatly assisted me in finding my way
through the bureaucratic tangle that seems
to separate all anthropologists from their
work; they also helped prepare me for life
in an Indian tribe. Paulo Rôlo and Miller
Hudson of the American Embassy were especially helpful in obtaining the documents
needed for my research and in assisting me
in many other ways.

Upon my arrival in the Upper Xingu at
Posto Leonardo Villas Boas of the Brazilian
Indian Agency, I was privileged to meet the
administrators of the Post, Claudio and
Orlando Villas Boas. These courageous
brothers virtually single-handedly established
the Xingu National Park (Parque Nacional
do Xingu) and protected its frontiers from
diamond miners, otter hunters, land speculators and other threats to the Indians' land.
Throughout my stay in the area, Claudio and
Orlando Villas Boas generously gave me the
hospitality of the Indian Post, the help of
their staff, and their encouragement for my
work.

I am also indebted to Bernd Lambert and
David J. Thomas for their critical sugges-

tions, and to Jane Hinshaw, Christine Tichy, and Katrina Vanderlip for the artwork.

Finally, I mention the assistance of my family. My father, Arthur S. Gregor, is the ace of editors and critics to whom this book is dedicated. My wife Elinor accompanied me on the first trip to the Mehinaku, is gifted in languages, and has a natural talent for field work. She maintained my good disposition as well as her own through occasionally trying conditions and times when the whole project seemed hopelessly mired. This book is therefore in large measure a joint endeavor.

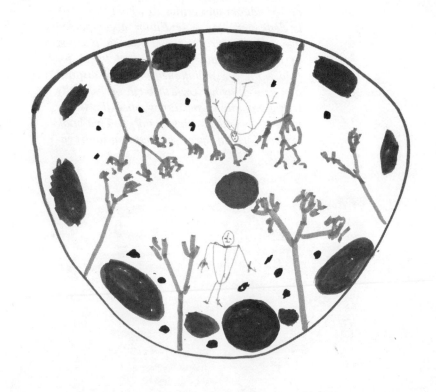

1

My intention in this book is to describe the way of life of the Mehinaku, a little-known tribe of Indians living in the Mato Grosso of Brazil, by viewing them as performers of social roles.

The first chapter in this introduction examines the validity of the view of life as theater and considers the usefulness and dangers of the dramaturgical metaphor. The second chapter rings up the curtain on the Mehinaku and describes my research among them.

Part 2, "The Setting for the Drama," takes the first steps in a dramaturgical analysis of the Mehinaku society by detailing the physical characteristics of the village-theater—how the physical environment, construction materials, house plans, and village layout affect the setting for social relationships. In this section of the book, I examine the village as a theater in the round, one with splendid acoustics and unobstructed seating. The dramaturgical problems and opportunities for the actors are very different from those in our own society with its emphasis on privacy and other barriers to communication. In the Mehinaku village everyday conduct—whether gossip, formal speeches, extramarital affairs or children's play—is shaped by a spatial setting that compels each individual to become a master of stagecraft and the arts of information control.

In part 3, "The Staging of Social Relationships," the focus is on the actors and their participation in social engagements. To take part in everyday relationships, the villagers must be adept at make-up, decorating themselves with the body paints and the ornaments that comprise almost all of their wardrobe. Once adorned and ready to engage their fellows, they will follow guidelines that make for orderly interaction, such as the rules for greetings and farewells that circumscribe each social encounter. In the course of interaction all villagers will attempt to project an image of themselves that identifies them as good citizens: cooperative, generous, and sociable. Finally, the continuing drama of Mehinaku social life will be shaped not only by such encounters but also by patterns for avoiding interaction. Villagers who are ambivalent about social situations need defined ways of disengaging themselves from their fellows. The last chapters of part 3 describe the institutions that separate the Mehinaku and allow them to remain aloof from social encounters.

Part 4, "The Script for Social Life," examines the roles that the actors perform. Kinsmen and in-laws, tribesmen and foreigners and shamans and clients are the major parts depicted in this final section. As we relate the formal demands of these roles to the theatrical problems involved in staging them, we will also discover that the Mehinaku are not mere puppets manipulated by the demands of their culture but are at times the conscious authors of their own lines.

In each of the major sections of the book, I have attempted to present Mehinaku culture from a definite theoretical point of view, the analysis of the setting, staging, and script of Mehinaku social life. Without losing sight of this purpose, I occasionally take leave of the dramaturgical metaphor to provide necessary background material and a reasonably full description of a little-known people.

Throughout this work I offer translations of Mehinaku words, phrases, and extended passages of speech. Unless otherwise indicated, the translations are free ones, designed to convey the sense of the material rather than its literal meaning. In all direct quotations of speech I have worked from tape recordings or notes taken at or near the time that the passage was spoken. The names of the Mehinaku to whom I attribute these quotes—or who are otherwise mentioned in the book—are usually pseudonyms.

Mehinaku words used in this report are written in a simplified phonetic script adapted for the economics of publication. Consonants have values that approximate English, though the "j" is always soft, as in the "dg" in "judge."

Vowels are represented below.

IPA symbol	Symbol used in text	Approximate English equivalent
ɑ	a	a as in father
ε	e	e as in bet
i	i	i as in machine
ɪ	ɪ	i as in bit
ɨ	ɨ	no English equivalent; a high, central, unrounded vowel
o	o	o as in note
ʊ	ʊ	o as in wolf
u	u	u as in rule

Several Mehinaku dipthongs have rough English equivalents, including *ai* as in *ai*sle, *au* as in h*ou*se, and *ei* as in v*ei*l. A tilde over the vowel indicates a nasalization of the vowel or of the entire dipthong. Unless otherwise indicated, the accent is on the next to last syllable.

1 The Dramaturgical Metaphor

The role concept in social science is based on the perception that life is like theater. Going back at least as far as the Greeks, the idea was given memorable form by Shakespeare:

All the world's a stage,
And all the men and women merely players:
They have their exits and their entrances
And one man in his time plays many parts.

"Shakespeare's metaphor," writes sociologist Ralf Dahrendorf, "has become the central principle of the science of society" (1968: 30). Certainly the culture of every society provides the script that defines the rights and obligations of "all the men and women," while the "many parts" of each actor permit him to adapt his conduct to the rest of the cast, thereby giving him a position in the larger drama. The impact of this position on modern social anthropology may be seen by glancing at the table of contents of a typical ethnography. The standard chapters on kinship, marriage, and the division of labor are usually descriptions of the roles of blood relatives, husbands and wives, the old and young, and men and women: the role concept is the organizational framework for presenting anthropological data.

The definitions of social roles that influence anthropologists (notably those of Linton 1936, Nadel 1957, and Banton 1965) are normative. A role is a part of culture that prescribes rules for getting along with others, a set of obligations and privileges or rights and duties acknowledged by the members of a community. The task of the ethnographer is to describe the terms of the contracts and the extent to which they are honored. This contractual, "who owes what to whom" approach to relationships, however, is only the beginning of good ethnographic description. The American social scientist Erving Goffman has systematically expanded the traditional role concept, following the work of G. H. Mead (1934), Kenneth Burke (1945), and the "symbolic interactionist" school of social psychology. In *The Presentation of Self in Everyday Life* (1959), Goffman sees roles not simply as rights and obligations that bind actors, but as prescriptions for actual performances; they are the script and stage directions as well as the contract for social life.

Like their theatrical counterparts, the real-life performers act out their parts in a spatial setting whose physical characteristics mold the course of the action. Preparing their performance backstage with the help of teammates and presenting it to an audience whose response further affects their conduct, they do not simply repeat their lines, but dramatize or overcommunicate them so that the audience will be sure to know who they are in the drama. Moreover, the rhythm of exits and entrances, the costumes and props, and the demeanor of the actors are all as much a part of the drama as are the lines of the script.

To illustrate how the dramaturgically oriented observer looks beyond the traditional perspective to include considerations of setting and staging, let us glance briefly at an encounter between a doctor and his patient. Consider, for example, that a patient has only a very partial view of a medical office. Backstage areas in which the physician informally interacts with his colleagues and subordinates must be kept off bounds to patients so that the doctor will not display an image antithetical to the one he projects up front.

To be perceived as a good doctor, a physician must provide more than competent treatment. He must stage the part, overcommunicating his status by means of a reassuring bedside manner, an impressive array of diplomas and gadgets, and the presence of immaculately clad attendants. Make-up, costuming, scenery, and the timely appearance of bit players all contribute to the necessary stagecraft.

A dramaturgical perspective also looks at the implications of the script for the performance of the roles. How rigidly are those roles defined? Do they leave room for improvisation when lines are ambiguous or contradictory? A physician is both a disinterested professional and bill-collecting entrepreneur. Are there spatial and dramatic devices that can reconcile such contradictory roles?

The strength of the dramaturgical metaphor is that it can open avenues for research not contemplated by the traditional approaches of social anthropology. There is a danger, however, in the temptation to forget that life-as-theater is an analogy, not an homology. So apt is the terminology of theater for describing the human condition that the analyst can easily be taken in by it, especially if his subjects are from a culture whose dramatic conventions are different from his own. Stating the limits of the metaphor will tell us where the analogy breaks down and give us an idea of what we can reasonably hope to accomplish by applying it to a society like the Mehinaku. Let us begin by examining how relationships are defined, both in real life and on the stage.

Unless viewed through the organizing lens of culture, reality is chaotic and random. A thousand roses are different from each other in a thousand ways, yet we share a cognitive slot that enables us to classify them all as "roses." In a parallel fashion, our culture provides us with a way of organizing social experience. A group of people sitting around a table may be a deliberating jury, a seminar in progress, or a meeting of the President's cabinet. Which it happens to be depends not only on the facts of the matter, but also on the point of view of the participants. It might be difficult for them to transform their meeting from one kind into another, although we have all taken part in seminars that gradually became social gatherings, and we have read transcripts of presidential meetings that degenerated into criminal conspiracies. The definition of the social situation thus depends on the consensus, usually unspoken, of those who participate in it.

Human beings interpret or "define" each other's actions instead of merely reacting to each other's actions. Their "response" is not made directly to the actions of one another but instead is based on the meaning they attach to such actions. Thus, human interaction is mediated by the use of symbols, by interpretation, or by ascertaining the meaning of one another's action. This mediation is equivalent to inserting a process of interpretation between stimulus and response. (Blumer 1967: 139).

By defining the situation we are able to occupy a multitude of realities, each socially built from a consensus that is ratified in speech and demeanor and reinforced by the characteristics of the setting. Taken together, these conventions communicate the definition of the situation and the roles of the actors.

If reality is a social rather than absolute construct, we may approach the contrast of theater and everyday life from the perspective of how both define the situation and establish a sense of reality or authenticity in the beholder.

The theater establishes a reality of its own, though this reality is based on conscious artifice. The play takes place in a room minus a wall and ceiling and is performed by characters who position themselves at odd angles and speak with unnatural clarity. What is remarkable about such dramatic conventions is that they work. Audiences seem to have an extraordinary capacity to "engross themselves in a transcription that departs radically and substantially from an imaginable original" (Goffman 1974: 145).

An experiment by Harold Garfinkel suggests that in real life as well as in theater we strain to accept and participate in the definition of a social situation, no matter how outlandish that situation may seem. In the experiment, students described a serious personal problem to an unseen counselor and then asked a question that could be answered yes or no. Though the responses the counselors gave were chosen randomly and were often inane or contradictory, the students strove mightily to make sense from nonsense: "The answers given . . . had a lot of meaning to me. I mean it was perhaps what I would have expected from someone who really understood the situation" (1967: 85).

Garfinkel's experiment illustrates that, like an audience in a theater, we are willing to invest the most flimsily constructed social situations with authenticity and imagined meaning. In everyday life, as in theater, we are called upon to narrow or "bracket" our attention to the situation being presented and to ignore whatever does not further the supposed reality. Hence we are unperturbed by settings that are not grossly discrepant, willing to forget in the course of a medical examination, for example, that we abhor our physician's taste in furniture or politics. We are always under strong constraint to accept the consensual definition of the situation even when we are not happy about it. Like actors in the theater, we act not as we are or as we would wish to be, but as if we accepted the role assigned to us. None of this is to say, however, that there are not fundamental differences between life and the stage. One of those differences—the alienation from role of the theatrical performer, as contrasted with the engagement and sincerity of the ordinary individual—has been particularly vexing for the dramaturgically oriented observer, and we must now deal with it directly.

Only occasionally does a participant in ordinary interaction feel compelled to assume the perspective of the stage actor. Goffman's sociology introduces us to pool-hall hustlers who cannot show their true skill, furniture salesmen who bilk their customers with extravagant claims about shoddy merchandise, and girls who feel obliged to play dumb on dates to convince their boyfriends of their femininity. Sheldon Messinger and his colleagues (1962) report that a few persons, including the very famous, are seldom off stage. As Sammy Davis puts it, "As soon as I go out the front door of my house in the morning, I'm on, Daddy, I'm on."

Theatrical self-awareness may from time to time fall to the lot of the not so famous as well. The essence of the dramatic perspective, as Elizabeth Burns (1972: 34) has pointed out, is composition: the conscious planning, staging, and arrangement of social events. Each time we relocate furniture, decorate our houses, buy clothes, or apply cosmetics we are moving stage properties or putting on costumes. Architects, clothes designers, and other engineers of appearances and impressions are, in this sense, fellow troupers of actors, directors, and playwrights.

Dramatic self-consciousness may also crop up in ordinary interaction. When we assume a new status (the first day at a new job), when our roles clash or are undefined, or when we engage in moments of self-reflection or fantasy, we take a perspective similar to the stage performer.

Nevertheless, we may reasonably conclude that a real-life actor is not chronically self-aware of the performance of his roles. People are not *dramatis personae* whose actions are make-believe and inconsequential, but participants in a real experiential world where the stakes are high and the play is for keeps. Erving Goffman, writing on the dangers of overextending the dramaturgical metaphor, warns that "Whether you organize a theater or an aircraft factory, you need to find places for cars to park and coats to be checked, and these had better be real places, which incidentally, had better carry real insurance against theft" (1974: 1).

The language and concepts of the stage are useful, however, because the ordinary individual, like the actor, is in the business of impression management. No matter that he may only occasionally be aware of the stagecraft that goes into performance, it is nonetheless there. By encouraging his audience to focus their attention on some aspects of his performance, while diverting their attention from others, the individual, like the actor, seeks to establish a social situation that his audience will accept as authentic. Operating within a physical setting that shapes his conduct, he conveys his message by means of speech, dress, demeanor, props, and other messages that sustain the definition of the situation. His performance is normally spontaneous only because the roles he acts are habitual ones, ratified by many previous encounters and part and parcel of familiar settings. The very fact that his conduct is not deliberately staged, however, means that he makes a poor informant. The theatrical metaphor provides the observer with a set of concepts ideally suited for isolating those communicative acts that establish and define relationships. The success of dramaturgical analysis must not therefore be measured by whether ordinary persons consciously put on a performance. The approach is not a theory of psychology intended to expose the subjects' view of the world, but a device for appreciating those subtle and often neglected aspects of interaction that define the social situation and confirm the identity of those engaged within it.

In practice the dramaturgical approach turns our gaze in new directions, focusing our attention on the expressive aspects of social relationships as well as on their economic or political significance. It leads us to describe subtleties of demeanor and dress normally neglected in standard anthropological accounts. It requires that we give special attention to community design, not just as a bow to general ethnography but as a setting for social relationships. It demands that we be sensitive to the shape and boundaries of communication networks, looking not only at the content of messages but also at the rules of privacy and discretion that control their movement. The dramaturgical approach provides us with a new perspective in social anthropology, an approach that has only just begun to be applied to the ethnography of tribal societies.

The Tribes of the Upper Xingu and the Mehinaku Indians

*Tell the Americans about us. Tell them we are
not wild Indians who club people. Tell them we
are beautiful.*

Shumõi, to the anthropologist

The Mehinaku Indians of Central Brazil are
one of a number of very similar tribes that
live along the upper reaches of the Xingu
River, a major tributary of the Amazon.
Waterfalls there block navigation and until
recently have kept out all but the most in-
trepid explorers and hunters. Even today the
nearest permanent Brazilian town, Xavan-
tina, is nearly 175 miles to the southeast.
Because of this isolation, a small enclave
of tropical forest Indian culture has managed to persist almost completely intact.

The distribution of this culture is limited
by definite barriers. About twelve degrees
south three rivers meet to form the Xingu.
Together with their numerous tributaries
they drain a well-watered, low-lying basin
of some twenty-five thousand square miles.
Living only in the northern corner of this
vast territory, the Xingu Indians exploit several ecological zones. The first is a narrow
line of trees along the rivers, trees whose
roots are adapted to the periodic flooding.
Further inland from the rivers are flood

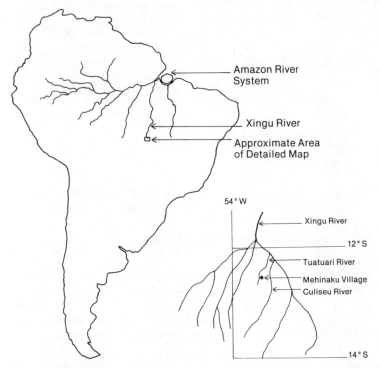

Fig. 1. Map of Brazil showing the location of the Mehinaku village

plains, a few feet to a few miles in width. Past the flood plains are miles of forest along whose margin, still never far from the rivers, the Xingu Indians have established their villages and cut their manioc gardens. Beyond the forest are other flood plains, other lines of flood-resistant trees, and yet other rivers, as figure 2 illustrates.

The appearance of the Xingu basin changes radically through the year. In August, at the height of the dry season, the rivers are very low and the banks in many places are fifteen feet high. The flood plain is baked flinty dry, so that walking barefoot is painful for someone used to wearing shoes. The wet season begins with the late September rains and by the end of December the rivers have overflowed their banks. From the air, the Xingu basin appears half swamp, half forest. As the flood plains become inundated, it is difficult to locate the main channels of the rivers. Walking from village to village is extremely unpleasant as the forest is crisscrossed by streams and brooks. Yet one can still travel by canoe over the flooded plain and sometimes right through the forest.

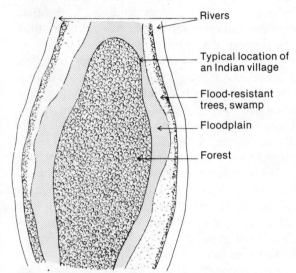

Rivers

Typical location of an Indian village

Flood-resistant trees, swamp

Floodplain

Forest

Fig. 2. Xingu topography

The Xingu seasonal round is fixed to the cycle of rain and drought. When the rains end in May, the gardens are cut and left to dry. During the remaining months of drought, fishing is extremely productive, since the fish are distributed very densely in the shallow rivers and streams. In August and September large numbers of fish are trapped by the receding waters and easily caught by the Indians who drug them with a vegetal poison (*timbó, Paullinia pinnata*).

In September, just before the dry season ends, the gardens are set afire. In October, the rains having begun, the gardens are planted with manioc and maize. These are the months of plenty in the Xingu. Fish are abundant and wild fruits ripen, particularly the *pequi (Caryocar butyrosum)* and *mangaba (Harcornia speciosa)*; all help to enrich the usually monotonous diet.

In January the rainy season is at its height. The fish catch is poor and the fruits are exhausted. The corn, however, is ready for harvesting. Stored away in the rafters of the houses, it will provide the villagers with a small amount of food throughout the year. Though the manioc that was planted in the October gardens will not be ready for another six months, the Indians can harvest the crop from other gardens producing at this time. In addition, they can call upon reserves of manioc flour stored away during the previous dry season.

Most observers of Xingu economic life have been impressed by its seeming abundance (Oberg 1953: 1). It is apparently so rich that the Indians can afford to taboo many of the game animals, including deer, wild pig, tapir, and *paca*. The only animals they will eat are fish, birds, and monkeys. Even fish, the principal source of protein in the Xingu diet, is not as avidly sought as it might be. I have discovered from keeping records of fishing expeditions throughout the year that the Mehinaku do most of their fishing when the chances of bringing home a big catch are brightest. During the rainy season when fishing, while less rewarding, is still well worth the effort, everyone tends to stay home and grumble about the lack of fish.

The Xingu basin is in fact an area of relative abundance, but we must recognize that both the environment and a simple technology impose significant limitations on the production of food. The Xingu farmers are slash and burn agriculturalists whose fields produce well for three or four years but then are either choked with weeds or must be abandoned for fresh soil. Eventually, the forest land available nearby is exhausted and the villagers pack up and move elsewhere.

In an important article Robert Carneiro (1956) offers an elegant mathematical model of this system, showing that one of the Upper Xingu tribes, the Kuikuru, could grow more food and have a much larger population than they do and still live at the same location. I believe that given favorable circumstances the Mehinaku could also have a permanent village, but thus far their experience has been quite different.

Much of the area around the Mehinaku (and many of the other Xingu tribes) is not suitable for agriculture. During the wet season it is inundated by the rivers, and some of it is permanently swampy. Nearly half of the land around the Mehinaku village cannot be cultivated. Further, the Mehinaku are unable to use almost a third of the remaining dry forest surrounding their community because of large colonies of destructive ants (the leaf cutter, *sauva, A. Cephalotes*). Several gardens planted on the periphery of the infested area were completely stripped by long columns of these ravenous insects. Perhaps for this reason the village is named "Leaf Cutter Ant Place" (*Jalapapu*), though the villagers say they have encountered the same problem in other locations.

The lack of suitable land is not all that limits the productivity of Xingu agriculture. In addition to the ant invasions, blights, plagues of grasshoppers, or the depredations of wild pigs can wipe out a crop. These disasters do not occur often, but combined with the limitations inherent in slash and burn agriculture, they have kept past Mehinaku villages small and essentially nonpermanent.

Research among the Tribes of the Upper Xingu

At present there are ten single-village tribes living in the Upper Xingu, representing four different language groups: the Carib-speaking tribes, including the Kuikuru, Kalapalo, Matipú, and Nahukua (who live with the Matipú); the Tupi-speaking Kamaiurá and Auití; the Arawakan tribes, including the Mehinaku, Waura, and Yawalapití; and the Trumaí speakers represented only by the Trumaí.

Despite the linguistic differences, the culture and social structure of all these groups is very similar. Their small villages have a number of haystack-shaped houses surrounding a central plaza; in the middle of each plaza is a men's house. All the groups have similar bilateral kinship, classificatory cross-cousin marriages, and affinal avoidances. Many of their myths and ornamental patterns are identical. All the tribes are firmly linked by intermarriage, ceremonial events surrounding the initiation and death of the chiefs, and barter of specialized trade goods. There is a rich intertribal culture involving ceremonial ambassadors, protocol, and a common song language used at rituals.

Xingu Indians have been the subject of studies by a number of anthropologists, including those of Von den Steinen (1885, 1940, 1942), the first European to leave us a written record of his entry in the area, Meyer (1897), Schmidt (1942), and Petrullo (1932). More recently Oberg (1953), Murphy and Quain (1955), Carneiro (1957), Basso (1973), and Zarur (1975) have described the Auití, Kamaiurá, Trumaí, Kuikuru, and the Kalapalo, while Harald Schultz (1965) and the Villas Boas' (1970) have provided us with a description of Xingu culture and a collection of myths from the Waura and the other tribes of the region. In addition to these books and monographs we have a large number of articles on many aspects of Xingu life, including Galvão's (1953) important comparative article identifying the Upper Xingu culture area, da Lima's (1955) examination of population distribution, Carneiro's studies of Kuikuru ecology (1956, 1961) and sexual behavior (1958), Dole's publications on Xingu culture history (1962) and Kuikuru social organization (1958, 1964, 1966), and Freikel and Simões' (1965) and Junqueira's (1973) research on culture change and the influence of Brazilian civilization.

Despite this work, there is still a great deal to be learned about Xingu Indians. Much of the older material listed above consists of anecdotal information, vocabulary lists, and descriptions of material culture. A few of my own articles (1970, 1973, 1974) have helped to acquaint readers with the Mehinaku, but otherwise they remain all but unknown in the enthnographic literature. Although this study is intended as an exploration of a theoretical approach rather than as a general or comparative ethnography, I will nonetheless try to provide sufficient detail both for the specialist and for the social scientist with a broad range of interests.

History, Culture Change, and the Community Today

The Mehinaku are not historians or record keepers. Within four or five generations the past begins to fade into mythic time. According to the older men, the Mehinaku have lived between the Tuatuari and the Culiseu rivers since the time of creation.

They have frequently moved their village sites for reasons of subsistence or warfare, but they never have lived outside the region they now inhabit. The first records we have of Mehinaku contact with the outside world are from Von den Steinen's visit to the tribe in 1887. Today the Mehinaku recall their first contact with a white man (though perhaps not with Von den Steinen) as follows:

Everyone was very frightened and fled to the forest leaving only the best bowmen in the village. When the *Kajaiba* (white man) came he gave everyone lots of gifts, and the bowmen called the people back from the woods. The young girls covered their bodies with ashes so they would be unattractive and not carried off by the *Kajaiba*. The people were given knives but didn't understand them, and they cut their arms and legs just trying to see what these new things were for.

At that time the Mehinaku were living in two villages. Subsequently severe epidemics of measles and flu so reduced their numbers that the villagers were forced to consolidate. Today's Mehinaku are the descendants of the inhabitants of the former villages, plus a few refugees from now defunct Arawakan tribes called the Yanapuhu and Kutanapu. Today only a few of the villagers keep track of whose ancestors came from which village, though one of the oldest Mehinaku does remember a childhood among the Yanapuhu. Actually the social and linguistic differences among all three groups are very slight.

Contact with Brazilian Civilization

The most visible results for the Indians of contact with outsiders have been the introduction of steel implements and depopulation. Steel tools have changed Xingu life in subtle ways, but without basically altering it. Carneiro (1957: 111) has pointed out that the men now have far more leisure time than in the past because steel axes can clear gardens much more rapidly than stone ones. The women's work of processing manioc, however, has not become more efficient with steel tools and still requires many hours of daily drudgery.

Depopulation has also changed Xingu culture. It has been estimated that when Von den Steinen visited the area at the turn of the century there were about three thousand Indians living in the Upper Xingu basin (Levi-Strauss 1948: 326). At present, there are approximately seven hundred. As population levels have fallen, villages have been consolidated and then moved closer together so that relations within and between communities persist much as they did in previous times (see Agostinho da Silva 1972). Depopulation, however, has played a significant role in the deculturation of the tribes.

Many lines of evidence suggest that the Xinguanos once had a more complex culture than they do today. The Mehinaku themselves say they are "bare shadows" of what they were in the past. Although we may discount some of their rueful comments about the good old days, we can also point to a number of important ceremonies and customs that are now defunct or passing away.

In former times, there was an elaborate intertribal ritual and game played with a latex ball made from the *mangaba* tree, but it has now lapsed. Chiefs used to be tattooed as part of their initiation to the post, but no more. Young men invariably had their ears pierced at an important intertribal ritual, but today an increasing number of fathers are piercing their children's ears at birth and bypassing the ceremony. The list could be extended, but it is enough to suggest that some elements of Xingu culture are disappearing.

The main point of contact with the outside world is the Indian Post, which today is only a three-hour walk or canoe ride from the Mehinaku village. The Post was established in 1946 by the Villas Boas brothers. As the directors of the Xingu National Park, they have protected the Indians' land from encroachment by backwoodsmen and speculators and at the same time have respected native culture and tribal autonomy. Today, thanks to Orlando and Claudio Villas Boas, Indian lands and culture remain essentially intact. Even while protecting the Indians, however, the Post itself has inevitably become an instrument of culture change.

In addition to providing steel tools and medical care, the Post has opened up a new social world for the Xingu Indians. Traditionally, contact between the tribes was limited to intertribal ceremonies and visits to kinsmen. Today the Post serves as an interactional free zone where the Xinguanos can make casual contacts with their neighbors in a setting that does not circumscribe their relationships. Intertribal news, gossip, and communication are facilitated as never before.

Fig. 3. The fascination of the outside world. The Mehinaku have an intense curiosity about the lands and peoples beyond the frontiers of their reservation. A visitor to the tribe is especially welcome if he brings a magazine or illustrated book. Here the villagers examine a book of photographs and puzzle over what they may mean.

Some of the effects of contact with the Brazilians are difficult to document, such as the psychological changes that have followed exposure to civilization. To appreciate the significance of this impact, the reader must realize that before the arrival of the Brazilians the Xinguanos lived in an isolated, self-contained world. They knew that Indians lived beyond the Xingu basin

but contemptuously dismissed them as wild, subhuman creatures. When the Brazilians came, however, they were very different from other outsiders. They came in peace, offering gifts and
a glimpse of a technologically incredible culture. In recent years,
some of the Xinguanos have actually been sent to São Paulo
and Rio de Janeiro for medical care. All of them have seen
photographs of these cities. Finding their way into the Mehinaku
village are trade goods such as transistor radios which constantly
play songs by Roberto Carlos (the current pop favorite in Brazil) and absolutely incomprehensible news broadcasts. The flow
of visitors to the Indian Post represents the most intellectually
sophisticated levels of Brazilian and international society, including biologists, medical researchers, anthropologists, and
government officials. Akanai, a young Mehinaku man, was be-
friended at the Post recently by several foreign ambassadors.

It is not easy to measure the effect of such contact on the
Xinguanos. At the simplest level new versions of myths have
been developed to explain the presence of the white man and
his superior technology (see chapter 18). Theories of cosmology
are in flux as the Xinguanos grapple with the fact that Americans have visited the moon, which has always been conceived
as a spirit, and sent up earth satellites that are visible on many
clear evenings. None of the tentative efforts at explanation,
however, seem satisfactory to the Mehinaku themselves. As is
true of the other Xingu tribes (see Junqueira 1973) they have
yet to evolve a world view to account for the white man and his
incredible technological feats.

Exposure to Western culture has created an anomaly. On the
level of subsistence, social organization, and culture, the Mehinaku live very much as they have in the past. On a psychological
level, however, there is growing insecurity about themselves
and the world around them. They have heard that the Brazilians
are building highways nearby that will slice through their preserve, and they fear the demise of their own culture. I asked
one young man what he wanted to be when he grew up: "A
great fisherman and wrestling champion like your father? A chief
who speaks well to the people? A shaman like your uncle?" He
thought for a while and then said, "I would like to be all of

these, but I will be none of them. The Brazilians are going to come and everything is going to end."

The Community Today and the Daily Round

The Mehinaku village is located on a swampy affluent of the Tuatuari River, about three hours by canoe during the wet season from Posto Leonardo Villas Boas. In June 1976 there were seventy-seven Indians living in the village's six houses. Of these, seventy-three were Mehinaku, and the rest were Indians who had married into the tribe. Although the Mehinaku have been hit by epidemics of measles and influenza, their population has entered an upturn, and they have unquestionably begun to recover. During the last ten years, only three adults have died natural deaths, and two others have been killed as witches. In the same period, twenty children were born. As these data suggest, the population is young; more than half of the tribe is less than eighteen years of age.

Aside from foreboding about the future, the morale of the village is good. Group activities such as ceremonies and work projects take place virtually every day. Houses are maintained in good repair, the central plaza is kept clear of weeds, and the main paths to the river and fishing areas are regularly cleared and widened.

The daily routine begins early each morning, about an hour before sunrise. The Mehinaku begin to wake and huddle shivering close to their fires. Then as the sky lightens, they go down to the river to bathe. Upon their return, small groups of women go out to the fields to work before the heat of the day. By midmorning they return carrying large baskets of manioc on their heads. They will spend part of the day processing the manioc to make flour, stopping only to take care of their children and prepare their meals. They follow the same schedule almost every day, especially in the dry season when they labor assiduously in order to accumulate a large surplus of flour.

The men's daily routine is much more varied than the women's. Freed from much of the work on their gardens by the efficiency of steel tools, they will spend most of their day hunt-

ing monkeys and birds, fishing, wandering through the forest in
search of root medicines, playing flutes in the men's house,
working on their bows, arrows, and canoes, and loafing in their
hammocks. Insofar as they have a schedule, they frequently
pair off to go on short morning fishing trips, returning by noon
for a meal of fish and manioc cakes.

On fine days midafternoon is wrestling time. The men gather
in front of the men's house in the center of the village and rub
themselves with charcoal and a red paint made from *urucu*, the
fruit of the annatto tree (*Bixa orellana*). Then, while the women
look on from inside the doors of the houses, challenges are
exchanged and the matches begin. Strict rules govern the sport
and, though the wrestling is aggressive and spirited, there are
few injuries other than cuts and scratches.

In late afternoon husband and wife pair off to tend their
gardens, gather firewood for the night, and have sexual relations.
They may also go down to the river to get water and bathe.
Frequently, the Mehinaku will have a second meal about this
time, especially if a kinsman has brought in fish.

In early evening, just after the sun has set, the older men sit
smoking around a small fire in the center of the plaza and discuss noncontroversial topics such as the quality of their tobacco
and the activities of the white man at the Post. The young men
stroll about the plaza arm in arm, making ribald jokes. Occasionally one of them will shout in a falsetto whoop, "Grab clay!"
meaning, "Go have sexual intercourse!" This is, in fact, the time
for liaisons between young men and their girl friends.

By eight o'clock the smokers return to their houses to chat
with their wives and families. Sometimes one of the men will
tell a story, or two of the older women will join in singing songs
about forest animals. Gradually the conversation dies out and
the Mehinaku sleep.

Some Notes on Field Methods and the
Limitations of This Study

Anthropology is unusual among the sciences in that its results
are difficult to verify. Reproducing a study of a preliterate tribe
requires energy and personal dedication that is more likely to

be directed toward research among a people who are still un-known. Since the Mehinaku are unlikely to receive systematic attention from another anthropologist in the near future, the reader is entitled to information about the field situation and how the data was collected.

My wife and I arrived in the Xingu National Park in Central Brazil in February 1967 and, except for a break of four weeks in July, lived there until December of the same year. All but a few days of this time was spent in the Mehinaku village, where we lived in the house of the chief and his family. I subsequently returned alone for seven months in 1971 and 1972, for an additional month in December–January 1974, and for a final trip to check my data in May and June of 1976. In all, I have resided in the village for eighteen months.

The Mehinaku have been good hosts. They, like the other tribes in the area, are hospitable and routinely provide visitors with water, firewood, manioc cakes, and a place to tie up their hammocks. Although this formal hospitality wears thin during an extended visit, the Mehinaku were glad to have us among them, for reasons both of sentiment and self-interest. We not only brought into the village hundreds of dollars of useful gifts, which were periodically distributed by the chief in a grand pot-latch, but we were able to provide limited medical assistance

Fig. 4. (See following page). A Mehinaku view of everyday village life. When Amairi painted this view of the community he occasionally stopped to chuckle over his characterization of a particular villager's appearance or comportment. There, in front of the men's house, for example, is Itsa, the most inept wrestler in the village—flat on his back. Just to the left we find Ahira, by far the tribe's best dresser, being carefully decorated with the red *urucu* pigment that is so essential to proper adornment. Watching the passing scene and waiting to wrestle, several men and boys look on from the bench in front of the men's house—but notice how stooped over Epyu is on the left. Near the extended family houses the women have finished their work, such as carrying water from the river, and sit outside to groom each other for lice, talk over the day's events, and watch the wrestling. Ever playful, a group of Amairi's younger kinsmen convert an unfinished house into a jungle-gym, while Kama, that club-wielding spoil-sport and village grouch, chases them away. Amairi's watercolor not only captures the hum and bustle of late afternoon activities, but does so with a deliberate sense of humor.

and occasionally act as a liaison between the Mehinaku and the reservation authorities.

During the initial phases of field work, my wife and I tried to learn about the Mehinaku by acting like them. Each morning at dawn my wife went to the gardens with the women. She would return several hours later carrying a heavy basket of manioc tubers on her head and spend the rest of the morning in the drudgery of processing them. Meanwhile, I would be off with the men, fishing, hunting monkey, or wandering through the forest in search of root medicines.

This approach was good public relations. It made sense to the Mehinaku that I should spend my time hunting and fishing with the men while my wife processed manioc with the women. Unfortunately, we were not learning very much. Each day I would come back from treks through the forest numb with fatigue, ill with hunger, and covered with ticks and biting insects. My own work was difficult to pursue, for fishing and hunting are serious business and there is no time to pester men at work with irrelevant questions about their mother's brothers. Meanwhile, my wife was faring little better with the women.

The time came when we stopped pretending we were becoming Mehinaku and instead began to collect information systematically. We started with census material: genealogies, residence patterns, hammock arrangements, maps of the community, and demographic data on births, deaths, and marriages. As we gained the Mehinaku's confidence, we were able to collect more delicate information, including patterns of friendship, accusations of witchcraft, and inventories of personal possessions.

Although we were ultimately able to collect survey material of this nature from the entire tribe, we found that only a few of the villagers were reliable and articulate informants. Several of these had some knowledge of Portuguese. Gradually, with their help and with the assistance of some linguistic studies of a similar Arawakan language (Richards 1973, Jackson 1971), we began to learn Mehinaku. Mastering the language has been a slow process, but at last I can effectively conduct both informant interviews and ordinary conversations in Mehinaku.

The topics the villagers like to discuss best are witchcraft and sex. It was relatively easy to get information on these subjects but considerably harder to obtain data on less colorful material like kinship. Genealogies do not much interest the Mehinaku and the obligations and privileges of kinsmen are regarded as being so obvious and inevitable that they are often difficult to elicit. Nevertheless, several of the villagers showed considerable sensitivity to their own culture and insight into the motives of their fellows. Much of the information we have on Mehinaku society derives from their observations.

We were especially successful in obtaining information from informants who were in seclusion. A villager in seclusion could speak to us without fear of being overheard. Cut off from ordinary social contact and with time heavy on his hands, he would generally welcome our presence and devote long hours to answering our questions.

Our ability to penetrate seclusion barriers and the relative ease with which we obtained data on such delicate topics as witchcraft and sex underscore a critical feature of our position in the community: we were outside Mehinaku society. Few of the expectations that guided Mehinaku conduct applied to us, for we took no active part in the political or religious life of the community. It is true that ties of affection, respect, and fictive kinship grew up between us and many of the villagers, but there always remained an apartness, an estrangement. Since we were outsiders who one day would leave the community, we were entrusted with information that was necessarily concealed from other Mehinaku. Quarrels and other shameful activities occurred in our presence without the participants fearing our censure. We were what Simmel (1950) has called *strangers*—persons in many ways outside the system, yet in a remarkably good position to observe it.

The Limitations of this Study

Anthropologists are in a position to be their own best critics. Unlike the reader, they were there and know what loose ends remain. They cannot lightly dismiss the uncertainties that arise in their minds as they contemplate the conclusions drawn from their field work. Those who study the Mehinaku, for example, must content themselves with a narrow range of informants. They are a small society, and though their population is normal for a tropical forest farming village, they have not provided as many informants as ideally I would have wished for. In part to make up for their small numbers, I have attempted to select informants who were both sensitive and conscientious and to cross check their accounts as often as possible.

A second caveat relates to the peculiar flexibility of Mehinaku culture. Social relationships, as we shall see, can at times be altered by individual negotiations, or role bargaining, while the religious system is freely open to experimentation and innovation. Contradictory myths explaining the origins of hallowed institutions circulate through the community and may even be recounted by the same person. In short, the Mehinaku are not easy to pin down and apparently thrive on a measure of ambiguity and playfulness in their relationships and institutions. Although I have tried to define the limits of flexibility in Mehinaku society and to keep the reader informed about my own uncertainties, it is well to post a reminder here that their culture is not all of a piece and often eludes facile generalization.

(On following page). Constellations: the jaguar, the tapir and the anteater. "In the night sky," say the villagers, "there is a jaguar and his prey, the tapir and the anteater." But try as I might, I could never make the stars resemble Kuyaparei's watercolor. At last I came to understand that the Mehinaku view of the sky is different from ours. Rather than connecting the stars with imaginary lines to form shapes, they see shapes in the spaces between the stars, for from Antares to beyond Altair a band of blackness blots out the tropical night sky. Outlined by the glow of the Milky Way, these black spaces form some of the villagers' major constellations.

In the illustration Kuyaparei's many-toed tapir (a relative of the horse having three- or four-part hoofs) appears on the left, while the jaguar looms over the anteater on the right.

The Setting for the Drama

2

The Mehinaku village and its environs are a theater for the enactment of everyday social relationships. Like all theaters, the community has spatial and physical properties that both reflect and affect the course of the performance. Thus the layout of the village and the architecture of the houses are simultaneously a spatial representation of Mehinaku social organization and a traffic pattern for the flow of information and interaction.

The chapters that follow examine the dramaturgical characteristics of the Mehinaku village-theater. We have noted that it is a theater with splendid acoustics and few obstructed seats. In fact, the visibility and audibility of social action and the efficiency of the institutions that broadcast information create special problems. Managing everyday social activities, from children's games to extramarital sex, requires the villagers to become masters of information control and stagecraft. I begin the discussion of the village as a theater with an introduction to Mehinaku space, settings, and designs.

Now it is a real *pot.*

Kuyaparei, after painting the bottom of a tub for processing manioc flour

Recently anthropologists have been increasingly attentive to the way a people design their communities and use the space around them. Edward Hall (1968) and others regard the use of space in interaction as part of a largely unconscious gestural system that communicates a person's background and view of a social situation. The spatial design of communities and houses is interpreted as both an expression of important cultural values and a force that helps create those values (Rapaport 1969, Sommer 1969). The study of space should be as revealing among primitive societies as it is in more advanced cultures.

There are tribes in which the design of a village or house clearly becomes a kind of social and cosmological map depicting the relations among men and between men and spirits. In South America, for example, the Bororo Indians live in a great wheel-shaped village whose northern and southern halves spatially locate their moiety system and model their concept of an afterlife (Levi-Strauss 1963). Even when village layout is less complex, space may still reflect social organization and religious life. Recent research among the Yekuana (Arvelo-Jimenez 1971) and the Desana (Reichel-Dolmatoff 1970), for example, has shown a rather precise relationship between house form, tribal social life, and cosmology.

Although the Mehinaku do not spatially represent their culture in their architecture or village design as elegantly or directly as do these other South American tribes, there is still a great deal to be learned from their use of space and form. In this chapter I shall present a basic ethnography of the Mehinaku's use of space to see how their social world shapes and is shaped by the layout of their village and the architecture of their homes.

The Mehinaku Interest in Space and Form

The significance of space as well as the shape and location of things has special interest to the Mehinaku. Most obviously, this interest is evident in their language, where nouns reflect the form of objects and some verbs must be modified to indicate the distance between speaker and event. Nouns, for example, are often tagged with "shape markers." Hollow things—such as baskets, and even the entire village—carry a morpheme (*yaku*) that labels them as different from things that are solid. Linear things—vines, necklaces, cotton thread, benches, and cord—carry a morpheme (*pi*) that denotes their linearity. There are ways to express these spatial distinctions in all languages, but among the Mehinaku they are not optional. They are required by the grammar. There is simply no way to talk about vines (*impi*) without classifying them with other linear things that take the same shape marker (*pi*).

The vocabulary of space is regularly used as a metaphor to communicate other concepts. Time, for example, is often expressed spatially. The Mehinaku tell time at night by stating the location of the moon or the constellations. During the day the villagers inquire about the hour by asking "where is the sun?" (*atenãisepyai kama*), the answer usually indicating the height of the sun from the nearest horizon: "the sun has just come out," "the sun is straight up," "the sun has begun to fall," "the sun is over the trees," or "the sun is entering his house." Intervals longer than hours and days are also spatially expressed. The passage of a month is described both by the position of the moon at dusk and its changing size. Future and past events are located in time by reference both to the position of important constellations at dawn and the cycle of wet and dry seasons, which are seen as having "edges" and "midpoints."

It is not surprising that notions of time among the Mehinaku incorporate notions of space, given the celestial progressions that are used as a natural measuring stick. It might have been possible, however, to represent the movements of sun, the moon, and the stars more abstractly, using a nonspatial vocabulary. There are a few such time words, including those for a day ("a hammock or sleep"), early morning ("gardening time"), late afternoon ("wrestling time"), the names of seasons, and others. Nevertheless, many of the discriminations of time actually heard in ordinary speech have an explicitly spatial component.

Metaphors of physical distance are employed in still another important way that happens to parallel our own usage. Ties of kinship that are uncertain or genealogically untraceable or that relate individuals who have little to do with each other are spoken of as being "far" or "distant." These are opposed to relationships that are "close" and thus more important.

The significance of space and form to the Mehinaku appears not only in their language but also in their everyday activities and conduct. Take the matter of art and design. The Mehinaku have a limited inventory of designs (*yana*) that they repeat on a wide range of media, including the human body, baskets, benches, and house poles. One of the most popular designs, derived from the shape of the *kulapei* fish (Portuguese, *pacu*), is used to decorate the backs of ceramic pots, the masks of spirits, and even women's legs. Designs such as *kulapei yana* are carefully applied and subject to criticism if they are done poorly. No mere embellishment or ornamentation, they become an intrinsic part of the object that is decorated. The designs applied to a man's hair, torso, back, and legs, for example, identify his social position and express his personal moods. In a sense, the design makes him a social person.

Decorating an object can be just as important. Painting an ordinary piece of wood can turn it into something potentially dangerous. Although a mask may safely be carved anywhere in the village, it may only be painted in the men's house, which is considered a temple of the spirits. Once a mask has been painted, it can attract a spirit because it now resembles him. Even a mundane object like a pot is regarded as incomplete without its appropriate design. Nor does it matter that the decoration is often painted at the bottom of the pot, where it will be invisible while in use and rapidly charred by the smoldering fires.

In this case no magic attaches to the design; everyone knows that an undecorated pot will cook as well as any other. It is merely that a pot lacking a traditional design is undesirable. No one wants it, as we would not want a car bereft of the usual paint job. Everyday objects among the Mehinaku, of whatever description, are not really complete or desirable unless they are properly decorated.

The appearance and reappearance of the same designs on different materials serving different functions help to give Mehinaku life visual harmony. Their artifacts, their religion, and their system of interaction are woven together by the same stylistic code. I will have more to say about this code in discussing adornment, but for the moment it is enough to note that Mehinaku language and art reflect an interest in the use of space and design. Let us see how this same interest is expressed in the Mehinaku's view of the cosmos, the natural world, their village, and their homes.

Orientation in Space: The Cosmos

The cosmos, from the villagers' point of view, is an intimate place. The moon and the sun are regarded as being somewhere between a few hundred yards away from the village (the distance to the river) and a few miles (the distance to the Indian Post). The Mehinaku have two theories to explain the movement of these celestial bodies. Although contradictory, these theories are in no sense rivals, since the villagers take no great stock in speculative cosmological debates. The more popular theory is terracentric. The sun, a spirit, travels once a day across the sky and along the great roads leading east and west of the village. During the dry season when the women are busy out-doors washing the poisonous juices from manioc pulp, the fumes give the sun a headache and he speeds across the sky to get home quickly. During the rainy season, when days are longer, the sun is not disturbed by the women who usually work indoors at that time of year.

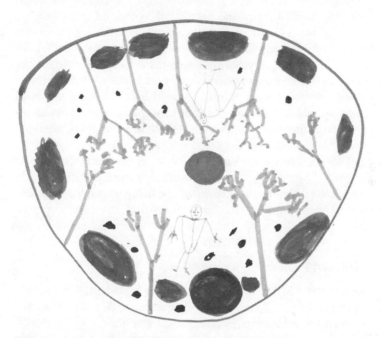

Fig. 5. A heliocentric cosmology. In Kuyaparei's watercolor, the universe is a great hollow ball lined with houses, villages, and trees. The sun is suspended in the center of the ball and the stars (represented by black spots) are scattered among the trees.

The second theory is heliocentric. The universe is a great hollow ball lined with villages, paths, rivers, and forests. The stars are set in among the trees claim the proponents of this position, but at such great distances that no one has ever come upon them. The sun and the moon float in the center of the ball, which gradually revolves around them. Day and night occur because the sun and moon shine in one direction only. No matter on which side of the ball you happen to be, you still believe that you are looking up at the sun and the moon. On the side of the ball opposite your own are the "villages in the sky." A path from the burial ground in front of the village men's house leads up to these villages, the first of which is the "village of prurient death," the second the "village of murdered witches," and the third the paradisical "village of one's father." The first two villages provide the proper afterlife for those who have died revolting deaths. Whatever the circumstances of his death, however, everyone must pass these villages before he can reach the home of his father. As he goes by he is offered a bowl of pus extracted from corpses. Should he drink from the bowl thinking that it holds manioc porridge, he is condemned to remain with the witches and the corpses throughout eternity.

In this second cosmology a network of villages, paths, rivers, and forests carpets the entire universe. Even places as fantastic as settlements of witches and prurient corpses are designed in the same fashion as the villages of the living. For the Mehinaku, the universe spatially replicates the world they know at first hand.

Maps and Plans of the Known World

How do the Mehinaku label and give shape to the lands that surround them? To answer such questions, I must direct the reader to a series of maps and plans drawn for me by the Mehinaku. These maps and how they were obtained tell something about the Mehinaku sense of space and geography.

The villagers are given to the use of visual aids in teaching. Whenever I failed to follow an explanation of a ritual or custom, I was urged to wait until I could see it; then I would understand. The Mehinaku teach physical skills, such as making arrows or weaving baskets, by having the pupil look on as the work is performed. There are, to be sure, occasional verbal explanations, but these are a relatively small part of the teaching process.

My own teachers would often try to help me understand what they were talking about by drawing maps or pictures, a *patalapiri*. A *patalapiri* is a representation of something that is real, but the representation also has a reality of its own. The picture of a spirit can be dangerous because, like all pictures, it includes at least some of the features that define real, substantial things, such as form or shape. A map or a plan is therefore a handy way of getting at the categories by which the Mehinaku divide up space in the world around them.

The maps and plans that follow were made at my initiative, but they are still the Mehinaku's own creations. I tried to make my requests as broad as possible, asking for a picture of "the village," a "house," or even "everything around." The Mehinaku chose the features to be included and their arrangement.

The first map (figure 6) is only partly reproduced and depicts the natural and social world around the Mehinaku village (Jalapapu). It was painstakingly sketched with reasonable accuracy by a young man in response to my request for a map of everywhere he had been. This map is therefore in no sense a representation of all the Mehinaku's knowledge of their immediate environment, but it probably includes most of the major features.

Perhaps the first thing to notice about this map is that it covers very little area. The world as seen at firsthand by this young man is a lozenge-shaped strip of territory between three rivers, the Tuatuari, the Culene, and the Culiseu. A few of the villagers have traveled beyond this region to the Indian Posts at Bacairi and Diauarum and to the small ranch of Tanguru on the Culuene, but their knowledge of the vast area beyond the boundaries of the map is still minimal. Much of the west side of the Tuatuari, for example, is mysterious and impenetrable. One myth of this far bank tells of a monster spirit that eats men. After it ate a child who ventured into the territory, an expedition of men slaughtered the demon with specially barbed arrows. Nevertheless the Mehinaku avoid much of the "far side" of the river because "there are no men there."

The region to the east is somewhat better known, at least up to the villages of the Carib-speaking Kuikuru, Kalapalo, and Matipú. Far to the east, it is vaguely understood, lie the impor-

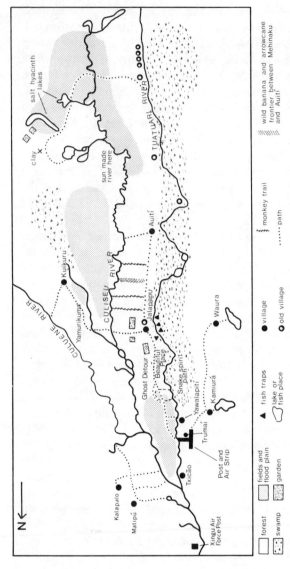

Fig. 6. Akanai's map of the known world. Akanai's map (redrawn by Jane Hinshaw) shows all the places he has visited. The area he knows best extends in a narrow band between the Tuatuari and Culiseu rivers from the Indian Post in the north, past the present Mehinaku village of Jalapapu, to the old Mehinaku villages in the extreme south, a distance of about twenty miles. Included in this territory are a variety of natural and social landmarks and old villages. Considering that the map was drawn freehand and from memory, it is reasonably accurate but it is not to scale and makes many obvious errors. The Waura village, for example, is shown located on a lake when it is actually on the Tamitataló River—a fact known to Akanai but not included on his map since he had always traveled to the Waura on foot. The map should be regarded as a social document rather than a representation of physical environment.

tant Kajaiba (Brazilian) "villages" of São Paulo, Brasília, and Rio de Janeiro. The northern and southern portions of Mehinaku territory are better known than the east and the west because the affluents of the Xingu make them easily accessible. Most of these regions are dangerous to explore, however, since warlike "wild Indians" (*wajaiyu*) live there (notably the Suyá and Txicão). Even if the Mehinaku were not frightened of these "wild" Indians, it is very doubtful that they would undertake to explore unknown territories. All of their traditional and even mythical villages have been located in a narrow fifteen-mile band between the Culiseu. and Tuatuari Rivers. They have no serious interest in any regions other than their own or peoples other than their immediate neighbors.

The territory covered by the map is well known to the Mehinaku. Even eight-year-old children are familiar with the bewildering maze of streams and eddies through the swamp to the west and north of the village. I have been along these waterways dozens of times, and no matter how I concentrate I often find that I am at a loss not only about the path back to the village but even whether the village is upstream or down. The forests are equally disorienting, since they permit no long view of the surroundings and the trails are often so overgrown they appear nonexistent. The Mehinaku, however, never lose their way.

Some of the cues that guide them through the woods and along the waterways are the natural features shown on the map, including lakes, rivers, swamps, narrow estuaries, fields, and forests. The names given to these features are occasionally arbitrary, but usually they reflect the Mehinaku's economic interest or esthetic observations. Hence, a lake near the traditional Mehinaku village is labeled "salt hyacinth lake" (*lapataku*) since it is there that the Mehinaku burn the leaves of this plant to make native salt (KCl). "Palmwood place" (*itsautaku*) is the general name for the swampy, permanently-flooded regions where the Mehinaku obtain palm fiber for their cords, bow strings, and hammocks. Many places on the map are identified as the haunts of desirable animals, such as fish and monkeys. Special attention is given to small lakes, which can be dammed and poisoned for fish, and narrow estuaries, which can be barricaded with lines of fish traps. Such areas are often simply called "fish place," having no other special name.

Some regions on the map are named after their prominent species or natural features. The Indian Post is located on what was formerly "the place of the otter," a high bank down which the otters used to slide. A small resting place along the trail linking the post to the Mehinaku village is called "beautiful place" because of its flowering shade trees, dry banks, and lovely setting.

A somewhat different set of landmarks (not labeled on the map) are the boundaries between natural regions, which are identified as "the beginning" (*tepu*), or end of the forest, the field, or the swamp. The location so mentioned is a precise one, because it is understood that the spot in question is an intersection of a path or waterway with the edge of the natural feature. Areas within the forest, field, or swamp are located by their proximity to "the middle," that is, the middle with respect to a known journey through a portion of the area. The flow of the rivers provides one more referent, so that a villager in search of honey, for example, may be given exact directions: "The Auití trail to the edge of the banana grove; the monkey hunting trail to the tree across the path; the upstream fork of the trail to the honey."

The Natural World and Social Landmarks

Although the Mehinaku differentiate many natural features of the land around them, they also make use of an impressive set of social landmarks. Some of them are mythological. Near the junction of the rivers that form the Xingu is *Morena*, the spot at which the sun fashioned the very first human beings out of wood. Further south, not far from the present village of the Auití Indians, is the very place where the sun broke a great ceramic pot of water, which then flowed out to form the Culiseu River. Other areas are associated with spirits or recent historical events. Children, for example, are cautioned about bathing alone in the river close to the village because they might be eaten by the monster spirit of the leafcutter ant, Jalapakuma, that haunts the stream. Other areas to be avoided by the circumspect are the habitation of the "shadows" (*ĩyeweku*) of executed witches. The map shows one such spot where the Mehinaku cut an extensive detour ("ghost detour") through the forest to avoid the path where a witch was slain in 1971.

Another set of social landmarks are abandoned villages and trails. The southern portion of our map shows no less than eight abandoned village sites which are still recognized by the Mehinaku. Some are merely of historical interest, while others are regularly visited. Many of the Mehinaku families return each fall to Ulawapuhu, their traditional village, where they harvest the fruit from their *pequi* orchards. Although the village itself was abandoned over ten years ago, one man still retains a garden on the site today. Other deserted villages, such as Wajatapuhu, an old Auití village, are used to break the long trip to the Mehinaku salt-making area. Even after a village has been abandoned for many years, it is likely to remain a resting spot, since travelers can only stop where there is solid ground. In the great swamp (*itsautaku*) that borders the western part of the Mehinaku territory, the ports of abandoned villages are often the only such places. These traditional homes thereby live on in Mehinaku memory where they might otherwise have been forgotten.

The trails that crisscross the Mehinaku territory vary in quality. Some, like the well-used path to the Post and the trail to the fishing port on the Culiseu, are well-maintained. During the dry season even I have no trouble finding my way along these trails. During the wet season, however, most of them will be under several feet of water. The monkey-hunting trails and those that connect the Mehinaku settlement with the villages to the north are so choked with foliage that I simply cannot make them out at all. The trail to the Auití tribe, for example, is virtually impassable in places and, although it is possible to reach the Auití village in one day, the traveler usually arrives totally exhausted, lacerated with thorns, and blanketed with blood-sucking ticks. Nevertheless the trail exists, and the Mehinaku know how to follow it.

The Question of Tribal Territory

The Xingu tribes are so dispersed, and the land and fishing places so abundant, that there is simply no serious question of whose land is whose. It is true that a Mehinaku when questioned on this subject will tap the ground and talk possessively of "Mehinaku earth," but he can seldom state with any precision where this earth begins and ends. Some say that the boundary between the Mehinaku and the Auití tribe is roughly as far as a man can go before he has to turn back in order to arrive at home before nightfall. Others point to a grove of wild banana trees as a boundary line, but their verdict is not unanimous. For most of the Mehinaku, the concept of a tribal territory as a single bounded region simply is not important.

The Mehinaku become more precise about tribal ownership, however, when resources in limited supply are in question. For example, in the no-man's land between Mehinaku and Auití territory, there is a small grove of trees producing a hard wood especially suitable for arrow shafts. Everyone agrees that this grove belongs to the Auití. It is true that the Mehinaku exploit the grove, but they do so only clandestinely. Surprised on the spot by an Auití, they will feel obliged to offer him a small gift. Other examples of important tribally owned territory shown on the map include the old villages and their surrounding orchards of *pequi* trees, deposits of clay, plantings of water lily for the manufacture of salt, and the small streams especially suitable for dams and fish traps. The Mehinaku mental map of tribal territory is less an enclosed block of land than a mosaic of owned resource areas.

The Land Around the Village

Were we to fly over the Mehinaku community at an altitude of about one thousand feet, we would notice that the village is circled by a wide network of trails, gardens, and ports. This area, which includes the land within a two-mile radius of the village, supplies the Mehinaku with virtually everything they need for subsistence.

The principal natural areas about the settlement that are recognized by the Mehinaku are the scrub woods (*walapá*) surrounding the village, the worn-out former gardens now covered with grass and useless bushes (*chumpei*), and the true forest (*yakakwĩ*). The longer a village occupies a site, the wider the ring of barren ground and the more distant the forest. When the Mehinaku initially moved to Jalapapu in the early 1960s, they had forest and gardens at their doorstep, but as the years have gone by they have gradually exhausted the nearby land. This worn-out land, however, is not totally unproductive. The abandoned gardens continue to yield *pequi* in fairly good quantity and the scrub woods are scattered with wild and semiwild fruit trees and bushes that include *mangaba*. Nevertheless, as time goes by the villagers will have to go further and further into the forest to locate food or firewood in abundance.

The most reliable source of food is the gardens, which are reached along well-worn and cleared paths called "garden paths" (*uleikyanapu*). The location of each villager's garden follows an interesting pattern, since not all garden sites are equally desirable. A woman unlucky enough to work a distant garden may have to walk thirty minutes with a forty-pound basket of manioc tubers balanced on her head before she reaches home. Nevertheless the Mehinaku work ethic calls for cutting gardens a considerable distance from the village, partly because the soil there is somewhat richer. This work ethic is very much a male-oriented system; it is relatively little extra work for a man to cut a distant garden, but it is a great deal of work for his wife to transport the harvest home. The location of the gardens suggests that factors of age, residence, and kinship help to determine the choice of a plot. Older men have gardens closer to the village than younger men because the burden of carrying the baskets of manioc is great for elderly wives. Villagers who live on the northern side of the settlement tend to cut their gardens on that side of the village circle. Close kinsmen and residence mates like to have adjacent gardens, since they are less likely to pilfer each other's ripening fruits and corn and related women can conveniently work together. Once kinsmen have established adjacent gardens, the system perpetuates itself, since a new plot is cleared at the beginning of each dry season simply by extending the boundaries of the old plot further into the forest. An aerial view of the gardens would show a great quadrilateral of cleared space that gradually enlarges each year as the margin of the forest is pushed back.

The most important sources of food close to the village are the fishing areas and ports along the Culiseu River. The port on the Tuatuari River is used as a place to moor canoes, as a water hole, and as a swimming area. The Mehinaku bathe several times a day, and the social encounters along the path leading to the port provide frequent opportunities for interaction between individuals who live in different residences. Occasionally small boys catch fish in the area of the port. The men, however, do most of their fishing in the network of streams and pools that border the western side of the village. During the wet season when it is difficult to catch fish either with bow and arrow or hook and line, these small streams are dammed and lined with fish traps. Older men who enjoy exclusive rights to a number of dammable streams share their catch with residence mates and kinsmen.

The Village

Let us resume our imaginary flight over the village and examine the layout of the community (see figure 7). The village is in a cleared area roughly a half mile from the border of the Tuatuari swamp, and appears to be bisected by a great diameter crossing from east to west. This line is the major road that leads to the bathing area and the port along the Culiseu. No matter of chance, the precise orientation of the village to the road is firmly dictated by tradition. Since the time of creation, say the Mehinaku, their villages have been located and designed according to the following pattern. Each village lies between the same two rivers, the Tuatuari to the west and the Culiseu to the east. When the sun rises, its path across the sky should parallel the great trail from the canoe port on the Culiseu to the center of the village. The men's house must bisect the path of the sun, and the bench in front of the men's house must offer an unobstructed view east along the road through the forest. As the sun passes over the men's house, it should follow the great trail west to the bathing area where it finally sets. The ground plan of the village reflects the architecture of the sky.

Fig. 7. Aerial view of the Mehinaku village, May 1976. The great trail from the Culiseu to the Tuatuari (off-camera, upper left) forms the east-west axis of the community. Scrub trees and bushes surround the village, a field of thatch grass (upper right) marking the location of gardens abandoned in the early 1960s. Some of the wider paths are visible in the photograph, as are the numerous manioc-drying racks shading manioc processing equipment, and the two small out-buildings used for craft-work or occasional seclusion retreats.

Since 1972 (see figure 8), all but two of the houses have been rebuilt to replace delapidated homes, a process that continues today, as may be seen from the frame of a new house that is under construction. A surprising addition to the village circle is a new house (an earthen *mehehe*, built in the style of a backwoods Brazilian home), which was constructed to accommodate a family that had broken away from its kinsmen. The harpy eagle cage shown in figure 8 is gone, its resident having died after giving up many of its feathers for the villagers' headdresses.

As the plane flies over the village, the men and boys, in typical Mehinaku fashion, rush to the center of the plaza to have a better look and to discuss the meaning of the event.

The houses in the village are placed in a roughly drawn great circle which surrounds the men's house. As figure 8 shows, the houses fronting the men's house are set back further than those located behind it. Within each house, the house owner (the person who initiated its construction) sleeps closer to the path of the sun than any of the other residents.

The precise location of the houses in relation to each other depends on a number of factors, the most important of which are the location of residences in the previous village circle and their relation to the houses across the way from them. The rule is that houses in new villages should be "opposite" (*ipalupei*) the same buildings they faced in the old community, although there is no other special social relationship based on being opposite another house. Despite these rules the actual ground plan of each new community is reshuffled somewhat because the builder of the village (*putakanaku wekehe*) usually chooses to locate his new house in an area that faces the men's house, the most desired spot on the village circle.

Status is closely associated with house location, because the houses of chiefs are built only by a major roadway on one of the cardinal points of the compass. Further, the chiefs responsible for the maintenance of the major roads must live alongside the trail for which they have primary responsibility. Commoners build their homes between the chiefly residences.

Let us now look at the village from ground level and examine the community from the viewpoint of the Mehinaku themselves. When the Mehinaku are asked to draw a picture of their village they often produce circular designs like those in figure 9. The area within the circle is the "inside of the village" while the area beyond is referred to simply as "the outside" (*paiyumá*). The word for village, *putakanaku*, incorporates both a morpheme meaning village (*putaka*), and a shapemarker (*naku*) applied to hollow containers, such as villages, houses, and baskets. One idea behind drawing the village as a circle, then, is that a village is a closed region that contains things, for example, a plaza (*wenekutaku*). Although the last word refers to the entire central portion of the village, it is usually applied in a more limited sense to a public region in front of the men's house where the villagers make decisions, speeches, conduct rituals, and socialize. A literal translation of the word for plaza is "frequented place." Other subareas of the plaza are also linguistically discriminated. These include the "wrestling ground" (*kapĩtaku*) for wrestling matches in the afternoon and the "shamans' circle" (*yetemá*) where the shamans of the tribe meet each evening to smoke and discuss the day's events. Finally, the village burial ground is also located on the plaza and is connected, the Mehinaku say, by means of an invisible road to the village in the sky.

Another area of the plaza identified by the Mehinaku are the regions just outside the doorways of the houses. Each house, ideally, is oriented so that it faces the center of the village, directly across from its "opposite" on the other side of the plaza. The front door of the house faces the plaza, and the area just in front (and just inside) is called the "mouth of the plaza." Here the women sit in the late afternoon and early evening to gossip, groom each other's hair for lice, and watch the men wrestle.

The area just in front (and just inside) of the back door is called the "mouth of the trash yard." Used not only as a place to dispose of garbage, the trash yard behind each house is an area for a wide range of everyday activities, including processing manioc during the dry season, cleaning fish, weaving baskets, carving wood, socializing with members of one's own residence, and (for males) clandestinely soliciting sexual relations with women from other houses.

Fig. 8. (See following page). The Mehinaku village, January 1972. In this scale drawing we see that the village conforms closely to the ideal Mehinaku model of how a community should be laid out: the path of the sun as it follows the eastern trail from the Culiseu River passes between two chiefly residences, bisects the men's house and finally follows the western trail to set over the Tuatuari River. Some features of the community, however, are not part of the formal groundplan. One house, for example, is built according to backwoods Brazilian rather than Mehinaku tradition, and is located in the trash yard of a more standard house (lower right). All the buildings are interconnected by a maze of narrow pathways (not all shown) that circle the village and facilitate both open and surreptitious movement through the community.

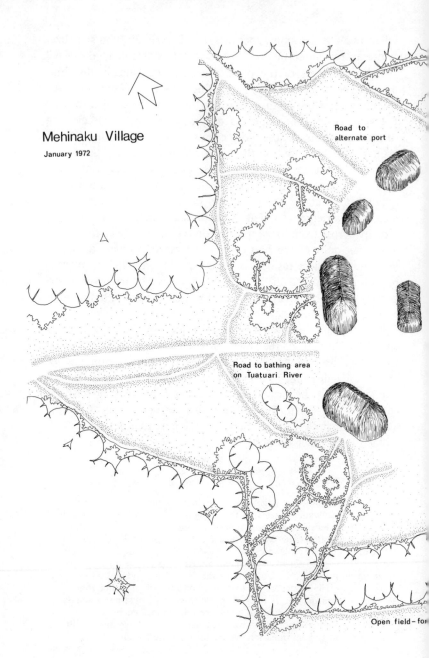

Mehinaku Village

January 1972

Road to
alternate port

Road to bathing area
on Tuatuari River

Open field - for

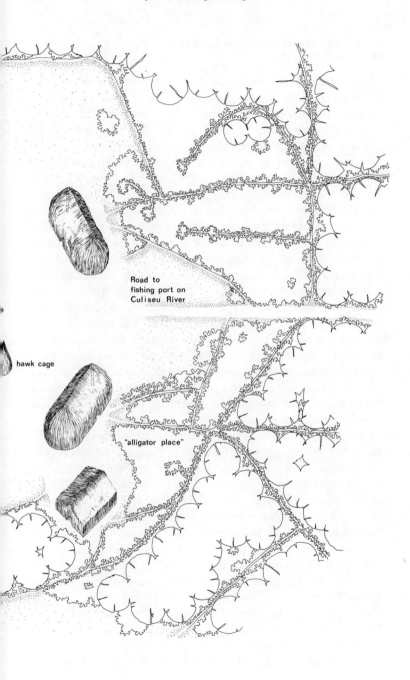

Road to
fishing port on
Culiseu River

hawk cage

"alligator place"

Village and House Design as Models
of Community Life

The ground plans the Mehinaku have drawn for me suggest that the villagers have several cognitive maps of their community, no one of which can really stand as *the* model of the village. One important model is based on the contrast between the realms of nature and men. Here the Mehinaku see village as the innermost of a set of concentric circles, labeled forest, scrub trees and played out gardens, and village (see figure 9). Since the root of the word for village (*putaka*) also means "men," (Xinguanos) this interpretation is especially persuasive.

A second Mehinaku view of their village categorizes social relationships and symbols within the community rather than contrasting the village with the world of nature. In this view, the villagers draw two concentric circles which bound the plaza and the trash yard (figure 9b). This contrast is significant, for the plaza is associated with the public sectors of Mehinaku life —the activities of men and sacred rituals. The trash yards, on the other hand, are the settings for domestic life, women's activities, and ordinary conduct. This distinction provides the basis for a metaphor that assigns status in the community: a man who is of little account, who takes no part of the public life of the tribe, and who seldom participates in ritual is appropriately called a "trash yard man" (*miyeipyenuwanti*).

A final map of the village presents it diametrically divided along the axis of the sun (figure 9c). Here the village is split into two halves by the path of the sun and the roads to the Culiseu port and the bathing area on the Tuatuari. This model of the village is unlike the first two plans, where concentric circles divide and separate relationships and symbols that are fundamentally unlike and often unequal. Played-out scrub forest is separated from the world of men in figure 9a, just as women, trash yard men, secular events, and private activities are contrasted with men, good citizens, rituals, and public conduct in figure 9b. In the final diametric model, however, the village is divided into regions whose associations are equal. Notice, for example, that the men's house is cut along its perpendicular axis in this ground plan so that neither of the resulting halves of the village differs from the other. Relationships across the diameter formed by the road are also equal, since chiefs live on each side. Similarly, the houses "opposite" each other across the diameter have symmetrical relationships, since chief alone can confront chief and commoner alone can confront commoner.

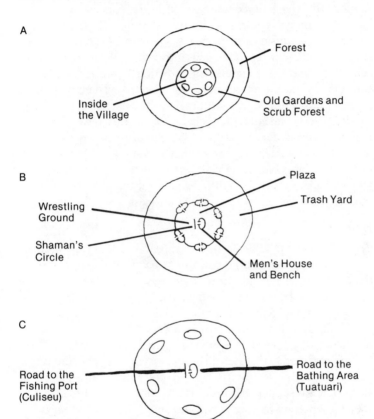

A

Forest

Inside the Village

Old Gardens and Scrub Forest

B

Plaza

Trash Yard

Wrestling Ground

Shaman's Circle

Men's House and Bench

C

Road to the Fishing Port (Culiseu)

Road to the Bathing Area (Tuatuari)

Fig. 9. Three views of the Mehinaku village. When the Mehinaku sketch maps of their village, they draw a series of concentric circles as in *A*, reflecting the contrast between the community and the natural regions around it. The artist may also be concerned with the opposition of the interior regions of the village and the surrounding trash yards, as in *B* or the contrast between opposed household groups as in the diametric sketch, *C*.

Since the Mehinaku maps from which this illustration is redrawn are idealizations of the actual community, the details of the figures (the number of houses, etc.) do not correspond to the scale drawing of the community, shown in figure 8.

Which of the three models is the correct one? Clearly no single one of them. Each is a partial expression of spatial, social, and symbolic relationships among the Mehinaku, and none in any sense contradicts another. The choice of model depends on whether the village is being regarded in the context of ecology, inequality, or symmetry of social relationships. These comments would be unnecessary except that Levi-Strauss (1963) has published an analysis of both concentric and diametric dualism suggesting that the apparent contradiction between them is resolvable by means of a more complicated geometric model incorporating both concentric and diametric elements. Maybury-Lewis (1960), however, has characterized this resolution as a kind of optical illusion with little real meaning. I essentially agree with this criticism, for symbol systems are often ambiguous and inconsistent. Resolving "contradictions" with geometric models unlikely to have the slightest meaning to the natives themselves is bound to be a sterile business.

Houses

The Mehinaku take pride in the appearance and size of their houses. A house is the biggest thing that men make, the standard against which all other enormous things are measured. One of the villagers, for example, was prepared to believe that the moon was big, even gigantic, but he was incredulous when I told him that it was bigger than a house.

There are at present eight houses in the Mehinaku village. Six are residences, three of them built according to a traditional pattern whereby heavy crisscrossed poles are planted deep in the ground to support the roof. These houses are called *pãi*, and they are opposed to houses built by any other kind of construction, which are known as *mehehe*. In general the true house, *pãi*, has a higher status than other buildings because it is built collectively, often in the name of a spirit or a village chief. A *mehehe*, although it may be constructed by a number of men working together, has no special association with spirits or chiefs.

The *mehehe* houses show a willingness to experiment with a wide variety of designs. One house, for example, is modeled after the backwoods Brazilian home, with a thatched roof and mud walls. A second *mehehe* was deliberately designed to resemble the houses built by the Carib-speaking Txicão. Given that the Mehinaku were at war with the Txicão until recently and still regard them as subhuman, the use of their house design shows a considerable architectural adventurousness.

If we look at houses according to the function they perform rather than from the perspective of their structural differences, we find that there are three basic types, each with its own separate location. In the center of the village is the men's house (*kwaukuhe*). Though often built with two front doors, the men's house is considered a *pãi* or true house. In addition it has a long bench (*jepitsi*) at the threshold on which the men sit. The construction of the men's house is a solemn enterprise from which members of other tribes are excluded. Women curious enough or bold enough to watch the building of the men's house would be subject to gang rape.

Used for additional work space, a second type of dwelling stands in the trash yards of the Mehinaku residences. It provides good light and shelter for women processing manioc, and on occasion it serves as a temporary residence for people in ritual seclusion, villagers who have been publicly disgraced, menstruating women, and others who for some reason cannot sleep under their own roof.

The Mehinaku residence, the third type of house, is invariably built along the village circle and ideally stands opposite its partner across the plaza. A true house, it is a large thatch haystack-shaped affair up to one hundred feet long, thirty feet wide, and thirty feet high. On first entering through the low doorway, the visitor is immediately struck by a sense of vast and gloomy spaciousness, for the floor area is obstructed by very few supporting poles. Since there are no windows and the low front and rear doors admit little light, the contrast between the dazzlingly bright plaza and the murkiness of the interior forces the visitor to pause for a while to get used to the darkness. In the evening, after the doors have been closed and locked against the mosquitoes and the witches who are said to prowl about in gloom, the only light comes from the small fires the Mehinaku tend by their hammocks.

The floor area of the house is divided into a number of zones, each associated with a set of social activities (see fig. 10). "The mouth of the house," the area about the doorway, has a variety

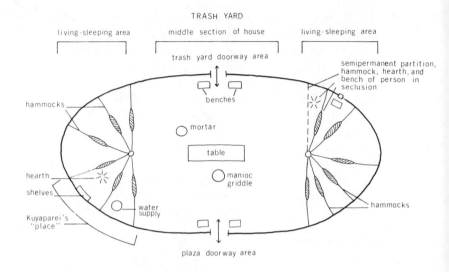

Fig. 10. The true house (*pāi*). The true house contains regions for public and private activities of a social, domestic, or ritual nature. In the diagram, each region of the house, as linguistically recognized by the villagers, is labeled by an approximate English translation.

These areas include the doorways to the plaza (*wenekutaku kanatɨ,* literally, "mouth of the plaza") and the trash yard (*miyeipyenu kanatɨ,* literally, "mouth of the trash yard")—points for casual socializing and working on handicrafts. The space just inside the plaza door is used to entertain visitors and, along with the middle section of the house (*ĩkatɨ*) is used as a stage and dancing ground for ceremonies. Within this area, too, are found the mortar (*ana*) and manioc griddle (*hehe*) areas, frequented by those who are making or just hoping to eat manioc bread.

The living and sleeping areas of the house (*iyepi*) are private regions, respected by all but the most boorish. Within these areas are the named but unwalled family "apartments," such as "Kuyaparei's Place" (*epʊgʊ*), containing hammocks, storage shelves, hearth, and water supply.

of uses. Residents sit before the door to work on crafts, watch their children, or keep tabs on what is occurring in the plaza. Here they greet and entertain visitors from other houses or other tribes. Here too a visitor is seated and offered food and drink. A well-bred guest will never go beyond the doorway except on ceremonial occasions when the house is opened to the public for dancing and trading.

The midsection of the house is a storage, work, and kitchen area. A large shelf at the base of the main house poles, occasionally used as a work bench, supports several tall manioc silos. In this area, using the nearby clay griddle and wooden mortar, the housewives prepare their fish and manioc-flour bread.

The sleeping areas of the house take in the space beyond the two main hammock poles, the heaviest posts in the framework of the building. Nuclear families tie their hammocks close to each other, share a common hearth, and either store their personal possessions on common shelves or suspend them from the rafters on long cords. Never lightly intruded upon, the sleeping areas are the only private portions of the house. As a token of intimacy, however, a resident may invite a good friend into this area and seat him on his own hammock. Some of the other tribes of the Upper Xingu, particularly the Carib groups, are regarded as boors because they will walk right past the entranceway and barge into the hammock area as if they were old friends or kinsmen.

To an outside observer, the Mehinaku household lives in a large unpartitioned and undifferentiated space. From the perspective of a resident, however, there are separate areas for receiving guests, preparing food, doing craft work, conducting rituals, managing family affairs, sleeping, and securing a measure of privacy. In short, we find in the Mehinaku house the entire range of public and private, sacred and secular, and recreational and utilitarian areas that we might find in a multiroom house in our own society.

Can we legitimately regard the house, like the village, as a metaphor about social relationships and symbols? I believe we can, for the house is associated with femininity, in opposition to the plaza and the rest of the village which are linked with masculinity. Men who spend too much time in their houses are called "women" in village gossip. Male children who loiter within the house are chased outdoors by their parents. In large part the identification of men with the world outside the home and of women with the home arises because the division of labor tends to disperse men and to localize women in and around the domestic unit. Every good Mehinaku knows that men should be outdoors, whether they are fishing, hunting, working, socializing, or wandering through the forest.

A second metaphor links the house to politics; a house is not only a home, it is a symbol that stands for its occupants. A chief's house must not only be located at a particular spot on the village circle, it must be built by the entire community. Its doorpost must be made of heavy "chief" wood, the supporting rails and crossbeams painted and the roof decorated with long poles and sticks called "earrings" that point in opposite directions. Such a house is a symbol of political office.

The occupants of even nonchiefly houses come closer to forming a bounded political group than any other social unit in Mehinaku society. The cluster of related individuals who live in a house are referred to as the "house owners" (*pāi wekene*), which not only identifies the residents of one building but also a significant unit in political discourse. A chief in a public speech for example, may invite the "house owners" of a residence to participate in a collective activity, or he may denounce them as gossips and slackers. Houses, then, are units in political action and village activities.

Mehinaku Space, Settings, and Designs

Nowadays an anthropologist working among Brazilian Indians inevitably becomes an applied anthropologist. Even though his initial interests may have been wholly theoretical, he can not help being horrified by the effect of the rapid encroachment of roads and settlers on Indian lands. From this point of view, one of the conclusions to be drawn from my discussion of Mehinaku space is that to relocate the Mehinaku is to destroy them.

Since mythic times when the Sun created the tribes of men, Mehinaku villages have been oriented in precisely the same way. The roads across the village from the Culiseu in the east to the bathing area in the west have always faithfully followed the path of the sun. This orientation is built right into the Mehinaku language; to go west and to go bathing may be expressed identically (*iye waku*). The location of the village also has important social and religious significance, since the road-chiefs have always lived alongside the eastern and western paths, and it is believed that a path leads from the center of the plaza to the village in the sky. The lands surrounding the village are equally alive with meaning. History lives for the Mehinaku because they still use their ancient and traditional villages and still visit the very places where culture heroes and spirits created animals, men, and even the geography of the Upper Xingu. Every time a child walks through the woods with his father, he receives a lesson in tribal history, mythology, and religion.

The Mehinaku's land is also the basis of tribal subsistence and material culture. In examining a map of the Mehinaku territory with me, my teachers were able to point out the distribution of such important resources as monkey, fish, honey, salt, palm wood, *pequi*, and wild fruits. This list, however, is only a very partial one, since there are other plants and animals that are important to the Mehinaku because of their medicinal properties and value in trade. One such plant, found only in a small area, has an important role in the great intertribal ceremony for the initiation of chiefs. In addition, we shall see that the uneven distribution of resources among the Mehinaku and their neighbors goes a long way toward explaining specialties in tribal manufactures, trade, and the cohesiveness of all the Xinguanos.

When a tribe like the Mehinaku stands in the way of the network of highways now crisscrossing the Amazon basin, the government solution is often simply to move them where no one else wishes to go. This response may seem responsible and even humane from the point of view of the bureaucrat who finds himself perfectly capable of moving from São Paulo or Rio to Brasília "in the national interest," but it will not do for the Mehinaku. To relocate the villagers would destroy the base on which rests their pattern of subsistence, their political organization, their religion, their mythology, and their sense of history and continuity as a people.

A more theoretical conclusion that I have tried to promote in this chapter is the importance of the ethnography of space. Normally this topic is given only passing attention unless spatial relationships are an elaborate and conscious metaphor for social and symbolic relationships. I have tried to show, however, that although the Mehinaku do not self-consciously formulate precise statements about the relationships of space and culture, these statements are implicit in the ground plans of their community. Their drawings reveal spatially visible distinctions between the realm of men and nature, between the public and the private, between the sacred and the profane, between men and women, between good citizens and "trash yard men," between chiefs and commoners, and between separate but similar political groups. The use of space among the Mehinaku as among other peoples can therefore be regarded as a metaphor expressing the relationship between nature, men, society, and symbols. Looking at space and designs is both a way of describing a people and summing up much that is important about them.

4 The Design of the Community and the Flow of Information

Papá just went by . . . I know the sound of his feet.

Akanai

In the previous chapter I argued that the layout of the Mehinaku community reflects their world view and important social relationships. I believe it is possible to make a stronger statement, for community design not only says things about the way a people live but also influences the way in which they live. This influence is inevitable, for social events occur in a setting whose physical attributes must have an effect on the course of everyday life.

Perhaps the most significant characteristic of any social setting is the degree to which the activities occurring there will be observable or insulated from public view. Accurate knowledge of the conduct of others is of course a prerequisite for organizing social life. The Mehinaku, for example, must know who is going fishing so they can make sure that everyone will have a canoe. Somewhat less obviously, a villager's reputation in the community is in part dependent on the visibility of his activities as a good citizen. A man should not only be generous with his possessions and sociable with his fellows; he should also be these things conspicuously. Public areas of high visibility within the Mehinaku community are well suited to such display.

On the other hand, there are certain kinds of information that a Mehinaku must conceal from the community. Misconduct is best hidden if the villagers are to preserve their self-esteem and merit a reasonable level of confidence from their friends and kinsmen. Mystification, obscurity, and limitations on the free flow of information must be as actively cultivated by the Mehinaku as are their efforts to publicize their good citizenship. For these reasons public areas of high observability and private regions of concealment are likely to lend themselves to very different kinds of performances.

Let us return to our description of the village and attempt to see how its layout, its physical setting, and even the materials used in its construction both expose and conceal important social events.

The Village as a Theater for Social Life

If the Mehinaku village can be regarded as a theater for the presentation of social performances, a quick glance at the village map (see fig. 8) tells us that it is a theater in the round. The area just in front of the men's house, the geographical center of the village, is stage center for the spectators. In fact this area of the plaza (*wenekutaku*) is used as a stage for major public events, including daily wrestling matches, rituals, and public speeches. It is situated so that all the Mehinaku, except the occupants of the residence directly behind the men's house, can see what occurs there from their doorways. Even when no formal activities are occurring on the plaza, it remains a highly visible area.

It is virtually impossible to walk across the plaza during the day without being seen. Someone is almost always seated at his or her doorway fashioning arrows, plaiting baskets, braiding cord, or just staring out at the passing show. People enjoy keeping an eye on the plaza because that is where the action is. Not only is the plaza center stage in being highly observable but it is also the interactional hub of the village. Here the main paths from the bathing area, the Indian Post, and the Culiseu converge, bringing people into the center of the community. The Mehinaku greet visitors and casually interact as they move from one part of the village to another. The plaza is a social nexus as well as the focal point of the villagers' attention.

Fig. 11. A mother grooms her daughter. The area in front of each door is used for casual conversation and watching what goes on in the public areas of the village. Toward late afternoon, groups of women preempt the doorways to groom their children and watch their kinsmen wrestle in front of the men's house.

A second public region consists of the main paths themselves. Nominally the property of the chiefs whose houses are built next to them, the paths are maintained by the men of the village in exchange for a "payment" of fish. The Mehinaku take immense pride in these roads and build them long, wide, and straight. The trail to the northern port, currently the most impressive, is wide enough to accommodate two small cars traveling side by side and extends nearly two miles through the forest as though drawn with a ruler.

The motive for maintaining these trails so meticulously is not only to impress visitors but also to find out as soon as possible who is approaching the village. When a neighboring tribe is scheduled for a ceremonial visit, many of the young Mehinaku will spend hours staring down the road in order to be the first to see them arrive. I recall that on one occasion when the Kuikuru were expected, they were first spotted at a distance of almost two miles from the village, a full thirty-five minutes before they arrived.

Even on days when no visitors are anticipated, the villagers often glance down the trails to see who is coming. In some of the houses tiny windows have been opened at strategic points in the thatch walls so that the residents can keep watch on movements in and out of the village. On occasion a great shout goes up: "Visitors! Visitors! Visitors!" (*putaka*), and men and children come racing out of their houses. Like as not, the visitors turn out to be Mehinaku returning from a fishing trip or a herd of wild pigs so distant that it looks like a group of men. Everyone then retires to his house and quiet once more descends on the village of the curious.

Mehinaku houses are more insulated from observers than are the plaza and the main paths. Though they are poorly lit and nonresidents are not supposed to enter without permission, the houses hardly qualify as fully private regions, for they are normally unpartitioned and doors are left open all day. Access is unrestricted to occupants and their kin, and admission is unannounced. Within the house the most public region is just inside the door, an area used for social activities and craft work. In this part of the house, both interaction and observation are inescapable. Socially available in this location, a Mehinaku must respond courteously to his residence mates who are working near him or walking by on their way outdoors.

Like the residences, the men's house has both public and private elements. On one hand it is a back region for masculine interaction, since women are absolutely excluded upon pain of gang rape. On the other hand it is a public region, since admission is unrestricted to all the men and boys of the tribe; there is no formal process of initiation.

With the exception of the bathing areas and the gardens, observability drops markedly outside the village. The bathing area along the Tuatuari River is visited from dawn until twilight, when the last bathers return home. Even when the river appears deserted, however, a canoeist may silently and unexpectedly come paddling around a bend. The gardens are also somewhat public, especially after they have been burned over. Until the crops return, it is possible to see what is going on across contiguous fields. As the corn and manioc grow and obscure visibility, however, the gardens gradually become a setting for back region activities.

By now enough evidence has been adduced to support the contention that the village, as theater, is one with relatively unobstructed seating. Each individual's whereabouts and activities are generally known to his relatives and often to the community as a whole. A Mehinaku has little chance of staying out of the public eye for any length of time.

The Acoustics of Social Action

One of the more remarkable things for an urban American about the Xingu forest and savannahs is their silence. To be sure, there are sounds, the sounds of insects, wind, rain, birds, and small animals. Nevertheless, to one accustomed to the continual sounds of venting fans, air conditioners, telephones, radios, televisions, and street traffic, a tropical forest village is a very quiet place. Because of the minimal background noise, the sounds made by people become highly noticeable. The acoustics are excellent in the Mehinaku theater-in-the-round; it is an amphitheater for sound. The circle of houses and the enclosing wall of vegetation seem to act as a sounding board for the human voice, so that a person who shouts in the center of the village will actually hear the trace of an echo a moment later.

Conversation can be overheard almost anywhere. Thatch walls are not soundproof, and villagers occasionally communicate with neighbors in nearby houses simply by raising their voices. At times when the village is very quiet, a conversation inside a house can be picked up as far away as the bench in front of the men's house, a distance of one hundred feet. To conduct a private conversation, people must whisper; and even then they can not be certain that another person is not listening wrapped unseen in a nearby hammock or pressed against the outer wall of the house.

There are sounds other than speech that convey significant information about the villagers. At dawn each day the boys and the younger men of the tribe whistle through their hands as they go to bathe in the Tuatuari. The rhythmic whistling sounds strange and beautiful as it echoes between river and village. A kind of alarm clock, it tells those still asleep that their fellows are already up and about. Associated with masculinity and youth, group whistling binds the boys closer together. Among the relatively few songs is one that reflects the solidarity of the young men. Called the "Piercing Song," it is whistled by those who have undergone the ear-piercing ritual together.

Some of the adult males often play small flutes on their way from the river to their gardens. Since each player has a distinctive style, the sound identifies those who are on their way to the fields. The playing of other musical instruments is also revealing. The style of those who play the sacred flutes in the men's house and their repertory of songs helps to identify at least the lead instrumentalist and often his accompanists as well.

Nonverbal sounds constantly alert the Mehinaku to each other's presence. One dark night Akanai, a young man whose hammock was next to mine, turned to me and said, "My father just went by on the plaza." Though I expressed incredulity, he insisted that he could identify a passerby by the sound of his footsteps. Since the Mehinaku go about barefoot, I was skeptical, but after several opportunities to check the accuracy of his observation I had to believe him.

After dark, sounds are an important clue to the activities of the Mehinaku, for once the doors are closed and the fires die down, it is pitch black. During these hours, thieves and lovers slink about in the darkness and sometimes the sounds they make with other people's possessions and female kin give them away. I will have more to say about how these night prowlers operate, but a brief quote from a Mehinaku ceremonial song illustrates the villagers' awareness of such activities:

> I hear my mother having sexual relations
> in her hammock
> I hear the hammock pole and the cords
> creaking
> *Pila, Kule, Pila, Pilaw Pila, Pila!*

The last line consists of Mehinaku onomatopoetic words for the sounds of sexual intercourse.

There are other night sounds to which I have often listened when I could not sleep. These include snoring, the creaking of ropes as a sleeper turns over in his hammock, the rustle of thatch as someone goes outside, and the stirring up of a fire as the chill of the early dawn creeps into the house. All these sounds are clues to the whereabouts and activities of the villagers, clues to which the Mehinaku attend.

The permeability of the houses and the community to sound allows the Mehinaku to signal to each other with high-pitched whoops. These calls are an important method of nonverbal communication, keeping the Mehinaku informed about daily events and activities. A male activity, whooping is part of the role assigned to men who are vigorous, social, and reasonably youthful. Women may "yoo-hoo" from time to time to attract their children, but the masculine whoop is another kind of sound altogether. It is a high-pitched falsetto call that carries great distances. On one occasion I heard it from two miles away when the Kuikuru were arriving for an intertribal ceremony.

Whenever food is brought into the village, the men whoop. There are distinctive calls for fish, monkey, honey, and *pequi* fruit. As soon as a returning fisherman is spotted on the trail, a great whoop alerts the community. The men rush to the doors to see who has caught the fish and to whose house it is being delivered. Even old men, who do not casually get up from their hammocks or leave their craft work, join in the whooping and excitement from inside the houses.

Despite the attention, the fisherman remains silent. He may be proud of his catch, but it would not be proper for him to acknowledge it. Further, he may not relish the acclaim. Once seen, he will find it very difficult not to share his good fortune with other households.

Marriages are also greeted with whoops; *"Wha! Wha! Wha! Whaa!"* the men call out as the groom's hammock is carried across the plaza to the bride's house. The calls are meant to announce the wedding to the tribe and to insure the fertility of the marriage by imitating the cries of a newborn baby.

Another signal announces and seals public agreements. When the older men of the village reach an agreement to organize a fishing expedition or an intertribal wrestling match, everyone whoops to punctuate the decision. Similarly, when valuable shell necklaces or ceramic pots are traded at formal bartering sessions, a loud call like an actioneer's hammer announces the culmination of the deal. As table 1 suggests, there are many other occasions for whooping (*utapai*). This list is only partial, but it contains sixteen entries divided for convenience of presentation into several categories. It is very difficult to indicate by orthography what these whoops sound like, but at least it is apparent that each of them is a separate and discernable signal that carries an important social message.

Other paralinguistic signals include the ritual weeping that follows a death and the songs women sing during the evening in the trash yards. These signals and whoops provide an efficient broadcast system linking the entire community. A Mehinaku can keep track of the major events of the day without stirring from his hammock.

Most of the audible clues to social conduct that I have described are carefully attended to, for the Mehinaku are as interested in them as their ethnographer is. A whoop announcing a visitor is enough to send the men and boys running to the center of the village to stare down the main roads. The women cluster at the doorways trying to guess who it might be. No matter that it is only someone coming back from his garden. The signal has served its purpose, making the Mehinaku a bit more knowledgeable about one of their fellow's whereabouts and activities. A seven-year-old child crying lustily sets off a chorus of questioning and speculation all around the village

Table 1   Whoops That Signal Social and Natural Events

Members of other tribes arrive in village
1. Xinguano (*putaka*) Indians seen on path: "Ka-ahoo."
2. *Kajaiba* (white men) arrive: shout and clap
3. *Waká* (ceremonial ambassadors) arriving from another tribe to invite the Mehinaku to an intertribal ritual: "Kaaku-wu!" The Mehinaku respond to this whoop by slapping their hands on their thighs and arms.
4. *Waká* (ceremonial ambassadors) arriving to invite the Mehinaku to the intertribal spearthrowing ritual (*jawari*): "Kaaku-woo!" Response: "Hu-ho-ho-ho-hu!"
5. *Waká* (ceremonial ambassadors) arriving to invite the Mehinaku to the ceremony of the sacred flutes: "Ke-ho, ke-ho, ke-ho . . ." (sound trailing off). The Mehinaku make no response, since the spirit of the flutes is a dangerous being.

Social and other important events within the village
6. Marriage: "Wa! Wa! Waa!"
7. Trading at public barter sessions (*uluki*): "Ahe-yooo!"
8. Choosing *waká* ambassadors to invite another tribe to the Mehinaku: "Hu-hu-hu-hu-wa-ho!"
9. Making public decisions: "Wa-hoo!"
10. Responding to a joke or clever remark on the part of one of the men: "Wa-ha!"
11. Men demanding pepper, salt, and manioc cakes from the chief's wife: "Ai ai ai ai!" (pepper, pepper!)

Food arriving in the village
12. Fish: "yu . . . pʊ, amanuya! Kupate, kupate, kupate!" (Wow, a lot! Fish, fish, fish!)
13. Monkey: "Wahu!"
14. Honey: "Wu, pʊ, mapa" (Wow, honey!)

Natural events
15. Thunderstorms: "unɨ!" (rain).
16. Meteors: "Wa!"

---

circle: "Who is crying? Why is she crying? Is her father scarifying her with a fishtooth scraper?" After a few moments of careful listening: "Ah-ha! Ui Etewe was bitten by a fire ant. Poor thing!" Everyone smiles and returns to work, sleep, or small talk.

Footprints and Other Telltales

Information can be conveyed in a number of ways. It can be directly seen and heard, as I have described, and it can be related, as I shall describe further on. Another method of learning about social events, however, is to observe them indirectly through the traces they leave in the environment. Footprints provide the Mehinaku with the most important of these traces and their absorption in reading and interpreting the marks left in the earth by their neighbors' feet reflects their extreme attentiveness to each other's activities.

Barefoot except when they are able to cadge a pair of sneakers from a Brazilian Air Force pilot or to fashion a pair of sandals from an old tire picked up at the Indian Post, the Mehinaku have strong feelings about the esthetics of the human foot. Oddly-shaped or outsized feet are considered ridiculous. One member of the Txicão tribe, for example, is held in special contempt because one of his toes splays out in a way the Mehinaku find laughably repulsive.

Feet are valuable telltales because they leave records of their owners' whereabouts and activities on the sandy village soil, records that the Mehinaku are remarkably adept at reading. At first I was skeptical when my companion looked closely at the path and said, "Auya has gone fishing with Iyepe. Maintyakalu went with them as far as the garden, but she has come back. They took Chilete (one of the village dogs)." Or again, "Look here! Kwalu had sex with Ahira. Here are her footprints, and here is where he put his buttocks. Don't come too close. You might step on the ejaculate and get a pain in your leg!" Remarks such as these seemed too much to believe, especially after I carefully inspected the place indicated and barely noted the outline of what might or might not have been a few toes. Whenever I had a chance to check, however, the villagers turned out to be surprisingly accurate.

I asked a number of the villagers to draw the footprints of their fellow tribesmen as clearly as they could in order to discover just what it was about feet that enables the Mehinaku to identify them. In all cases the villagers felt sufficiently knowledgeable about the appearance of other adults' feet to try to draw pictures of them. The details different artists noted about the feet they drew were roughly similar—their gross size, their length, their width, and the curve of the arch. The toes provided an especially important set of identifying characteristics. The degree to which they splayed, their relative size, their distance apart, and the size and pointedness of the large bone on the side of the big toe (the distal end of the first metatarsal) were particularly important markers.

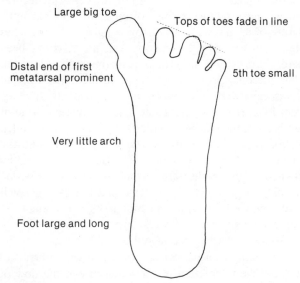

Large big toe

Tops of toes fade in line

Distal end of first metatarsal prominent

5th toe small

Very little arch

Foot large and long

Fig. 12. The chief's foot. Drawn and commented upon by one of the villagers.

All of my artists claimed that they were able to read the footprints of every adult, many of the children, and all of the dogs in the village. None of them claimed any familiarity with the footprints of Indians from other tribes, though they noted that both Xingu Indians and "wild Indians" (those outside the Xingu reservation) had identically formed feet. They pointed out, however, that the white man had narrow feet with closely spaced toes because he wore shoes. Interestingly, my artists were somewhat less adept at identifying each other's drawings than they were at reading actual on-the-ground prints. In gen-

eral, they were successful with each other's drawings of footprints when I asked them to choose from among a number of
possible villagers I listed for them. This assistance actually
corresponds to real life, since a Mehinaku reading footprints
on a path can always eliminate a number of possibilities based
on his knowledge of the whereabouts of his fellow tribesmen.

Footprints are not the only telltales that let the Mehinaku
keep up with each other. Most personal property is so distinc-
tively made that it can be identified with the owner. The decorative pattern wound around the shaft of an arrow, for example,
is the signature of its maker. A lost arrow caught in the branches
by the side of a river may therefore reveal just who has been
fishing there, information fishermen sometimes like to keep
secret. Other personal property that may be identified with an
owner includes canoes, paddles, and garden implements. A canoe
missing from its port usually indicates that the owner or one of
his kinsmen has left the village. Paddles are generally left hidden
near the canoe port; close relatives who know how to find the
owner's cache can discover whether he is on the river simply
by noting whether his paddles are in their usual place. Garden
tools left leaning against a stump indicate that the gardener will
soon be returning to work, since no Mehinaku will unduly expose his implements to theft.

Thus far I have described the layout and construction of the
Mehinaku community as a theater for social life whose arrangement maximizes the interaction of the villagers and the flow of
information. Actors in this setting are highly visible and highly
audible. The village is so permeable to sound that many of the
social events of the day are in effect broadcast to the entire
community. Those events that escape the spectator and listener
can often be reconstructed from footprints and other telltales
that the Mehinaku leave behind.

The physical attributes of the Mehinaku setting can carry us
only so far along the channels of information flow within the
community, since some ways of learning about social and natural events are not immediately connected to ground plans and
construction materials. In the next chapter, therefore, I shall
turn to some of the social institutions that also transmit information within the community.

5

Institutions and Information

Hush! I want to hear the news.

Kaialuku, quieting her children

In a small face-to-face society like the Mehinaku, everyone is naturally interested in learning about everyone else. The basis of this interest is that relationships between any two persons are wide ranging; they may simultaneously be kinsmen, work partners, and participants in ritual. No one can compartmentalize life as we do, insulating domestic conduct from outside relationships. As a result virtually everything the Mehinaku do is potentially interesting to their comrades; they are engaged in such a wide spectrum of common social activities that they cannot help but be curious about each other.

The openness of the community to the flow of information suggests that the villagers' curiosity is not likely to be frustrated. A number of important social institutions, including the smokers' circle, the program of public speeches, and the informal network of gossip seem designed to satisfy social curiosity still further. Let us look at how these institutions operate and at the categories of information they serve to distribute.

Categories of Information

The Mehinaku divide the category of speech into several kinds of linguistically recognized subclasses among which are greetings, myth, oratory, conversation, gossip, lies, and news. Table 2 will guide the reader toward an understanding of how the villagers classify information, though the table is not intended as a bounded taxonomic system (such systems are constructable, but tend to obscure the ambiguity and flexibility characteristic of Mehinaku culture).

Table 2   Categories of Speech

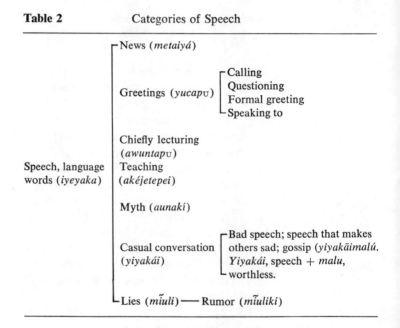

Telling the News at the Smokers' Circle

Metaiyá or news, is noncontroversial topical information. It is news about events in other tribes, the things the white man is doing at the Indian Post, and the more-than-ordinary activities of the Mehinaku themselves, such as killing a big animal or catching a lot of fish. It is generally assumed to be accurate unless it turns out otherwise, in which case it is a lie or a mistake (*mĩuli*). *Metaiyá* is always recounted publicly and it is understood that everyone is eligible to listen in. The villagers routinely hush their children in order to listen to news being told at the opposite end of the house. When a particularly choice news story is related in another house, nonresidents may legitimately wander over and listen in through the thatch wall. Or they may send a child over to collect the story and report back to his parents. The definition of *Metaiyá*, then, is news that interests everyone, offends no one, is presumed accurate, and is public.

Where is one most likely to hear the news? The principal formal institution for disseminating information is the circle of smokers who meet each evening in the center of the village. Although all the members of the circle are shamans (the word for smoker, *yetamá*, also means shaman), their main purpose in coming together each evening is to discuss the events of the day.

Toward early evening the smokers begin to roll their tobacco in leaves until they have a number of long thin cigars (*huka*). The chief usually finishes this task before the others since he is expected to be the first smoker. Placing his cigars behind one ear he picks up a sculpted wooden bench, goes out to a spot in front of the men's house, and starts a small fire. Gradually the other smokers arrive. Each man, carrying his own bench and his own quota of cigars, takes his place in the circle nearest his own home so that the smokers' circle reflects the location of the houses around the plaza. On a fair night, when the men have nothing else to preoccupy them, all eight male shamans will join the circle. On occasion, Kaiti, the chief's wife who is also a shaman, will sit behind her husband, but she rarely participates in the conversation.

The chief usually brings more cigars than he actually expects to smoke, because the etiquette of the smokers' circle demands that he share his tobacco. He lights a cigar, puffs on it vigorously until it begins to spark and burn, and then passes it on to a fellow smoker who takes the cigar and says, "Heh-heh-heh-heh!" in acceptance and appreciation.

Once everyone is seated and smoking, a member of the circle starts the conversation with a casual observation. Unlike other social gatherings, the interaction is focused; only one person speaks at a time and he holds to the same topic as the previous speaker. The conversations are usually dominated by the older men, the younger smokers confining themselves to brief remarks and interjections unless they have specific news to relate. Nonmembers stalk the circle from a distance or sit on the men's bench where they can follow the conversation even though they do not participate. Young boys are usually told to go on home and get into their hammocks. The hour is late and the smoke is dangerous to the uninitiated.

When there is no news of any consequence, the smokers' circle is a dispirited group and there are long lapses in the conversation. I recall one occasion when by my watch no one spoke for thirty minutes except to say "Heh-heh-heh!" upon accepting a cigar. At such times whatever sparks of conversation the smokers manage to keep alive concern the white man at the Indian Post, ceremonial activities in other tribes, and the quality of their tobacco.

When there is news to tell, the smokers' circle is an exciting gathering. The main source of news is the Indian Post where the Mehinaku have a chance not only to keep tabs on the ever-puzzling activities and customs of the *kajaiba* (white men) but also to meet members of neighboring tribes. A Mehinaku returning from the Post is briefly a minor celebrity, especially if he is the only one to have gone on that day. The Post is a three- to four-hour journey from the village, depending on the time of year. During the rainy season the trail is largely under water and the traveler must go by canoe. Even during the dry season, the trip is long and arduous enough that the Mehinaku do not go without some definite purpose. I have the strong impression that a major payoff for those who make the trip is to come home with a good newsworthy story that will guarantee them some attention. Happily the Post is usually alive with news and rumors if not actual occurrences, and a Mehinaku who goes there is seldom disappointed.

When he returns home the traveler jealously hoards the details of his tale until the smokers have assembled. Then, casually, he takes his place in the circle and waits until he is questioned about his trip. The other smokers have been fairly itching to find out what happened, since they may have already heard a brief sketch of the exciting events. Once the bearer of news begins to talk, he is stage center even if he is the youngest of the smokers. If he is a good storyteller, he punctuates his narrative with the many onamatopoetic words that give Mehinaku myths and stories much of their color and excitement. The listener hears the "puh-puh-puh" slap of the canoe paddle, the cries of birds, and the shrieks of spirits. The assembled smokers express surprise, amusement, or skepticism with appropriate interjections: "Wow!" "No!?" "My my!"

The most exciting stories concern the conduct of the white man, ritual, witchcraft, and spirits. For example: In early February 1972, Iyepana, one of the older men of the tribe, went to the Indian Post in the early morning. When he returned late that afternoon, he was carrying a fifteen-foot length of light-weight palm wood (Portuguese, *buriti*) which he had obtained at the Post from a Kamaiurá, a member of a Tupian-speaking tribe, one of the Mehinaku's near neighbors. Everyone began to ask what the palm wood was, until word spread around the village that it was an image of a spirit named Munu. If a man were to touch Munu, he would come down with fever and vomiting. An image of Munu is anything that is tall like Munu, such as an ant hill, termite nest, or length of palm wood.

There was great excitement in the village when all the smokers had gathered and Iyepana dramatically joined the circle, carrying his fifteen-foot image of Munu. Perched on his folding chair (which he obtained at the Indian Post and uses instead of a native sculpted bench), he told his story:

> Some of the Kamaiurá were canoeing through an unknown part of the swamp. As they were paddling by a clear area of high ground they saw two Munu spirits with hideous eyes and ears walking slowly across the clearing. Takama (the Kamaiurá chief) wanted everyone to see how big they were. He cut the palm pole on the spot and delivered it to me at the post.

The smokers received Iyepana's account with the utmost seriousness and interest. There were numerous expressions of surprise at the size of the spirits and admiration for the Kamaiurá chief who approached so close to the dreaded creatures.

Finally, after Iyepana had repeated and enlarged upon especially exciting portions of the tale and the listeners had exhausted their questions, the chief brought the session to a close. "Over?" he said. "Over," said the men, and each returned to his house to retell the story to those members of his family who had not had an opportunity to hear it.

The smokers' circle appears to function as a press service does in our society; it gathers, authenticates, and disseminates the news. We turn now to a Mehinaku institution that serves not so much to broadcast the news as to comment upon it.

Public Oratory: The Chief's Speeches

One institution, somewhat more elaborated among the Mehinaku than among other South American Indians, is the pattern of obligatory lectures given by the chief of the tribe. A Mehinaku chief (*amunão*, masculine, *amunuleju*, feminine) is an individual of chiefly descent who has been initiated into his status in the course of an intricate intertribal ritual. Ideally, he is a special sort of person, generous to his comrades, prone to neither anger nor frivolity, strong and imposing in his bearing: he is *káukapapai*, inspiring both fear and respect in his fellow villagers.

Above all, the chief is a public speaker. Unlike commoners, who are sometimes referred to in a nonpejorative sense as "trash yard people" (*miyeipyenuwantɨ*), the chief is a man of the plaza —a master of the archaic language used to address ceremonial ambassadors from other tribes, and skilled in delivering lectures at dawn and in the evening to his own people. Said to be his "children" (*yamukunão*), the villagers are instructed by the chief in the virtues of good conduct, just as a parent lectures his sons and daughters (the term for both parental and chiefly talks is *awuntapʋ*).

Akusa, the most prominent of the Mehinaku chiefs, is a particularly effective speaker, in full command of the repetitive phrasing and drawn out terminal vowels that constitute the chiefly rhetorical style. He urges his "children" to get up at the crack of dawn, to take cold baths, to work hard in the fields, to go fishing often, and to complete the roads leading into the village that are his special pride. Although Akusa delivers such inspirational addresses year-round, the festival of Amairi (the two southernmost stars in the constellation of Pegasus, and the Spirit of the Manioc Harvest) is the occasion above all others for his lectures on the subject of hard work. At 5:45 A.M., on January 30, 1972, when Amairi appeared over the eastern horizon, Akusa addressed himself to his people:

> Awake, my sons! Amairi has risen and the time for work is here. The time for work is here! Do not tell me, "I'm not going to do anything." A man is pleased to go to work. A long time ago when the people saw Amairi they went to work in their gardens. They were real workers, and their gardens were far from their houses, not in their doorways like yours! A long time ago my mother's brother made a garden very far off, almost as far off as the Post. In his doorway? I should say not! Not him!
>
> Here in our village the ants eat our gardens and everyone complains, "The ants are eating my manioc". I say to you, "Why then do you make your garden near the ants' house? Our ancestors cut their gardens far off and harvested an enormous quantity of food. Make gardens! Make manioc flour! Work!

As charming as this speech may seem to us on first reading, the Mehinaku have heard it many times before. They are all too familiar with the chief's bromides on the ethic of hard work, and as he rambles on, often for a half hour or more, fewer and fewer villagers appear to be listening. They are chatting idly with their spouses, joking with their children, or valiantly trying to get back to sleep in their hammocks. The chief, too, often seems to lose the thread of such speeches, permitting his thoughts to wander, following a process of free association. Gradually his material becomes more personal and his delivery more impassioned as he berates his subordinate relatives, sneers at his rivals (who are never named), or justifies his special position in the village. In the speech quoted above, for example, he also alluded to his experience with the warlike Txicão tribe and attempted to convince the villagers that he could not be a witch:

> Be like me. I am not a witch. At the Post there are many Txicão. They have said, "We will kill Akusa; we have already

shot him with an arrow!" I know they want to kill me. If I were a witch I would have killed them long ago, every one of them, but look: their women are pregnant and their babies are fat. I could not be a witch!

The chief not only uses his forum to deliver homilies on good conduct and to promote his interests but also to offer editorial comment on the events of the day, providing the tribe with interpretations and evaluations about matters of common knowledge. Sometimes the message is cautionary: In May 1972, two members of the Kamaiurá tribe who had previously been in good health died unexpectedly. Witchcraft being suspected, suspicion fell on an Auití Indian who was then waylaid and killed by the Kamaiurá. To make absolutely certain that any other witches responsible for the death of their fellow tribesmen were also punished, the Kamaiurá prepared a broth containing bits of their deceased kinsmen's corpse and cooked it over a fire. In this fashion the heat of the fire would be transmitted to the body of the witch and drive him mad with pain. The Mehinaku call the victim of this kind of sympathetic magic *peheke mei piya*, or "the grilled prey."

All of this was known to the Mehinaku when the chief walked to the center of the plaza one evening and made the following speech which (like the previous excerpts) I freely translate from a tape recording:

A long time ago my father was heating a pot to grill his prey. One day, while hunting, I shot at a bird, but I missed and left a mark on the ground so I could find the arrow. An old woman saw the mark and told everyone she had found the place where my father's "grilled prey" had danced in agony because of the heat of the pot. Everyone told my father to come and see. The old lady said, "There is the spot where the 'grilled prey' danced all night." My father was about to add dirt to the pot to burn the witch's feet. If I hadn't been there to stop him he would have done it and my feet would have been ruined!

When we "grill prey" we make mistakes. People lie to the man seeking revenge, telling him that they know who the witch is. If you go to the Post [where there are frequently Kamaiurá], act well. Don't run away when you see others there; don't be ashamed to speak to strangers or hide from them. The Kamaiurá are blaming all of us for the deaths in their village. They say a trail of the "grilled prey" runs through the woods near their village. Don't visit the Kamaiurá now or they will think that we are the "grilled prey." Act well at the Post!

The speech placed the events following the death of the Kamaiurá in perspective and reassured the Mehinaku by connecting the story to the experience of their chief. The warning at the end of the speech was particularly well taken because some of the younger people had given little thought to the dangers of visiting the Post.

We will have further occasion to quote the chief's speeches, since in exhorting the villagers to be good citizens, commenting on the news, or simply promoting his own interests, he offers his listeners information about himself, his fellows, and his understandings of the events of the day.

Informing the Village of Important
Events

The chief is not the only one who delivers speeches on the plaza. Any adult male responsible for the organization of collective tasks formulates his plans publicly by stepping onto the plaza and calling upon those who have an obligation to assist him. They in turn notify the other villagers when the work will be undertaken and urge them not to shirk their duty.

One evening in January 1972, when the Mehinaku had to build a new cage for a harpy eagle (*Thrasaetus harpyia*) which they, like the other Xinguanos, keep for its feathers, the man responsible for the maintenance of the cage stepped out into the center of the village and called to the owner of the bird, "My nephew, Kuyaparei, come here, I wish to speak to you." Kuyaparei, in his hammock at the time, immediately rose, walked to the central plaza, and asked, "Why have you called me, my mother's brother?"

His uncle then began to explain that they must build a new cage because the present one was too small for the bird and so flimsy that the wind might knock it down. Nominally between two people, the conversation was actually meant for the entire village, for the older man spoke in an oratorical style in which his voice rose and trailed off with each significant expression. Periodically Kuyaparei would come in with an "Ah!" or "Is that so?!" or "So be it!" Finally he responded that he had to have time to go fishing so that he could pay for the construction of the new cage.

Several days later Kuyaparei had caught enough fish, and his uncle summoned two other men to the plaza. Both agreed to join in the venture and then they simultaneously began to address the entire village:

> Tomorrow we build a new house for the eagle! Don't be lazy. Help us build a new house for the eagle. It's just a little work. Don't leave the village tomorrow to visit another tribe. Help us build the house for the eagle!

The next day the men of the village were out in force to construct the cage. Other tasks, whether economic or ceremonial, are organized on the village plaza in similar fashion. Speakers inform the community about the nature of their projects, justify them, recruit personnel, and set a working schedule.

It is apparent that the plaza is not only spatially the most exposed portion of the village, it is also the setting for a number of institutions that distribute important information. These include the smokers' circle, the chief's public speeches in which he comments on the news, and the oratory used in organizing and informing the village about collective activities. Still, these are not the only ways of distributing verbal information in Mehinaku society. In fact, much of such information is transmitted in casual conversation and gossip.

Casual Conversation and Gossip

Casual conversation and gossip transmit information to individuals rather than to the entire community and are therefore more relevant to the houses and trash yards than to the central plaza. Casual conversation (*yiyakai*) is informal talk about one's plans, current events, and the weather. Unlike a news story or a formal speech, it is not a focused narrative, and since it is nonpublic in character a passerby is not supposed to listen in on it. A good citizen may accidentally overhear casual conversation, but he will not silence his children in order to eavesdrop. Nor may he go prowling about the vicinity of houses hoping to pick up an interesting bit of conversation, as he may legitimately do in order to learn the news. Casual conversation as a means of distributing information is relatively inefficient, not only because it is private but also because its subject matter is not as interesting as a good news story. Casual conversation between villagers simply does not hold the neighbors' attention sufficiently to make it worth passing along. There is another variety of conversation, however, that the Mehinaku do find endlessly fascinating—gossip (*yiya-kãimalú*, literally "bad or worthless speech").

Gossip contrasts with ordinary conversation and news in a number of important ways. First, it is wholly nonpublic. Gossiping, it is said, occurs only when two persons are together in relatively private areas such as the house, the trails outside the village, and the trash yard. One of the derogatory terms for a gossip is *miyeipyenukanati* (literally, "trash yard mouth"). Gossip is also distinguished from other kinds of speech by the effect it has on the listener. According to the villagers, gossip is "speech that makes one sad"—since the hearer may learn things he might have preferred not to know, such as allegations that he is a witch or a thief.

Gossip not only "makes one sad," it makes one angry, because the tales are sometimes doctored to give pain to their victims. The Mehinaku call this process "adding pepper" and they have a number of derogatory epithets for those who practice it, such as "woman mouth" (*katenejukanati*), "trash yard mouth," and simply "gossiper" (*yiyakãimaluwekehe*). This last term is of particular interest since the affix *wekehe* usually marks roles of social importance. Thus, in contrast to the news reporter or casual conversationalist, there is a linguistically recognized social position for the gossip.

The gossiper is bad for those whom he "makes sad," he is bad for the community as a whole, and he is bad for himself. The man who gossips will not catch fish, he will fail as a lover, he will be rejected by his spouse and by his in-laws, and he will very likely lose his health. Or so the villagers claim. Yet despite all the sanctions against it, gossip continues to flourish—so much so that it is a source of serious tension and has more than once forced villagers who were the butt of malicious talk to leave the community.

Let us trace a choice tale as it moves through the community gossip network. Itsula, one of the younger men of the tribe, had just returned from the Indian Post with still another damning story about the tribal scapegoat, Ipyana. Itsula had heard that Ipyana had stolen a mosquito net belonging to the "chief of the white men." On discovering his loss, the "chief" (actually an air force pilot) vowed to send planes to drop bombs on the Mehinaku village.

Once Itsula had told his story, it was picked up by the groups of women who work together on the never-ending task of manioc processing. According to the men, women are the main pipeline for the transmission of gossip; hence the term "woman mouth" for a gossiper. At this juncture some of the women passed the story on to their spouses and male kinsmen, while others relayed it to relatives and friends as they chanced to run into them on the river and garden trails. Children who, like women, help keep the gossip network in good working order, were also instrumental in spreading the tale. Unlike adults, they can move freely from house to house and brought the story back home to their parents. Within a few hours there was not a single Mehinaku who had not heard the gossip, except the miserable Ipyana and his immediate family.

The Content of Gossip

The content of Mehinaku gossip tells us something about the kind of information that freely circulates in the village and suggests some of the individual motives and social functions of the gossip system. If we look at the cast of characters mentioned in the tales that move through the community, we note that although no one, except the very young children, is exempt from being mentioned, there are stars and super-stars whose names appear again and again. The most prominent of these was Ipyana, whose career came to an end in 1971 when he was killed as a witch. According to the gossip, which was largely accurate, Ipyana was an unabashed thief who stooped to steal-ing fish and processed manioc flour. Not even expensive property, such as a shell necklace or a heavy dugout canoe, was safe with him around.

Max Gluckman, in his classic article on gossip (1963), has suggested that gossip at once serves as a sanction to control misconduct and as a device to reaffirm the normative system by deriding those who violate it. The stories that circulated about Ipyana functioned in precisely that way. I often heard him cited as an example of how not to behave, and children were taunted for conduct bearing any resemblance to his.

Ipyana and others like him, however, are not the only targets of malicious tales. At one time or another almost every villager is the butt of gossip. At the present time reports are circulating that Ipyana's completely innocent ten-year-old nephew is as much a witch as his uncle ever was. Even my friend Kwaumutin, as solid a citizen as you can find anywhere, has been talked about as a witch.

How are such tales to be explained? Gluckman offers another helpful hypothesis. Gossip, he suggests, serves to mark the boundaries of factional groups within a society. The purpose of a story is not so much to say anything false or true about the characters involved as to identify friends and opponents. Hence, the villagers say that women ought to tell "little lies" about others in order to demonstrate their trust in their confidants. Gossip is thus a sign of friendship. Among men, gossip marks the boundaries of political groups. I notice that all but fifteen of the eighty-nine allegations of witchcraft that I have recorded were directed against men who belonged to residences, kin groups, and factions other than those of the gossiper himself (see table 14, chap. 12).

Some tales, however, are best explained by the personal motivations of the gossipers rather than as expressions of the boundaries of social groups and the continuity of values. The most common form of gossip, for example, deals with sexual escapades. These histories have a greater basis in fact than tales about witchcraft but, unlike witchcraft allegations, they are nonpolitical. The men speak critically about the behavior of the women during coitus and occasionally deride the size, color, and odor of their partners' genitalia. Though the amusement these stories arouse is not shared by those who are compromised by them, no one is seriously hurt. Any attempt to explain these stories must recognize that gossip is created by individuals who have a variety of motivations for their conduct. Sexual gossip seems designed to enhance or dramatize the status of the narrator. Part of appearing masculine is telling sexually oriented stories and responding to them enthusiastically.

A final explanation of gossip in the Mehinaku community is that it is a creative and even artistic activity. It flourishes because, like any good tale, it tells emotional truths even when it is factually wrong. Again we encounter the unfortunate Ipyana:

> Ipyana told the Waura that he wants to kill all of us because we have had relations with his wife. He brought a small box with him to the Waura which contained everything he needs to kill us all. In it were locks of hair from all the women, bits of Mehinaku arm bands, urine-soaked earth which he collected when no one was looking, wax balls to make mosquitoes, clay pigs to invade our garden, tiny arrows to kill us, and a ball of red paste for *kuritsi* love magic. The Waura saw all these things and they found that there was a device to kill each person here. Ipyana will live with us a while and then kill us all—unless he dies first.

Ipyana's reputed collection includes virtually everything used by witches to murder their victims. It is unlikely that any of the Mehinaku practice witchcraft, certainly not on the scale attributed to Ipyana. And if Ipyana were in fact a witch, he would not brag about it while visiting the Waura or any other tribe in the Xingu region. The story, then, must be dismissed as false. It grew from a general conviction that Ipyana was in fact a witch and a belief that he might very well have a collection of Mehinaku hair, arm bands, urine-soaked earth, and so forth. Since Ipyana was generally hated and feared, it was not difficult to attribute reciprocal hostility to him as well as possession of a witchcraft kit. The tale, then, is factually false but it is sentimentally true. The lurid embellishments of Ipyana's trip to the Waura serve to heighten the teller's and the listener's fear and malicious excitement. The more lurid the tale, the greater the enjoyment in recounting it. Gossip may be "speech that makes you sad" but it is often a sadness alloyed with other more pleasurable emotions.

Whether we interpret gossip as a sanction to control misconduct, as a device to outline group boundaries, as a presentation of self in a favorable light, or as a narrative art form, we can have no doubt about its effectiveness in the Mehinaku community. Despite the private nature of most of the tales and the relatively cumbersome person-to-person transmission, they speed about the village in only a few hours and brand their victims as thieves, witches, and adulterers.

It must be apparent that privacy is scarce among the Mehinaku. Not only does the design of the community maximize the observability and audibility of social relationships, but the villagers have also developed a number of institutions that make each man a public figure. The smokers' circle, the chief's speeches, and public oratory seem particularly designed to broadcast significant social facts to the community as rapidly as possible. There are many positive consequences of this communicational efficiency. Community activities, for example, are relatively simple to organize and coordinate.

There is, however, another side to efficient communications. A Mehinaku is never long out of the limelight. Wherever a villager goes, he may be seen or heard. When he speaks there is a chance he will be overheard, and in a short time everyone else will know what he has said. The most intimate details of his sex life may quickly become public knowledge. The pressures of living in this kind of situation can become unsupportable, for there are dangers in knowing too much. A man may be better off if he does not know that his brother-in-law has seduced his wife, accused him of witchcraft, or stolen his feather headdress. If these facts are hidden or merely suspected, they can be ignored. The gossip network and the openness of the community to communication, however, expose just this kind of information. The aggrieved villager may be tempted to sever his relationships with his kinsman by withdrawing from mutual economic obligations and by maintaining an uneasy sullenness in his presence. Broken relationships can be extremely disruptive, given the wide range of economic and social activities that bind kinsmen. Since the Mehinaku community is small, the social fabric cannot withstand the quarrels that would arise from the continual free flow of such information. Consequently, the tranquility of the village and the maintenance of vital social relationships require limitations on mutual knowledge.

Ingeniously, the Mehinaku have found methods of restricting information about themselves in spite of their highly public and exposed setting. I will next describe some of the strategies and institutions the villagers employ to conceal information, protect the boundaries of back regions, and gain a measure of privacy.

6

The Institutions and Strategies of Concealment

Follow Yuca's trail to Yanapa's path. Look down the river trail to make sure no one is in sight. Run across as fast as you can and keep your head low!

Atala, teaching the anthropologist how to enter the village unseen.

The best evidence that the Mehinaku need to limit exposure are the lengths to which they go to secure privacy. In this and the following three chapters I will describe some of the institutions and personal stratagems that limit the flow of information in the community. I shall discuss the use of falsehood, extramarital affairs, theft, and even children's games. I begin with a second look at the spatial design of the village and the houses.

The Hidden Village: Regions of Low Observability

In my description of the layout of the village and the architecture of the houses, I emphasized the highly public character of Mehinaku social life. The reader, however, should not be left with the impression that the Mehinaku live in a goldfish bowl. There are, in fact, a good many natural and man-made zones of low observability in and around the village which insulate a wide range of activities from public view.

Let us locate some of these areas by reexamining the map in figure 8. A quick glance will show that a Mehinaku can be easily seen on the main paths, in the plaza, or near the primary bathing area. In the regions around the circumference of the village, however, just beyond the "trash yards," visibility is poor because of the profusion of shrubs and trees. An intricate network of narrow paths in this area connects the houses with the main trails and with each other. There are at least twenty-two of these paths, most of which are named after their builder or the owner of the house where they originate. In addition there are numerous so-called "alligator" (yaká) paths leading to small cleared spots behind each house that are used to conduct extramarital affairs. The entire network of low-visibility walks is so interconnected that with care a Mehinaku can make a complete circuit of the village without being visible.

Some of these paths, it is true, have clearly utilitarian functions. The quickest route, for example, to the port or the bathing area is not across the plaza but along the shortcuts beginning at the back door of each house. Consider, however, the paths for which there are shorter and often better-kept alternate routes. One explanation for the existence of these trails is that each time a new house is built (every five to seven years) a new network of paths is built up while the old one is largely retained. The same process occurs when the village is moved. The hidden path leading to the alternate bathing area, for example, is a leftover from the early 1960s when the village was a hundred yards south of its present location.

Still, why have these paths been retained and not allowed to grow over? Why are others deliberately cut through the underbrush? In essence, it is because they permit the Mehinaku to move about unseen on a variety of devious and ordinary errands. Consider the most remarkable hidden trail of all, Itsa's Path (Itsa Napu—not shown on map). I have paced off Itsa's Path, which winds for over two thousand feet through thicket and forest. It was built for only one reason, to bring fish into the village unseen. This path connects the backdoor of Itsa's house with the main trail to the northern port on the Tuatuari, where he has a chain of fish traps which produce a small but regular supply of fish during the wet season when the catch is poor elsewhere. If Itsa were to enter the village along the main path with his catch, the whoops of the villagers would immediately alert his kinsmen in other houses. Unwilling to share with anyone but his own residence mates, however, Itsa built his path so that he could remain unseen.

When the trail was first cut, everyone quickly caught on to its purpose. "He is very cheap (*kakaianumapai*)," they said. Nevertheless, Itsa is not the only one who uses it today. There are a good many fishermen who have taken to sneaking along this path whenever they want to get home unseen. One of the Mehinaku, who has taken me on a tour of Itsa's path and the other hidden trails around the village, has demonstrated that it is possible for a fisherman to reach the back door of any of the village houses with little risk of being observed. There are a few harrowing moments when he must dash across one of the main paths with his fish and gear in tow, but even this risk can be minimized by carefully peering down the trail beforehand.

These examples suggest that one of the uses of the hidden paths is to conceal conduct antithetical to the self-image that the Mehinaku publicly promote. Itsa insists he is the most generous of men and as evidence thereof he will on occasion openly enter the village carrying his fish and gear for all to see. Unfortunately, his public relations ploy hardly works because everyone knows he has used the hidden paths excessively.

Were one to leave the village by way of the hidden paths, he would come upon other areas of low observability such as the infrequently used ports along the Tuatuari River and the "alligator places" (*yaká epʊge*), small clearings in the forest that are used for privacy in sexual intercourse and as a temporary refuge from fellow villagers when social pressures become intolerable.

The persistent explorer of the hidden paths will also stumble on the family gardens used by spouses during the growing season for private conversations and sexual relations. Like the closed bedroom door in the American middle-class home, the tall vegetation shields the sights and sounds of marital intimacy from general scrutiny. Elsewhere outside the village, safe from the prying eyes of their fellows, the Mehinaku like to hunt for secret herbal medicines, prepare materials for rituals, and call upon the spirits. In the forest they secrete possessions that might be stolen or that they do not care to share with others. The villagers have an amazing faculty for recovering the articles that they have hidden away in the forest. One day I watched one of my friends retrieve as if by magic his father's paddle from a patch of weeds. His father had told him roughly where the paddle lay in relation to a big log that had fallen across the trail; the exact spot was indicated merely by a few bent stalks of tall grass.

The Houses as Private Areas

Areas of low observability exist within as well as outside the village. Within the community the Mehinaku have physically and symbolically established zones of privacy by discouraging nonresidents from intruding into their homes. Houses are considered semiprivate domains informally restricted to a resident and his close kinsmen. No adult Mehinaku feels comfortable in someone else's residence unless on the occasion of a barter session or ritual. Even close friends will not casually enter each others' houses. A man who wants to speak to his friend locates the approximate spot along the outside wall of the building where he sleeps within and conducts the conversation right through the thatch wall.

It is difficult to convey the intensity of a Mehinaku's reluctance to enter another's house. Just the phrase "other households" (*kala naku*, literally, "other insides") carries unpleasant associations. A man is shamed by spending time in another's house. He hears too much gossip and inevitably becomes a conduit for it himself. Chronic visitors are potential threats to members of their own household for it is feared that as they become intimate with their neighbors they will grow apart from their residence mates.

The frequent visitor to other people's houses is called a "*kujuma*," a kind of oriole. I only came to understand how extraordinarily expressive and derogatory the term is when the Mehinaku captured several *kujuma* in the forest and brought them back to the village to keep as pets. Never caged, the *ku-*

juma flits from house to house, eats whatever it can scavenge, and indifferently defecates on peoples' heads and manioc silos alike. The arrival of a *kujuma* in our house was always the signal for the young men to shout at it, attempt to dislodge it from the rafters by hitting it with blocks of wood, or shooting at it with blunt arrows. One Mehinaku *kujuma* was recently killed this way, much to the sorrow and anger of its owner who had been hoping to pluck its feathers for his headdress. Everyone else was secretly pleased, however, since like human visitors, *kujuma* are not welcome in Mehinaku households.

The only villagers who freely move from house to house are young children. Taking advantage of their offsprings' mobility, parents use them to deliver food and messages to neighbors and to bring back information about what is going on elsewhere in the village. Boys and girls are not deliberately recruited to keep tabs on neighbors nor are they systematically pumped for information when they come home. Nevertheless children have the spotlight when they tell their parents the news and gossip about other houses. They are thus implicitly encouraged to act as informants though their parents may deny responsibility.

Around the age of nine or ten, a child discovers that his welcome in other houses is wearing thin. At the same time his mother and father begin to discourage him from getting around. He is told that he ought to feel ashamed when he enters another's house and, as an object lesson, his parents place in his hand the larva of a moth which curls up in a tight ball when disturbed. "Curl up in shame like the larva," the child is told, "whenever you think about intruding into someone else's house." Whenever necessary, the lesson is reinforced by scarifying the child with a fishtooth scraper.

The rules against intrusion do not apply during formal public events, such as trading sessions, when outsiders may freely enter houses. Still there are certain houses located in the trash yards that are almost never entered by visitors. At present (1976) there are two such houses in the village, both of them set up in the trash yard of the chief. One shelters a family that has separated itself from the chief's residence, much to his annoyance. On occasion he makes public speeches expressing his anger about kinsmen who have chosen to live apart from him, but

there is little more that he can do about it. The second outbuilding is used by the members of the family of the chief when
one of the women is having a menstrual period or when they
want to escape social pressures. In a situation where several
families live in close contact under one roof, the trash yard
buildings serve as a refuge from unwanted interaction and communication.

Areas of Low Observability
Within the Houses

Interaction and communication is limited in the Mehinaku community not only by separate residential buildings but also by
low observability within the houses themselves. Because of lack
of fenestration, almost all of a house except for the area about
the doorways remains in perpetual semidarkness. Since the
houses are long and cavernous, it is difficult to see with any
acuity what is happening on the other side of the building.

The least observable portion of the house is a narrow crawl
space between the thatch walls and the house posts. Too low to
stand up in, this alleyway is usually infested with thousands of
tropical cockroaches, inumerable spiders, and the other vermin
that make their homes alongside the Mehinaku. The wooden
bar about a foot off the ground that parallels this corridor is
accurately called the "mouse rail" in Mehinaku construction
parlance because it serves as a runway for the hundreds of mice
that infest an older dwelling. Normally used only for storage,
the crawl space is occasionally frequented by boys armed with
toy bows and arrows in pursuit of the vermin—but even children do not make a habit of spending time there. Witches,
thieves, men bent on extramarital liasons, and óthers engaged
in surreptitious pursuits, however, are said to crawl along this
corridor when they enter their neighbor's houses at night.

Other limitations on observability are symbolic as well as
physical. Restrictions connected with affinal kinship, for example, divide living space almost as effectively as ceiling-high
partitions. Bound by stringent avoidance taboos, parents and
children-in-law may not pass through a doorway together nor
casually enter each other's dwelling space, even though they
live on very close terms. Since younger people possess a large
number of classificatory parents-in-law, including their spouse's

parents' siblings and cousins, a newly married husband may be restricted in his movements about the house to the immediate area of his hammock and hearth.

In addition to the explicit taboos regulating conduct between in-laws, there are informal rules that establish a measure of privacy for residence mates. Families occupying opposite sides of the house, even when they are not affinal kinsmen, are somewhat cut off from each other. Visiting is infrequent and shouting across the house except during periods of story-telling and joking is improper. When such families interact, it is usually at the work areas and hearths in the center of the building. In contrast, families who reside on the same side of the house customarily live on close terms, are aware of each other's activities and are usually free to participate in them. During meal times, however, a family will be left undisturbed as it sits down to eat around its own fire.

The Trash Yards

As the limitations on interaction within the houses suggest, privacy is not entirely a matter of cutting off sight and sound. Areas that are both visible and audible can become settings for "back region" activities, their privacy guaranteed by convention rather than by walls and doors. The trash yards (*miyepyenu*) behind the Mehinaku houses are examples of such areas, for although usually visible from the main paths and only partially screened off from the plaza, they are nonetheless the focus of a variety of nonpublic domestic activities. Here, during the fine weather of the dry season, the women sit in small groups of friends and relatives to process manioc flour. Here too, the men carve wooden benches, help make *urucu* dye, playfully tease their children, or just sit quietly while their wives groom them for head lice and ticks. At twilight both men and women assemble in the trash yard to drink a hot sweet beverage made from manioc (tapioca), talk quietly, and take note of the position of the moon and evening stars.

The prevailing ethos of the trash yard is informality. Unlike the front yard, which is regularly swept and weeded, leavings from the manioc process and garbage from the house are all unceremoniously dumped in the bushes surrounding the trash yard area. Householders eating in the back door of their homes

Fig. 13. Come and drink *nukaiya!* In the late afternoon and early evening the women prepare *nukaiya*, a hot sweet beverage made from manioc. As the sky darkens and the air chills, the residents of a house gather around the steaming pot for a dipperful of the drink and conversation. Uleiru's informal appearance (uncombed hair, lack of an *uluri* garment or body paints) is typical of the trash yards as is the litter of baskets, bowls, and refuse under the manioc loaf drying rack.

casually flip fishbones outside with a vague hope that the village dogs will tidy up. A sour smell occasionally permeates the area, for the trash yard is also the place to urinate.

Even the most casual observer notices the differences in comportment between persons sitting in the front of the house and those in the rear, differences that define public and private demeanor in Mehinaku society. Greetings in the trash yards, for example, are informal or dispensed with entirely. Villagers from other houses may be ignored as they move about on adjacent pathways, well within range of a salutation that would have been mandatory on the public plaza. To greet a man while passing by his trash yard is slightly strange, a violation of an unspoken rule of "civil inattention"—rather as if a boor in our own society were to lean through an open window to accost an acquaintance.

Dress, like other aspects of interaction, has an informal "at home" quality. A man may be unclothed and unadorned in both the public plaza and the trash yard; but only in the plaza is his nakedness an unambiguous symbol of withdrawal and aloofness. In the trash yard, though clothing still retains many communicative functions, virtually any style of dress or undress is acceptable.

Despite the informality of trash yard conduct, not everyone is welcome to participate. The observer need only tick off the names of the select few who freely enter a trash yard and he will have a roll of those who share close relationships with the householders—kinsmen, friends, and work partners. All others must arrive through the front door announced by a formal greeting—if they are to arrive at all. The trash yard thereby enfolds those whose relationships are intimate and separates those who are socially distant. The barriers that provide the villagers with this domestic back region rely not only on obstacles to· perception but also on conventions. Like the black-pajamaed stage hands who move about the players in the course of the traditional Japanese drama, the action in the trash yard may be seen by the audience, but it is unwatched and uninterrupted.

Although I have argued that the Mehinaku community is relatively open to the flow of information, there are also limitations. The hidden paths, the isolated bathing areas and ports, the trash yards, the separate residences, and the rules against intrusion—all indicate that the villagers have ways of defending regions of low visibility. Later I shall examine still other institutions that conceal information, such as disengagement from interaction and the extraordinary practice of ceremonial isolation. For the moment, however, I would like to redirect the reader's attention to the gossip network and the system of verbal communication, for barriers to observation are not the only devices that limit the flow of information within the village. The Mehinaku have also developed a number of techniques that allow them to limit the efficiency and compromise the reliability of the network of gossip, news, and conversation.

Spies, Eavesdroppers, and Verbal Communication

One of the major limitations on the flow of information within the Mehinaku community is a set of rules that limits the way in which the villagers can learn about each other. The first of these rules is that any furtive conduct is wrong. A Mehinaku cannot creep about the village spying on his fellows without risking serious repercussions, the least of which is that he may get a reputation as a spy. As far as I know, there is no word in the Mehinaku language for "spy" or "eavesdropper," but there is a way of referring to them. Such people are celled *nitséi*, that is, a person who likes something to excess. Hence an *itsi nitséi* is someone who loves *itsi* (genitals), that is, a sex fiend. A person overly interested in the conversations of his fellows is a "conversation hound" (*yiyakái nitséi*), a "news hound" (*metaiyá nitséi*), or a "back-of-the-house lover" (*pãutsukiri nitséi*). The last phrase refers to someone who hangs around at the back of houses hoping to pick up a bit of conversation through the thatch. With the exception of "sex fiend," which is a joke, calling someone a *nitséi* is often a genuine rebuke and is taken fairly seriously.

The Mehinaku who is unabashedly furtive risks even more serious consequences than simply being called a "news hound." His conduct may gain him a reputation as a witch, for witches as everyone knows are just the kind of people who creep about unseen. Armed with tiny arrows, the witch stalks through the village in invisible guise and shoots his victims through holes in his house walls. Villagers who feel themselves especially susceptible to witchcraft keep the walls of their house in good repair and their doors carefully secured.

Perhaps the best evidence of the association of furtiveness and witchcraft is the distinction made between a witch and a sorcerer (see table 13, nos. 1, 2). Both the witch and the sorcerer kill their victims by similar magical means. The crucial difference is that the sorcerer is a witch who has decided to operate publicly. He not only announces his role to the community, but he displays his magical equipment openly. Unlike the furtive witch, the sorcerer is held in high repute and is paid large sums for his services. The danger of being mistaken for a witch is a strong sanction that discourages the Mehinaku from syping and eavesdropping upon their fellows. A man who has to rely on stealth and concealment to gather information has good reason to hesitate long before he gains a reputation as a "news hound" or a "back-of-the-house-lover."

There are other effective barriers to the circulation of information, even though they are not as dramatic as the fear of being called a witch. These are the rules that place limits on the kinds of topics the villagers can discuss and the kinds of questions they can ask.

Limiting Verbal Communication

In some cases the rules that restrict conversation are explicit, governing what may be said in particular relationships and social situations. Fathers and sons-in-law, for example, may converse only in exceptional circumstances and then only about immediate and practical problems. Conversation in the men's house must be restricted to informal and noncontroversial topics. Although joking is permissible and even required in this setting, it should be inoffensive. Witchcraft is an acceptable subject only in the abstract. It is proper to say that the Auití tribe must have many witches since they have suffered from so many epidemics. On the other hand, it is very bad form to speculate on who is responsible for the plagues of mosquitoes among the Mehinaku.

Conversation in the evening smokers' circle is governed by similar restraints and must be, above all, inoffensive.

Perhaps the most socially important limitations on speech are the restrictions on free discussion of witchcraft and sex. These restrictions tend to curb the hostilities arising from sexual jealousies and disagreements about who is and who is not a witch. Gossip about witches is usually limited to persons who trust each other; in practice, they tend to be close blood relatives of the same sex. From a man's point of view, these include his father, brothers, and sons. From a woman's perspective, they include her mother, sisters, and daughters. Husbands and wives may hesitate to confide in each other when they believe that their in-laws are witches. Since children learn about witchcraft primarily from the parent of their own sex, brothers and sisters can have slightly different ideas about who is and who is not a witch. Having a somewhat distant relationship that usually does not permit talk about witchcraft, however, siblings are able to maintain such differences without conflict.

Sex is a much more open topic than witchcraft, yet there is a strict limitation on talk about sexual relationships. No one should ever speak to a cuckold about his spouse's unfaithfulness. Not even brothers or sisters of the cuckold may divulge what they know; a conspiracy of silence keeps the truth from the injured spouse.

In addition to rules governing what may or may not be said, Mehinaku communication is restricted by a code of politeness that is best described as discretion. Just as a Mehinaku does not reveal socially damaging information about himself, neither does he expose such information about others. Personally intrusive questions are considered to be in bad taste and unless one has a good reason it is improper to inquire into a person's whereabouts, his plans for the next day, or his personal property.

Truth and Falsehood

One limitation on verbal communication is the Mehinaku's healthy skepticism about much of what they hear. This skepticism is based on hard experience. They know that much of the news and gossip that circulates through the village turns out to be untrue. Much of the misinformation comes from news picked up at the Post. The most distorted (and often the most pathetic) of these tales are the villager's efforts to understand the white man. In 1967 the Mehinaku chief, filled with anger and uncertainty, came back to the tribe after a brief stay at the Post. He explained in a public speech that the chief of Brasília and the chief of São Paulo had gone to war, and that the Mehinaku village was in danger of attack. The kernel of truth in this rumor was the report of the June War between Israel and the Arab States.

Even more frightening stories regularly sweep the village. Boatloads of white men are coming to give the Mehinaku poisoned candy. Planes are going to drop bombs on the village. One bomb, "monster fire" (*itseikumá*) will burn everyone to death; the other, "monster razor blade" (*gilletekumá*) will cut down everything in the village at a certain height—people, houses, and even trees. The first of these rumors clearly has its origin in the massacre of Brazilian Indians conducted with the complicity of the old Indian Protective Service (S.P.I.). The second and third probably came from accounts circulated at the Post of the American use of napalm and cluster bombs during the Vietnam War.

The most obvious source of confusion in all these tales is the language problem. Very few Mehinaku are fluent in other languages. Stories overheard at the Post are only partly understood, inviting the hearer to straighten out the confusion to his own satisfaction. Since white society and culture are even more of a mystery than the Portuguese language, the reports describing the white man are interpreted according to what makes sense to the Mehinaku—a war between two nation states becoming a quarrel between two chiefs and their local factions.

News about neighboring Xingu tribes and the Mehinaku themselves is less liable to this kind of distortion but errors are still often introduced in the transmission of the story. This last source of misinformation arises from the reception given to bearers of interesting news or hot gossip. Their story is always told as vividly as possible and on occasion the plot is deliberately embellished for dramatic effect. For example, Yuma, who is notorious for his wild stories, returns from the Post to report that a great plane load of white men has arrived, ready to trade guns, bullets, and flashlight batteries, and to give away sugar candy. The next morning the Mehinaku dust off their feather earrings, baskets, and ceramic pots and lug them to the Post to trade with the white men.

The villagers have been had again. Yuma's plane load of whites turns out to be two reporters sent down to the reservation to do a fast "Naughty-Children-in-the-Garden-of-Eden" photo essay for their weekly magazine. They have nothing to trade but the shirts on their backs, they are complaining about the heat and the mosquitoes, and they want to get home as fast as possible. The Mehinaku return to the village later that afternoon vowing never to believe Yuma again.

I have noted a number of sources of error in the communication of news, including misconceptions based on language and culture and errors more or less deliberately introduced by some of the villagers. All these distortions may be compounded if a news item is repeated many times before it reaches the entire community. Studies of serial transmission of information in our own society have found that 70 percent of the information in a message may be lost after only five or six successive repetitions (Allport and Postman 1947: 75). It is reasonable to assume similar losses among the Mehinaku, especially as the tale passes from tribe to tribe and person to person. Chains of transmission are often quite long; the Mehinaku may not learn of a news story until it has gone through retellings among several Xingu tribes who speak different languages. Understandably, the final report bears little relation to the original.

Although the Mehinaku are not aware of the sources of error in the transmittal of news, their principal explanation for defective communication is deliberate falsehood. News that turns out to be incorrect is usually called *mĩulikí*, a lie or intentionally false rumor. Much of the misinformation communicated in gossip, casual conversation, and even public oratory is said to have the same origin. Villagers often speak disparagingly of their fellows' mendacity and are derisively skeptical of stories that appear to conceal a damaging truth. Children are forever accusing each other of lying; the Portuguese word for liar (*mentiroso*) is one of the first the Mehinaku learn after they have picked up the terms for basic trade goods.

The Mehinaku conception of the lie (*mĩulí*) is very much like our own. A lie is a deliberate attempt to deceive. A liar (*mĩulitsí*, masculine; *mĩulityeju, feminine*) is an individual who lies chronically and maliciously. A trickster who sends a comrade on a fool's errand, however, is not a liar even though he obviously told a lie. Lies are further differentiated from mistakes. A villager who passes along a rumor that someone is a witch is culpable only of a "*mĩyulitãi*," or a little lie, since he only made a mistake and did not fabricate the tale. A person who makes a completely innocent mistake, such as misreporting the number of canoes at the port, is not guilty of any lie at all.

Under what circumstance do the Mehinaku use falsehood? According to the villagers, malice is a primary cause of mendacity. As with gossip, villagers sometimes deliberately set out to hurt each other with hateful tales. The liar "adds pain" or "pepper" to the story to make it sting. To illustrate, one of the villagers is known as a malicious liar. His tales are so effective that he is called "the one who makes it well" (*awushatuma-laitsi*), meaning that his lies are so skillful they cannot be distinguished from the truth. His principal method is to take a set of generally known facts and interpret them unfairly. On one occasion he saw a neighbor molding a wax ball, an innocent enough occupation since the Mehinaku use wax to haft arrow points. But the Mehinaku also believe that witches use wax to generate plagues of mosquitoes, and when the liar said that he saw his neighbor manufacturing mosquito larvae the tale took on a measure of credibility.

Lies like these are by far the most malicious use of falsehood in the community, but I do not think they occur as frequently as the Mehinaku claim. A far more common use of prevarication is especially significant to us because it seems to originate in the openness of the community to the flow of information. Thus certain kinds of lies are not intended to injure others but rather are defensive. Lovers, for example, must use prevarication to hide their extramarital trysts. They use other techniques as well, such as confining their liaisons to the nonpublic regions of the community, but many of the activities that accompany their relationships simply cannot be hidden from the cuckolded spouses. As I shall explain later, their best defense is to prevaricate about the meaning of their conduct.

Theft is another activity the villagers must lie about. In the open setting of the Mehinaku community, the thief must interact frequently with the villagers he victimizes. If he expects to use stolen property, the highly public character of everyday life will usually lead to his exposure and occasionally to a confrontation with his victims. On such occasions he is likely to employ mendacity to cover his tracks, denying all accusations and claiming that the loot was legitimately traded from someone conveniently outside the village.

These examples suggest that in the arena of the Mehinaku village, the free flow of information leaves the villager bereft of the barriers and distance he might wish to place between himself and others. Within this exposed setting, the lie functions as the last line of defense protecting his reputation as an upright citizen.

Static in the System

The net effect of deception and other misinformation is to introduce a large amount of noise into the Mehinaku communications system. Information concerning the activities of the villagers is frequently wrong or so seriously distorted that the core of truth is barely discernible. Misinformation generates uncertainty, and as a result the level of trust and confidence in verbal communication is low. I am not suggesting that the Mehinaku are a skeptical people, that they require demonstrable evidence before regarding a statement as true, but rather that their knowing the "truth" is not sufficient to motivate them to action. It may be rumored that a Mehinaku is about to bewitch a kinsman and run away with his wife. When word of this plan reaches the supposed victim, he may give some credence to the story. Yet, because he does not have total confidence in the gossip system, he will not be inclined to act decisively in a way he might subsequently regret. He may nurse a sullen resentment towards the alleged malefactor, but he will not sever the relationship. Only when he is confronted with indisputable evidence of misconduct, such as finding the adulterer in a hammock with his wife, is he likely to act. Until that time the unreliability of Mehinaku communications permit him to maintain a tranquil relationship, at least on the surface, with his wife and his kinsman.

In this chapter I have tried to show that there are limits to observability and communication in village life. It is true that the community is a theater in the round in which every member of the audience has a good seat, but it is also true that there is a backstage. In fact, there is a second village, a hidden village, that consists of a network of secret paths, secluded bathing areas, forests, thickets, clearings, and swamps. Within the village itself, the trash yards, the separate residences, the rules against casual intrusion, and the internal divisions within the houses provide a measure of privacy and freedom from interaction.

Verbal communication is also bounded by a number of restrictions. Certain topics are never casually discussed, certain questions are never asked, and certain subjects are avoided by in-laws and members of the opposite sex. Finally, the use of mendacity and frequent errors in the gossip and news that sweep through the village encourage skepticism about the spoken word. Even when the truth of a villager's misbehavior is revealed, there is hope that this "truth" will be dismissed as just another lie.

How effectively do these factors protect each Mehinaku's public reputation? The following chapters approach this topic by analyzing the control of information revealed in examples of everyday social conduct.

7

What Goes On Behind the Scenes: Games Children Play

You louse egg! You tiny penis! You player of children's games!

A returning fisherman, cursing a ten-year-old boy who stayed home

The previous chapters have examined the flow of information in the Mehinaku village and the system of verbal communications. I have tried to show that despite the openness of the community to the movement of people and messages, there are areas of relatively low visibility, areas suitable for backstage conduct. Except in passing, I have not given the reader a good idea of the purposes to which these regions are put. This chapter begins to remedy that deficiency with a brief study of children and their games.

Children and Their Games

If we could somehow keep all the regions of low visibility outside the village under surveillance, we would discover that it is not the adults but the children who use them most frequently. We should not assume, however, that all the children's activities in these areas are clandestine. Many are quite innocent. Close to the bathing area are trees that provide a diving platform from which the children leap into the water. On the river's edge is a bank of clay where the children sculpt alligators, jaguars, and other animals. Nearby, a field of grass provides cover for playing

Fig. 14. Playing outside the village. Boys spend most of their time in play in the areas of low visibility surrounding the community. Here Waku, accompanied by his younger brother, threads flowers onto a thin stalk to make a puffy white pennant.

"Jaguar" (*yanomaka*), a game in which one child ambushes his unsuspecting comrades. In the forest groves about the village the children divide into two groups to play a game they call "Monkey" (*pahi*): the "monkeys" climb the trees and bounce about on the branches whistling and clucking while the "hunters" throw sticks and try to knock them down. "Monkey," has only recently been eclipsed by "Tarzan," a game stimulated by a comic book that somehow found its way into the village. To the consternation of their parents, the village boys fling themselves from limb to limb in the tallest trees while shouting "Tarzan!"

Some play activities, however, are not so innocent and are kept carefully hidden from the scrutiny of adults. To understand why the children conceal a part of their world from their parents, we will examine the nature of the games they play, especially those games in which they enact the roles they will one day fill in Mehinaku society.

Games Played Alone

The closest word for "game" in Mehinaku is *mapampam*. This word also means "children's play," and includes very simple activities like doing headstands, climbing trees, or walking on stilts. During my most recent stay in the village string games were popular. Children take lengths of cord and perform various tricks with them. One favorite stunt is to loop the cord about the neck, appear to tie a knot in it, and then give both ends of the cord a sudden jerk. If the cord has been tied properly, the knot slips and the loop around the neck slides free. Like good showmen the children love to display their legerdemain before an audience, especially of adults if they can be persuaded to watch.

Older children are particularly skilled at making "cat's cradles." The abilities of the performers and the patterns they evolve far exceed anything I have seen among American children. The Mehinaku have an advantage since they use not only their hands but also their feet, toes, and teeth. Petuti, an eleven-year-old boy, with bewildering rapidity produced a series of ten designs representing fish, animals, houses, and abstract patterns (*yana*). The point of the game does not seem to be the ultimate design, which is displayed only for a moment and then released; it is rather the skill and speed with which the pattern emerges. Solitary games such as cat's cradle are faddish, enjoying a brief vogue in the village, soon to be replaced by others. Games that I have seen come and go include making and using stilts, wheeled carts, and kites. Inevitably these activities are initiated by older children who teach them to their younger siblings. After everyone has learned them, they disappear, perhaps to reappear months or years later.

Plaza Games

Towards early evening, when the heat of the day has passed and most of the little girls are freed of the tasks that have occupied them for much of the afternoon, the children gather on the plaza to play. In contrast to the largely solitary activities described above, the plaza games invariably involve at least two players and a number of onlookers. On occasion all the children of the village participate at the same time. One of the most popular games, especially among the younger children, is "Wasp" (*atapuje*). Several of the older children make a careful spiral design on the ground in replica of the pattern of a wasp's nest. One child attempts to trace the design as closely as possible with his forefinger while everyone else stands by expectantly with a handful of sand. Should the child fail to trace the line exactly as it is drawn, all shout and throw sand at him.

Other games played on the central plaza include human pyramids, wrestling, tag, and a variant of hide-and-seek, none of them very different from the versions our own children play. The anthropologist-theorist of games, John M. Roberts, has argued that games like these are a kind of model in which we can make out important aspects of the psychological and social organization of adult life (1959). Roberts' observation seems to be true of the relation between the Mehinaku children's games and the role system of the society. Both, for example, are simple. In Mehinaku games there are never more than two kinds of players. A sport like baseball with its nine different positions is far more elaborate than any game played by the village children.

Again, Mehinaku games, like Mehinaku social life, involve minimal stratification. There are no powerful leaders, although some of the children exercise informal authority in initiating and organizing activities. Further, Mehinaku games, like Mehinaku society, are noncompetitive. Although ability is important, the games do not clearly identify a "winner" who can then boast of triumph. A child demonstrates his skill rather than besting an opponent.

These conclusions about Mehinaku games are for the most part negative ones, in that a missing feature in the game correlates with the absence of the same characteristic in the organization of social life. There is another set of games, however, that more positively reflect Mehinaku society. What arouses our interest at once is that these games, which I have called games of role playing, are invariably played well out of public view in the hidden regions about the village.

Games of Role Playing

What is to me the most stirring of the games of role playing is "Women's Sons" (*teneju ɪtãi*). Held a good distance from the village where the children cannot be seen either by their parents or their other siblings, "Women's Sons," quite unlike most plaza games, is played by boys and girls together. The age of the players runs from about five to twelve years.

The game begins as the children pair off as married couples. The husband and wife sculpt a child from a clump of earth, carving arms, legs, features, and even genitals. They cradle the baby in their arms and talk to it. The mother holds the child on her hip and dances with it as she has seen her own mother do with younger siblings. After the parents have played with their child for a while, it sickens and dies. The parents weep and dig a grave for the infant and bury it. All the mothers then form a circle on their knees in traditional fashion and, with their heads down and their arms over each other's shoulders, they keen and wail for the lost offspring.

On the occasions that I have seen *teneju ɪtãi* played, the children were enormously amused by the entire enactment. When the time came to bury the "babies," the boys smashed them into pieces and the girls interrupted their ritual crying with bursts of giggling and shrieks of laughter. Nevertheless, "Women's Sons" provides a tragic commentary on Mehinaku life—death in infancy and early childhood is all too common in the village. The game helps the children prepare for the time when they may lose a sibling and, later on, an offspring of their own. It also teaches them how to express and cope with grief through the medium of ritual crying. A poignant amalgam of tragedy and burlesque, *teneju ɪtãi* will help the young villagers to face the bitter fact of death in future years.

A second game called "Marriage" (*kanupai*) is played, like the other games that enact adult roles, in the areas of low visibility outside the village. The marriage game begins as a child's version of the wedding ritual. An uncle takes his nephew's hammock and ties it a few feet over the hammock of the bride-to-be. All the children participating in the game pretend to be married in this way, although without scrupulous attention to the rules of incest avoidance and preferential cross-cousin marriage. The husbands then go hunting and fishing, returning from their trip with leaves that are said to be fish and monkey. The wives cook the "food" and distribute it to their men. The game now has several variations. In one, the husbands and wives pair off and go to hidden areas around the village to engage in casual sex play or, if they are capable, actual intercourse. The Mehinaku are sexually free, and most children have had some degree of experience by the time they are adolescent.

In another variation of the marriage game, called "Jealousy" (*ukítsapi*), the boys and girls take lovers while their spouses are away. When the cuckolded partner returns from a fishing trip, he discovers his wife and his friend together in the same hammock. In a fury he pretends to beat his wife while his friend runs off.

There is a game of tribal politics, "Chief" (*amunão*), which requires the participation of a large group of children. The players divide into two tribes representing the Mehinaku and one of their neighbors. Each tribe builds its own village and in each the chief comes forward on the plaza and delivers a public lecture to his people. The neighboring tribe visits the Mehinaku village for a formal intertribal barter session and, as in real life, the chiefs of the villages exchange gifts and the men wrestle.

The children then trade their clothes and other personal possessions, to their parents' subsequent annoyance and chagrin.

Finally, there is the role-playing game called "Shaman"
(*yetama*). One of the children pretends to fall ill and his kinsmen go off to solicit the services of the most powerful shaman
in the village. At the same time lesser shamans seat themselves
about the patient and smoke make-believe cigars made of twigs.
On occasion they suck the patient's body in order to remove
the sickness. When the powerful shaman (*yakapa*) arrives, he
smokes, falls over in a faint, and then rises and races about the
outskirts of the village as though he were a real shaman searching for evidence of witchcraft. After a short time he returns with
a bit of string and wood which he claims was made by a witch
to make the patient ill. In one ghoulish version of this game, one
of the children plays the witch and is executed by his comrades.

There are also games in which the children pretend they are
undergoing seclusion, a lengthy period of isolation believed necessary to the growth of adolescent boys and girls. There is even
a game in which a girl violates the privacy of the men's house
and the little boys in retaliation pretend to gang rape her. Virtually every vital adult activity seems to have its mirror image
in a game played by Mehinaku children.

Games As Life

Mehinaku children's games not only replicate adult society but
they do so with surprising accuracy and insight. No doubt there
is occasional misunderstanding, especially when the children
attempt to act out some of the more complex ceremonial roles.
On the whole, however, their portrayal of their parents' activities is surprisingly true-to-life, far beyond the level of American
children playing "Cops and Robbers," "Doctor and Nurse," or
"School." The accuracy of the role playing is most vivid in
games involving kinship relations such as "Marriage," in which
the children not only imitate their parents but their parents'
mistresses and lovers as well. The children are aware not only
of the public world of the village but also of the private world
their parents attempt to conceal from each other. In the shaman
game, for example, it is apparent that the players have caught
on to the surreptitious techniques used by shamans to plant or

manufacture evidence of witchcraft. In all cases the roles the children portray are acted with attention to detail and considerable understanding of the operation of the adult community.

This high level of comprehension has its origin, I believe, in the openness of Mehinaku social life. In our own society children have only a very partial view of social institutions and of their parents' nondomestic activities. Only a few of them, for example, will have regularly accompanied their mother or father to work. In the public world of the Mehinaku, however, very little can be kept from small children. They not only follow their parents through the day's activities but, because of their special status as youngsters, they have free access to regions forbidden to their parents, such as the residences of others.

The true-to-life nature of the games brings us to the question of why games of role playing are performed in secret regions, safe from the view of adults. According to the children themselves, the games are not played in the center of the village because everyone would be ashamed. But they have never been able to explain to me just why everyone would be ashamed.

I am convinced that these games are hidden in back regions because they are more than games. Although they may be called *mapampam*, like the games played on the plaza, they are far more elaborate, organized, and serious. Games like "Women's Sons" or "Marriage" are not so much games as dress rehearsals for roles the children will some day play in Mehinaku society. The children would be ashamed if their parents came upon them in the midst of a performance precisely because they would not be playing games but rather experimenting with future social roles. They would be embarrassed because they were assuming statuses to which they did not yet have a legitimate claim. Once they were observed by their parents, the world they had constructed with so much imagination and feeling would dissolve, leaving them not with an experiment in shaping identity but only a childish game of "Let's Pretend."

In fact, the children's play is seldom intruded upon, since adults have a stake in respecting their privacy. For parents as well as for children, a vague sense of shame attaches to the games— adults not only made poor informants about their own play in childhood but they barely concealed their irritation at my interest. I believe that in children's games, parents may see an all-too-accurate exposure of the very aspects of Mehinaku society they have been careful to hide. The spectacle of seeing themselves and their secrets through the indiscreet eyes of their offspring would be painful. Like most of us, the Mehinaku are content to keep certain sectors of their lives not only out of public view but out of their own immediate awareness as well.

Children sometimes frequent the hidden regions beyond the village for reasons other than games of role playing. There boys and girls occasionally hide small items they have pilfered from their friends and residence mates. There, too, boys and girls engage in clandestine sex play and some prepubescent girls enter into casual lesbian relationships. Since the participants in these experimental affairs are mercilessly teased if they are exposed, village children must become acquainted at an early age with the arts of concealment they will employ in adult life.

In the next two chapters I shall describe how the adults in Mehinaku society manage to conceal theft and extramarital affairs despite the highly public setting of their community.

8

Theft and How to Get Away with It

He takes it because he wants it.
Shumõi, explaining why a thief steals

Theft among the Mehinaku is an old tradi-
tradition. It is tempting to interpret it as a
recent response to the influx of Brazilian
trade goods, but in fact it is a native pattern.
According to the villagers there have always
been thieves. Stealing is described in myth,
and the very first recorded foreign visitor
to a Mehinaku community, Karl Von den
Steinen, the German explorer, was himself
a victim of theft. He recounts that in 1887
he visited a Mehinaku village only to be relieved of a surgical scissors, a small hunting
horn, a box of candy mints, a compass, and
a number of other small items. Angered over
his loss and genuinely concerned about the
compass, he decided to cow the savages into
returning his property: ". . . these people
had shown themselves to be so greedy and
demanding that I saw it to be indispensable
to teach them a lesson to maintain authority . . ." After loudly demanding his possessions and grimly refusing to accept concilia-
tory offers of food, the items were gradually
returned, but: "Unhappily the most important thing, the compass, did not appear. For
this I went directly to the house of the fat

old chief . . . I took him by the hand and brought him to the flute house . . . [and] startled him by firing my revolver into the central post. A great panic occurred among those who were outside who disorganizedly raced back and forth. . . ." Gunboat diplomacy, however, failed to get the compass back—and no wonder, for the following day Von den Steinen sheepishly admits, ". . . the compass could not have been robbed since I hadn't brought it with me" (1940: 136–137, my translation).

Theft and the Economic System

The Mehinaku "economic man" is a surprisingly acquisitive sort of individual. He evinces a lively interest in his fellows' economic standing and does his best to accumulate property by means of formal barter, collecting fees for healing and ceremonial services, and the everlasting exchange of valuable shell belts, necklaces, ceramic pots, and feather headdresses.

Despite the Mehinaku's acquisitiveness and materialistic attitude toward possessions, the economy is egalitarian. Houses are economic units in which the resident families share food and work. Differences in wealth are minimal and ownership of treasured goods constantly shifts back and forth. People who accumulate a lot of property fear becoming a target of witchcraft and invidious gossip. They are also discouraged from producing a large store of treasured items such as ceramic pots, canoes, headdresses, and gardens by taboos against their manufacture during certain adult years. In addition, a number of leveling mechanisms set limits on what anyone is able to accumulate. These devices, some of which can wipe out a man's possessions overnight, include the destruction of personal property at the time of death, bankrupting payments to the village shaman or *yakapa* for medical services, and, to a lesser extent, theft.

The openness of Mehinaku social life and the simplicity of their technology serve to encourage theft. Other than a few proud owners of cardboard suitcases, no one has a box that can be securely closed, much less locked. The bulk of a man's possessions are therefore on display and vulnerable during much of the day. His best strategy is to keep his valuables hidden in the woods or suspended from the rafters of his house. Yet such strategies can be self-defeating, for property such as a feather headdress or a shell belt has value only to the extent that it is openly displayed. It would make little sense to conceal such possessions so effectively that they would be out of public view as well as the reach of thieves. Chiefs, shamans, and others who accumulate and make a conspicuous display of their possessions also allow thieves to keep track of the ownership and whereabouts of valuable property.

The rich are not the only victims of theft. All the Mehinaku can list numerous possessions that have been stolen and several of their fellow tribesmen who they think are particularly culpable. Putting these allegations together, it appears that theft is not confined to "pros" who specialize in stealing the treasures of shamans, chiefs, and other accumulators of wealth. There are probably few Mehinaku who have not from time to time filched small items, even though they might hesitate to steal precious articles such as shell belts.

The villagers are fully aware that it is unsafe to leave personal effects unwatched for more than a few moments and generally try to keep a trustworthy residence mate in the house at all times. Whenever an entire household must be away from home for any length of time, the door is carefully tied and the most valuable possessions are hidden away in the forest.

The limitation of crop diversification offers interesting additional evidence of the extent of theft among the Mehinaku. No one steals manioc because it is so abundant. Bananas, watermelons, mangoes, and those vegetables introduced by the white man, however, are stolen so regularly that the gardener often must harvest them unripe if he is to have any kind of yield. Some of the Mehinaku refrain from planting such crops altogether because theft has made their efforts worthless.

The prevalence of theft among the villagers requires explanation. After all, the community is very much like other face-to-face folk communities where theft rarely occurs. Some background on the Mehinaku interest in possessions and the nature of the property concept will help explain the motives of the village thieves and the reactions of their victims.

Table 3   Difference Between Possessed and Unpóssessed
Forms of Mehinaku Nouns

1. *uléi* (garden), *nupeteje* (my garden)
2. *epí* (ax), *niyawa* (my ax)
3. *pãi* (house), *nupune* (my house)
4. *itséi* (fire, firewood), *nimya* (my fire or firewood)
5. *kupate* (fish), *numapiya* (my fish)
6. *papá* (father), *ınıja* (his father)
7. *mamá* (mother), *ınınu* (his mother)
8. *ite* (genitals), *pitsi* (your genitals)

The Language of Possession
and Ownership

A striking characteristic of Mehinaku grammar is the possessive
form of nouns. When possessed, nouns may change so much
that the learner of the language cannot immediately recognize
them. Richards's work (1973: 12) on a closely related Arawakan language (Waura) shows that this pattern is partly understandable as morphophonemic variation. For some nouns, the
difference between the two forms is so great that Richards
regards the possessive and unpossessive forms as two different
nouns (see table 3). It is my impression that words such as
these, including kin terms and words for body parts and other
basic objects, have a very close association with the individual.
In mentioning these words and, indeed, almost all other nouns,
a villager is obliged to call attention to whether the object
being talked about is possessed. The Mehinaku interest in ownership is thus built right into the structure of their language.

Things That Are Owned

Every man-made object in the vicinity of the Mehinaku village
is associated with an owner (*wekehe*). The rights that the owner
has over his property depend on the nature of his possession,
for some "owned" things are not strictly economic in character.
Hence, the owner of a road or house can neither trade nor sell
his possession, charge tolls or rents, or even restrict their use.
Movable objects, so-called *apapalai* (possessions, "things that
have a price"), however, come closer to our own concept of

property. Possessions are divisible into three classes—valuables (*apapaliyaja*, literally, true possessions), ordinary possessions (*apapalai* or *apapalaihete*, literally, mere possessions) and possessions of little worth (*apapalaimalú*, literally, worthless possessions). Valuables include four kinds of shell or jaguar claw necklaces and belts, feather headdresses, large ceramic pots, hardwood bows, and Brazilian manufactured radios and rifles. The reason that these things are valuable, emphasize the Mehinaku, is that they are not only desirable but also few in number. As in our own society scarcity is a measure of value.

Ordinary possessions, in contrast to valuables, are in good supply and easy to make. They include baskets, spun cotton, small ceramic pots, and wooden benches. Possessions of little worth include small amounts of wax, salt, *urucu* pigment, or anything else that the villagers happen to have stored away in large quantities.

Each of the three classes of possessions is exchanged in somewhat different ways. Valuables, for example, are given to shamans and others who perform important ceremonial services, and they are traded at formal barter sessions (*uluki*) for other valuables. In all cases the valuables are closely associated with their owner. He wears them (necklaces, belts, headdresses), regularly works with them (large ceramic pots), or carries them as symbols of authority during rituals (bows, guns); only the recently introduced transistor radio breaks this pattern. Stealing valuables is understandably the Mehinaku equivalent of grand larceny and does not occur often.

Ordinary possessions and possessions of little worth are less closely identified with their owners than are valuables. Although they too are frequently exchanged in barter sessions, they are more commonly transferred less formally. Someone who needs beeswax, for example, may simply "request" (*aiyátapai*) it. The owner may ask for "payment" (*epetei*) of roughly the same value as the request, but in the case of possessions of little worth, he is under pressure to give them away freely. A man who fails to do so will be asked sarcastically, "You can't give up this *valuable*?" A donor calls his gift his *epäitye* (the same term is applied to food reciprocally exchanged among networks of kin) and keeps only a rough calculation of where he stands with respect to his fellows. By giving in this fashion, he at once confirms his identity as a generous individual, cements a friendly relationship with the receiver of the gift, and establishes a future claim over that individual's possessions.

A villager has a right to expect that some payment of roughly equal value will be made for most of his ordinary possessions. Two characteristics of the trade, however, make it different from the sort of commercial transaction familiar to us. One of these is that the seller is under strong pressure to agree to the trade. One of the specific hallmarks of the generous man is that he agrees to barter when he is asked. Only valuables are properly held back, although even here a cautious man may think twice before refusing. He does not want to seem ungenerous and fears the jealous witchcraft of the man he turns down.

The second characteristic that makes Mehinaku trade different from a commercial relationship is that the seller retains an interest in his possession even after he has given up its use. A villager who is given or informally trades a pot, for example, can not barter it to someone else the next day. If he does so, the original owner will be angry: "Why did you demand it from me if you did not want it yourself?" he will ask.

Given the Mehinaku property concept, we are in a better position to understand what makes theft irritating to the victim and attractive to the thief. Curiously, the value of the stolen goods is the least important part of the equation to the victim. Ordinary possessions and possessions of little value are easily manufactured and replaced. Indeed, they are often available for the asking. The victim is robbed not so much of a possession but of the benefits of a proper transaction—the public confirmation of his generosity and the right to make similar claims in the future. Since the thief in the small Mehinaku community is likely to be an everyday companion, the victim therefore feels cheated, frustrated, and personally aggrieved.

The thief, for his part, gains what his victim loses—the use of a possession without shouldering any future obligations and perhaps the malicious pleasure of his victim's discomfort. The actual value of the item stolen may be especially important to the thief since the most notorious of the Mehinaku pilferers seem to be rather marginal individuals who are to a degree outside the network of reciprocity. For them, if not for their victims, the theft may be economically significant.

What To Do When Robbed

The small size of the Mehinaku community helps to explain the course of events after a robbery. Such are the overlapping relationships binding a thief and his victim that resentment can not be openly expressed. On too many occasions, for example, my friend Kuyaparei was relieved of his possessions. Beads, arrows, fishing gear, and bullets disappeared from his storage shelf with depressing regularity. Inevitably, the finger of blame pointed directly at that skilled thief, the resourceful Ipyana, but Kuyaparei never did anything but nurse a bitter resentment: "He is my brother-in-law; he is my sister's husband. He is very stupid to do this to me, but you see, I never mention his name, I respect (amunapatapu) him. We go fishing together. I would be ashamed to confront him and end all that."

Kuyaparei's dilemma was not untypical. The community is so small that in many cases of theft the victim will share relationships with the thief that would be seriously compromised by an expression of outward hostility. Detection, then, is not only a problem for the thief. In the setting of the Mehinaku community it is also a problem for the victim. Let us now examine the strategies available to the villager who has been robbed and see how both thief and victim handle the problem of detection.

The victim's simplest strategy is to confront the thief and demand the return of the stolen property. Let us say that our victim is unconcerned about his ties of kinship with the thief and does precisely that. He walks up to the thief, tells him he knows that he did it, and demands the return of his property. The thief cannot return the property under these circumstances, however, for to do so would be to admit that he is a thief. He responds therefore by prevarication, denies that he is responsible, and perhaps throws up a smoke screen by accusing another man.

A confrontation, then, not only does not achieve the desired result; it may also lead to a far more serious situation than the original offense. Among the Mehinaku a confrontation over theft or any other delict arouses acute embarrassment and may be considered a more serious violation of social ethics than the act that provoked it. Anyone who risks a showdown, especially a public one, runs the danger of being labeled an angry, sullen person. And in a small face-to-face community like the Mehinaku village, one's good name is worth far more than any piece of stolen property. This same logic does not restrain the thief because, unlike a man who risks a confrontation, he expects his activities to remain concealed.

A wiser strategy open to our victim is to enlist the good offices of an intermediary. The ideal go-between is a mutual relative who stands in a "strong" position in the kinship system, such as the thief's wife's brother, although an older blood kinsman can also be effective. If the intermediary is sufficiently ashamed of his kinsman's behavior, he will try to persuade him to give up the stolen item. Most intermediaries, however, take little pleasure in their job and by the time they get around to it the thief has probably disposed of the spoils.

Still another course of action is to steal back something of equivalent value. Given the nature of the system, I am surprised that this strategy is not used more frequently. But though some Mehinaku may not hesitate to pilfer small items, they believe that it is wrong to take anything of real value. Furthermore, stealing under these circumstances is risky and few men wish to take a chance of being themselves exposed as thieves.

The strategy most frequently employed by a victim is retaliation. One villager who was robbed of a number of fishhooks announced that he was going to have sexual relations with the wife of the thief just as frequently as he could. A more sophisticated type of revenge is to denounce the thief in a public speech, while only hinting at his name.

In May 1972, I tape-recorded the Mehinaku chief making such a speech after a machete belonging to a Kuikuru visitor had disappeared from a canoe anchored at the Mehinaku port:

Tell him, our guest, who did it! The Kuikuru chief has
sent him to me. He has no second machete. I don't know who
took it but several of you went fishing (he names the villagers
who went fishing and therefore were at the port) . . . Tell
who took the machete! . . . This old man does not wrestle;
all he does is make his garden with his machete. He isn't a
witch. He doesn't take our armbands and belts to tie up
like a witch.

You are all thieves; you hide your machetes in the gardens
because you fear each other. One of you has hidden this
man's machete in a garden. Return the machete!

Public oratory raised the incident from one of individual
concern to a problem for the entire community. The chief did
not single out the thief but hinted at his identity by naming
those who were at the port at the time the theft took place. At
this point the village gossips took over and began to bandy
about the names of those who might be guilty. Despite the
chief's emotional speech and the attendant gossip, however, the
thief failed to come forward and return the machete, and "this
old man who does not wrestle" had to return home empty-
handed.

Neither confrontation, the services of intermediaries, public
oratory, nor gossip are wholly satisfactory to the victim, because no matter what strategy he employs he usually does not
secure the restitution of his property. Fully aware that his efforts
are to be unavailing, he often announces that he is not really
interested in the return of his goods: "Let the thief keep them
if he wants to." At the same time, he makes it very clear how
he feels about the scoundrel, still making sure not to mention
him by name publicly. The robbery remains unsolved, the property is never returned, the thief goes scot free, and the victim
stews in his own bitterness and anger. And yet something positive has emerged. Because the thief has not been denounced
by name, the social and economic bonds that unite him and the
victim have not been severed. The Mehinaku community could
not long endure gashes and wounds caused by frequent public
denunciation.

How To Steal and Not Get Caught

When we consider the open setting of the Mehinaku community and the intimate knowledge the villagers have of each other's movements, it may seem that thieves face almost insuperable problems in concealing their clandestine activities. The "thieves' notebook" that follows describes the problems thieves face and the often ingenious methods they use to overcome them. The reader should be cautioned that these methods were not learned from a self-admitted thief, since no one in the Mehinaku community normally makes such confessions. Nevertheless, virtually everyone seems to have a good idea of how thieves operate.

Let us consider a case involving Ipyana, until the day of his death the most notorious of village thieves. One day Yuma discovered that Ipyana was loitering in his house near the place where Yuma stored his fishline and hooks. Subsequently Ipyana announced that he was going on a trip to the Auití, the Mehaniku's neighbors to the south. Before his departure with hammock in hand, he was again seen near the spot where Yuma kept his fishing equipment. Soon afterward Yuma discovered that his equipment was missing. The next day an Auití arrived and reported that Ipyana had offered hooks and line for trade when he came to visit.

Ipyana had carefully prepared for this theft. He had apparently cased the premises for several days before the heist and then had secreted the stolen goods in his hammock, the last a rather inventive idea. Nevertheless he gave himself away and everyone knew that he was guilty. His mistake was in allowing himself to be seen in Yuma's house, for no Mehinaku has the right, except on certain trading and ceremonial occasions, to enter another's house without a legitimate excuse. To be successful a robber must be prepared to offset the high level of observability and the efficiency of communications within the community.

One way to avoid being observed is to enter a house at a time when no one is likely to be at home, say, at about seven in the morning. At that hour both the women and children are cultivating manioc in their gardens. The men are likely to be out of the village, fishing, hunting, or just wandering through the forest. The children who are not with their parents are scattered about the village or playing in the river.

Even at such a time a thief runs serious risks. It is very difficult for him to enter a house without being observed from the plaza or trash yards. Nor can he be certain that a house is in fact vacant without actually going inside and looking around. A house may look empty and yet a resident may be present, wrapped unseen in his hammock. Children may be playing quietly in the building's dark corners, ready to report the intruder's activities to their parents. In addition, the fresh footprints of the culprit on the dirt floor can give his identity away. Although children may occasionally have the termerity to pilfer a small item, an adult thief will think twice before he robs a house during the day.

The very best time is at night. By ten o'clock virtually all the Mehinaku are asleep and, unless there is a full moon, it is almost impossible to tell who is walking across the plaza. Silently the thief gets up from his hammock and slips out the back door of his house. Should he be seen it will be assumed that he going to urinate or is on his way to sexual liaison. He takes a back trail and circles the village until he comes to the trash yard of the house he is going to rob. Carefully he eases open the door and steps inside. The house is virtually pitch black. The fires have died down to embers and it will be some time before anyone wakes up to blow on the coals and add more fuel.

Having surveyed the house sometime before, the thief knows just where to find what he is after. To avoid detection he slithers along the crawl space between the house poles and the walls. Any noise he makes will sound like the scurrying of the hundreds of mice and the chattering of all the insects that share the house with its human inhabitants. Ipyana, the most notorious of all Mehinaku thieves, was popularly known as "the mouse" (*makute*) because of the sound of his movements while on nocturnal raids through the houses.

The crucial stage of the robbery comes at the moment the thief reaches the basket he is after. Although sometimes stored on shelves that are easily reached from the crawl space, baskets holding valuable possessions are often suspended from the rafters by long cords to keep them safe from mice, children, and all but the most adroit thieves. Tampering with the contents could awaken the owner, but some thieves are so skillful that they are rarely surprised in the act. My wife and I were robbed on several occasions at night by a thief who had previously stolen the key to our trunk. In the course of a number of visits he managed to make off with our most valuable trade goods without ever awakening us. If he had been surprised, he would have run away and the cover of darkness might still have allowed him to escape detection.

Thefts such as these occurred relatively frequently when Ipyana, "the mouse," was alive. So dextrous was he that he was able to relieve the villagers of their most cherished possessions while they were sleeping. Given the hazards of navigating in the darkness undetected, everyone was at a loss to explain his success. Some of the villagers hypothesized that he crept about as we have described, and some believe that he used a blanket to carry off the loot and muffle the sounds he made while collecting people's possessions. Others claim he utilized an ingenious method of stealing from the houses, occasionally used by village thieves. This technique takes advantage of the permeability of the walls of the houses. A small dog can usually find a number of places where it can force its way in and out of the house by pushing aside the thatch. An old house in bad repair has many such areas. Ipyana, it was said, would locate the position of the item he wanted to steal and late at night force his way through the wall to withdraw the loot through the hole. Whatever techniques Ipyana employed, there are villagers who seriously insist that he must have been assisted by supernatural help such as the scalp of a magically slain female demon, and a special shirt that rendered him invisible and undetectable.

Although stealing within the houses is the most dramatic form of theft, it would be wrong to assume that most of the Mehinaku are second-story men. Only Ipyana practiced this form of burglary regularly; today just a few others do it on occasion. My impression is that these other thieves are not as professional nor as courageous as Ipyana. Normally they limit themselves to filching small items in other people's houses when the owner's attention is momentarily diverted, as in the case of Ipyana's theft of Yuma's fishhooks.

Theft Outside the Village

Most Mehinaku theft takes place outside the village in locations where visibility is low and the chances of getting caught are slim. Here the most annoying (and perhaps the most common) form of theft is the removal of fish from the lines of traps set up in the maze of streams around the village. These traps are the property of families and individuals who have expended a great deal of effort damming the streams and keeping the weirs in repair and clear of debris. Some of the traps are near a main canoe route, conveniently located for unscrupulous villagers looking for a quick lunch on their way to the Indian Post. It is a simple matter for them to empty a trap and grill the fish on high ground nearby. If they steal moderately the owner of the trap may never realize that he is being victimized, since he has no way of predicting just how much a particular trap will yield. Nevertheless, when the traps produce less than he expects and he can see no obvious reason for it, he is likely to believe that he is being robbed. Often members of other tribes are said to be culpable, but occasionally the finger of blame points at certain villagers. The evidence, however, is generally flimsy; the alleged pilferers were seen in the vicinity of the traps, or they had previously been suspected in similar robberies. There is little the trap owner can do except to retaliate through malicious gossip.

Stealing a canoe is grand larceny from the Mehinaku point of view and no one but Ipyana ever dared do it. Paddles, however, are quite another matter and the villagers take pains to hide them in the bushes around the port area, well away from possible thieves. Garden produce is also frequently taken, since there is little chance of being caught unless surprised in the act. As in other cases of misconduct, however, the Mehinaku do their best to avoid confrontations. Consider Kupatekuma's chagrin when he watched an older kinsman trespass in his garden:

> I was behind a tree and he did not see me. He picked a
> nearly ripe watermelon, slashed it open with his machete, and
> thirstily sucked it dry. He spat out the pits and the juice ran

down his mouth. I was too ashamed (embarrassed) to stop him.

Disposing of the Merchandise

Once a thief has taken possession of another man's property, his difficulties are not over, for somehow he must dispose of the goods. His problem is compounded by the open setting of the community and the ease with which many personal possessions can be identified with their owners. Even manufactured items obtained from the white man are often one of a kind in the village and known to belong to a particular individual. The thief's best adaptation to this situation is to take produce that can be quickly consumed, such as fish, fruit, and processed manioc flour. A more adventurous strategy is to take the stolen articles to a neighboring village where they can be traded with members of another tribe. Ipyana was famous for precisely this kind of maneuver, trading shell belts, headdresses, and on one still memorable occasion, that canoe, with neighboring Xingu villagers.

Another method for disposing of stolen goods is to hide them in the woods for a few weeks and then trade them to fellow villagers. Some trade goods of relatively low value—small pocket knives, ceramic pots, old shirts—move through the maze of the Mehinaku barter system so quickly that tracing them back to the original owner would be very difficult. If the stolen item is given to a mistress in return for her favors, the thief can usually count on her discretion to keep the owner from discovering what happened to his property. Even if the victim of the theft finds his property in the hands of one of his fellow villagers, it will be difficult for him to reassert his right of ownership. Although the Mehinaku believe it is wrong to steal, they have few scruples about accepting stolen merchandise. An owner's right to his property diminishes after it has been stolen and appears to evaporate altogether once it has been traded.

Despite the openness of the community to observation, we see that theft can be successfully managed in the Mehinaku village. By making use of a number of ingenious ploys and taking full advantage of the minimal concealment at his disposal, the thief is able to remove his neighbor's property and dispose of it undetected. When all else fails he can boldly assert his complete innocence: "Oh no, that's not yours; I got that from a Kamaiyurá . . . I traded it at the Indian Post." The public nature of Mehinaku social life may put difficulties in the way of a resourceful thief but it cannot write an end to his activities.

In the following chapter I shall describe an everyday activity that is potentially even more socially explosive than theft—extramarital sex.

Good fish gets dull, but sex is always fun.
Shumȭɪ

The greatest pleasure, according to my Mehinaku male companions, is sexual relations.
The men often discuss the opportunities for
pleasure in sexual relations, using such terms
as "delicious" and "succulent" (*awirintya-
pai*), to describe their sensations. Women
are evaluated as good or bad sexual partners
according to their physical attractiveness,
their activity during intercourse, the character of their genitals, and their general
sexuality.

Standards of feminine attractiveness do
not entirely correspond to our own. The
ideal female is a youthful woman with long
sleek hair and heavy yet firm thighs and
calves. She has large breasts, big nipples,
small close-set eyes, sparse body hair, and
tweezed eye lashes. In an effort to achieve
this ideal, adolescent girls make use of scarification and cosmetic drugs.

A man's pleasure in intercourse is enhanced if the woman is active and enjoys
herself. Only a few of the women, however,
move about in such a way as to maximize
the man's sexual pleasure. In the picturesque
vernacular of the younger men, the word for

such sexual movement is *ulutapai*. This verb normally is used to mean "scraping the skin off manioc tubers." In a sexual context, however, the word is a vivid and unmistakable metaphor to describe a woman's sexual proficiency.

A woman is especially desirable if her genitals are attractive. In practice this means that they are not overlarge, they are light in color, and they have no offensive odor. In addition, they must feel good or be *weiyupei*, a term which best translates in this context as "voluptuous itching."

The final criterion of the sexually attractive woman is less easily identified. It is my impression, however, that Mehinaku men are attracted to a woman who has a certain sauciness in her speech and carriage. The two most popular mistresses in the village, for example, are decidedly more forward, more inclined to joke, and far less docile than their sisters. A cognate of "*weiyupei*," *weiyeju* (sexy woman) is admiringly applied to a girl who meets the tests of appearance and conduct.

What constitutes masculine sexual attractiveness from the woman's point of view? Unfortunately my data are weak on this point, because the women are less outspoken about sex than the men and less overtly enthusiastic about sexual pleasure. This attitude may derive from the association of sexuality with procreation, which is known to be painful and dangerous. In 1967, one woman told me that the pain of her first childbirth was so great she would never have sexual relations again (a decision she must have reconsidered before she had a second child in 1971).

I do not mean to suggest that the women have no interest in the physical aspects of sex. Not only is there a word for appealing men (*weiyuteri*), but the women are openly critical of men who achieve orgasm too quickly or who are impotent. Nevertheless, the main focus of the women's interest in sexual affairs seems to be in the social or remunerative aspects of the relationship. Judging by the success of some of the physically least desirable men in the village, it appears that most of the women are willing to engage in casual acts of intercourse if they are offered payment in the form of fish, beads, or soap. This pattern is not prostitution as we know it, for a sexual act simply is not invested with the same emotional and social significance as in either our own or Brazilian society. Nevertheless, the willingness of some of the women to enter into this kind of transaction suggests that their interest in sex is different from that of the men.

Mehinaku men are very much aware of the women's feelings about sex. They say that only women are *kanatalalu*, persons who do not like sex. Women who do not care for sex are a threat to the men, putting into question their sexual attractiveness as well as the legitimacy of their sexual demands. One young man reports that he became angry with women who refused his overtures. On one occasion he threw such a woman to the ground, calling her *tenejumalú*, or "worthless woman." Although there is only one thoroughgoing *kanatalalu* in the village at the present time, the men believe that the nonsexual aspects of their affairs are uppermost in their girl friend's minds.

The Social Organization of Extramarital Sex

Unmarried men and women who regularly have sexual relations refer to each other by a special term which I gloss as boyfriend and girl friend (*pʊje, pʊjulu*). The first thing to note about boyfriend and girl friend relationships is that they are extensive. As may be calculated from the data in table 4, there are at least eighty-eight such relationships within the community.

This table was compiled by combining the information offered by several knowledgeable informants. The difference in their reports was fairly wide, deriving not only from failure to recall all of a particular individual's sexual contacts but also from disagreement over who are lovers. According to the villagers, a couple are lovers only if they have intercourse frequently and exchange gifts. Lacking definite standards about how frequently a couple must have sexual relations to be lovers or how many gifts they must exchange, there is understandably some disagreement about who are lovers and who merely engage in casual sex.

At any event, the table summarizes most of the relationships between lovers in the village. Eighty-eight affairs is an enormous number for only 37 adults. It is true that the number of statistically possible affairs is almost four times larger (340), but this figure must be reduced by the number of couples already married to each other, close relatives who cannot have sexual relations because of the incest taboo or rules of affinal respect, and individuals of different generations. I roughly estimate that given these limitations, the number of theoretically possible affairs is 150, suggesting that sexual liaisons are limited primarily by barriers such as the incest taboo and only secondarily by personal preference. In short, the Mehinaku have affairs with most of the villagers of the opposite sex who are not excluded from such relationships by considerations of age and kinship.

Table 4   Mehinaku Extramarital Affairs, 1972

Number of affairs per person	Number of persons having affairs	
	Men	Women
0	0	3
1	2	0
2	3	0
3	4	3
4	3	1
5	0	4
6	4	1
7	2	1
8	1	1
9	0	1
10	1	0
11	0	1
14	0	1
	20	17

The table shows that not only is the total number of sexual relationships large but the number of extramarital contacts enjoyed by different individuals varies widely. There are two factors that explain this variation, the most important of which is age. The young maintain the widest network of sexual affairs, while their elders have far fewer contacts. According to the Mehinaku, older men and women are unattractive as sexual partners; they are *ekejeke*, "ugly." In addition, they have less interest in affairs than do their juniors. Finally, affairs are not wholly appropriate for the older generation. It is considered somewhat ridiculous for an older man to pursue many sexual involvements, even with women of his own age.

The second factor explaining the range of variation in the number of extramarital partners is gender. My data demonstrates that women show greater variation than men in the number of their sexual partners. The average man engages in 4.4 extramarital affairs, and an inspection of the table shows that most of the men are fairly close to this average. The women, however, tend more to have either a very large or very small number of boyfriends. The three most sexually active women in the village account for almost 40 percent of the total number of liaisons in the community. The three least active women, however, account for none of the sexual partnerships in the village. This data contrasts markedly with the men's, for all of the men have one or more sexual partners, and the three most active men account for only 28 percent of the extramarital affairs.

This contrast probably reflects the differences in the meaning of extramarital affairs to men and women. The men's principal motivation for engaging in these affairs is sexual desire, and all the men desire. The women, on the other hand, value the social contact and the gifts they receive in the course of an affair beyond the mere physical relationship. The result is that women who do not excite men's interest, such as the aged or ill, have no opportunity to engage in affairs. All men, however, no matter what their age or physical appearance, can have an affair by offering a gift. Hence we find that all men have some sexual contacts, while some women have none.

The social and economic aspects of extramarital sex can encourage a woman to engage in many affairs. Consider Kuyalu, the most sexually active woman in the village. At present she has fourteen lovers whom she began to accumulate within a few weeks of her arrival in the village in 1967. Her initial status in the village was uncertain, since she had fled from the Waura tribe after her husband was murdered as a witch and she was forced to marry his killer. Though she was welcomed by her Mehinaku cousins and sheltered in their house, the men grumbled because she and her two daughters consumed a great deal of fish and produced none. Further, her daughters were mercilessly teased by some of the village children because of the circumstances of their father's death. After Kuyalu had resided in the village for a while, however, these problems largely abated. Gifts of fish from her lovers arrived with such regularity that it was apparent she was an economic asset, and some of her paramours took it upon themselves to protect her daughters against the more aggressive village children. Kuyalu's case suggests that the pressures and incentives for women to engage in extramarital affairs are not identical with those of men and sometimes leave them very vulnerable to male advances.

Privacy and Extramarital Sex

Sexual intercourse is regarded among the Mehinaku as a natural act. It is a frequent topic of light conversation in both mixed and unmixed company. Children from the earliest years hear their parents discussing sexual activity and frequently become the butt of their parents' sexual jokes. A father may laughingly claim that he saw his five-year-old son trying to have relations with a girl of the same age. In fact, beginning at this age children engage in various forms of sexual experimentation that their parents only half-heartedly discourage. One result of this relative freedom is that children are open in their discussion about sex, regarding it as one of a number of activities in which they will regularly engage when they become adults. One eight-year-old boy told me, "I haven't had intercourse yet, but when I am a little older I will." The subject is as matter-of-fact as that.

Given this casual attitude it may appear anomalous that sex requires privacy and to be seen having sexual relations is shameful. It is not that sex itself is improper. An unmarried girl will return from an act of sexual relations without bothering to wipe off her boyfriend's body paint that was smeared over her during copulation. Everyone in the village will notice her appearance and draw the appropriate conclusion, but this only gives her a sense of pride. Had there been a witness to the act, however, she would have been both ashamed and angry.

Even though the act of sex must be concealed, the villagers cannot always rely on each other's good will and discretion to secure privacy. Intercourse is not only pleasurable to engage in, it is also interesting to watch. Few of the Mehinaku will admit it openly, but I guess that nearly everyone has seen some of their comrades engaged in sexual relations.

There is another less expected reason for conducting affairs privately. Despite their permissive attitude towards sex and the high frequency of extramarital affairs, the Mehinaku do not want to be confronted with their spouse's intrigues. Men are especially inconsistent in their attitudes. They believe it is a good thing for them to have many girl friends but bad for women in general and dreadful for their wives. This attitude is even incorporated in the rules of Mehinaku kinship, for although it is proper for a man to have sexual relations with his wife's sister, it is both bad and disruptive for a woman to conduct an intrigue with her husband's brother.

Jealousy over extramarital affairs is an important source of tension between spouses. Husbands and wives "prize each other's genitals highly," to use the Mehinaku idiom, and don't like to see others take even temporary possession of them. A husband, especially a new one, may become so jealous of his wife's extramarital activities that he will publicly beat and denounce her. She, in turn, may destroy his property, cut down his hammock, and even swing at him with a lighted brand. On rare occasions the consequences of conducting an indiscreet affair can be more serious. The cuckolded husband may turn on his wife's paramour and thrash him with a stick. As the chief explains in an excerpt from an evening lecture I tape-recorded in 1971, male jealousy is never to be taken lightly:

> Women's vaginas are very dear to men, they prize them highly. No one lets his wife have sex with others. You must not let a husband see his wife while you are propositioning her. The Sun, in ancient times, made men kill with witchcraft when others had sex with their wives!

A measure of the hazards of extramarital adventures is a set of sexually oriented myths that function as cautionary tales for men who would cuckold their fellows. Consider the following tale which not ony graphically depicts the fate of an indiscreet lover but does so in terms remarkably familiar to readers of Greek mythology.

A husband was being cuckolded by one of his friends. One day, a bird told him what his wife and companion were up to and gave him a magical wax to get his revenge. That night, while his wife slept, he rubbed the wax over her entire body, but especially around her genitals. At dawn he went off on a long fishing trip.

Shortly after he left, his wife's paramour crept into the house. He found his girl friend's hammock and got in on top of her. As they were having sexual relations they suddenly realized that the magical wax had glued them together; struggle as they might they were stuck in a lover's embrace. At dawn the girl's mother in her adjoining hammock told the young man to get up and go, but neither he nor the girl were able to move from each other's arms or from the hammock.

Days went by and the lovers were forced to urinate and defecate in their hammock. Finally the husband returned home and saw what had happened. He angrily berated them and took them out to the plaza so that everyone could see them and laugh.

Although this story is only a myth, it is also a cautionary tale. Even the most mature and liberal spouses have the right to expect that their mate's liaisons will be conducted discreetly. The question is, how can this be done in the relatively open setting of the Mehinaku village?

Discretion and Concealment

Extramarital affairs are of intense interest to the Mehinaku community. Not only are such relationships intrinsically dramatic, but they are also important in shaping both the economic system and the network of kinship. All the villagers are therefore interested in learning the identity of couples who are conducting extramarital affairs, the gifts they are exchanging, and their chances of their having children by the relationship. This level of curiosity is virtually impossible to frustrate in the long run since all social relationships are rendered highly visible by the physical setting and the spatial design of the community.

Techniques of concealing sexual relationships are at best holding operations; their aim is not to obscure a sexual liaison
totally, but merely to make it possible to ignore it.
Normally, such discretion is sufficient. Mature husbands and
wives may be aware of the identity of their spouse's lovers, but
so long as they are not directly exposed to the arrangements
or effects of these relationships, there is little trouble. Indeed,
husbands demand that their wives discreetly ignore their extramarital involvements, almost to the point of cooperation. They
say that a good wife does not ask too many questions about her
husband's whereabouts and activities. If he puts on his feather
earrings and combs his hair in the late afternoon, she may suspect that he is preparing for a liaison, but she will say nothing.
Husbands as well as wives who question their spouses and
demand too many explanations are severely criticized. They are
said to be jealous (ukítsapai) and always picking fights with
their mates. Such persons are nicknamed after a bird (ɪtsula,
a kingfisher) that flaps about, scolding everyone. No one likes
such a label and only the younger spouses really seem to deserve
the title. Nevertheless, all husbands and wives feel compelled
to manage their extramarital liaisons as covertly as possible.
As soon as a young man decides to initiate an extramarital
affair, he gives thought to how he will conceal it. Since a rejection is regarded as a personal rebuff, he must not speak to the
girl anywhere in the community where her response might be
overheard. Instead, he waits until she is outside the village on
the way to her gardens or to the river. In this area of low visibility, he can approach her with some confidence that they will
not be observed.
A second method of initiating an affair avoids the possible
embarrassment of a rejection. The young man approaches one
of the lovers of the girl or even her brother. In exchange for a
small gift, one of these may be willing to arrange a liaison. Once
an extramarital affair has been established, the lovers will usually have sexual relations when chance permits them. The young
man notices or is informed by a friend that the girl has gone
down to the bathing area alone or is out gathering firewood.
If her husband is not about, he simply follows her out of the
village. If the husband is nearby, he meets the girl at her desti-

nation after taking a circuitous route through the woods. The couple may then have sexual relations right beside the path. Near the river, for example, there is a field interlaced with small trails often used for this purpose. Most of these trails are "defecation paths" (*akane apui*), but others lead to secluded areas where a couple can quickly have sexual relations and return to the main road with little chance of being seen.

If the couple wish to meet on a more regular basis, they must secretly prearrange a time and a place for each liaison. This problem is not easily resolved, since there are few opportunities for lovers to speak to one another privately within the village. A common solution is to use a child as an intermediary or to set a tentative date after each assignation. The preferred time is an occasion when the lovers' spouses are outside the village. A wife can predict with a fair degree of accuracy when her husband who has gone on a fishing expedition is likely to return. If a liaison has been prearranged in his absence, she waits until she sees her lover leaving the village. A few moments later, perhaps after telling the women of her house that she is going to defecate, she leaves the community on a different path from his and proceeds to the place of assignation. There are many cleared areas in the forest encircling the village that have been chosen because they are secluded, invisible from the main paths, and free of biting ants. Each of the Mehinaku men maintains several of these around the periphery of the community. The area selected by the lovers will be the one closest to the back door of the girl's house, so she will not be forced to cross the central plaza or take a circuitous route through the forest.

When the couple meet, they exchange small gifts, such as combs or cotton thread, and then have sexual relations. In the most common position, the couple sit on the ground facing each other, with the woman's legs over the man's thighs. In an alternate position, the woman lies down on a large log or on the ground with the man on top of her. After intercourse the lovers may sit together for a while, assuring one another that they enjoyed the experience, that they care for each other, and that they fear their spouses will discover their relationship. They may also proclaim their faithfulness by saying that they do not have any other lovers, though each realizes that such assurances are not to be taken seriously. They return to the village as they came and rejoin their families as if nothing had occurred.

Since the open setting of the community makes it virtually impossible for lovers to conceal all their preparations for a tryst, they routinely use mendacity to conceal the intentions that lie behind their conduct. In the late afternoon, when a young man puts on his best shell belt and carefully decorates his hair with red dye, his wife may have the temerity to ask what he is planning to do. He explains he is going to the men's house in the center of the village. Since the men often adorn themselves for this purpose, the wife is likely to credit this fabrication or at least to realize that she is not expected to inquire further. If the wife tends to be suspicious about her husband's activities, his efforts to mislead her grow more elaborate. He tells her that he is going fishing or gardening. He carefully dresses to suit the part, puts on bark ankle wrappings, rubs his body with oil, and goes off shouldering a gun, canoe paddle, hoe, or whatever other prop best suits his story. At the same time his mistress is keeping herself busy deluding her kinsmen into thinking that she is going off to bathe or harvest manioc in her husband's garden.

"Alligatoring" and Other Bold Strategies

Not all intrigues are conducted so discreetly. Frequently the lovers can not plan a rendezvous in advance or wait until a woman's husband is a safe distance from the village. Such circumstances call for a bolder strategy, called "alligatoring" (*aiyakátapai*), a name given by the Mehinaku to soliciting sexual relations from the area behind a mistress's house. The term is a reference both to Mehinaku mythology, in which the alligator (actually the cayman, *Caiman crocodilus*) is highly sexual, and to the animal's famous ability to lie motionless in wait for its quarry.

Behind the trash yards of each house there are bushes, trees, and thickets. In the midst of these areas are small cleared spaces (see figure 9) called "alligator spots" (*yaká epʋge*). Each man has his own set of alligator spots, although most are jointly used by a number of men. My companion Atala took me on a tour

Fig. 15. Alligatoring. Nearly hidden from sight by the foliage surrounding his "alligator place" (*yaka epʋgʋ*), one of the villagers calls ("alligators" [*aiyakátapai*]) his girl friend to have sexual relations. Preoccupied as her kinswomen are in boiling a manioc beverage, they do not notice as she slips off to join her lover. The watercolor picture by Akanai accurately captures the Mehinaku's sportative and humorous attitude toward sexual intrigues.

of his personal alligatoring areas around the village. He has twelve such spots, located behind his girl friends' houses. All of them are connected to the maze of small paths surrounding the village. The paths to his alligatoring areas (called "alligator paths" [*yaká apui*]) are in bad condition, but they are definitely visible, indicating that they are regularly used. According to Atala a good alligatoring area has the following characteristics: it is as close as possible to the back door of the girl's house without actually being visible; it allows the alligatoring man to stand and wait comfortably; and it permits him to signal to the girl when she steps out of doors.

Just outside his girl friend Ulawalu's house, Atala has an ideal alligatoring area that he cleared by hacking away at the surrounding vegetation until he had a leafy shelter. From the back door of her house he was completely invisible until the strategic moment when she stepped outside. Then he simply raised a few boughs and suddenly his face and arms were visible among the bushes, wildly signaling to his love.

Yuma gave me a vivid description of how he makes use of his own alligator spots. He waits until his mistress' husband goes to the men's house to wrestle or work on handicrafts. He then slips out the back door of his house and sneaks along the maze of paths surrounding the village to his alligator place a short distance from his girl friend's back yard. He does not dare call her or enter the house. Speaking to her publicly would give him away and entering a neighbor's house would be out of the question unless a trading session or a ceremony was in progress. An hour may go by as Yuma waits patiently. At last, the girl steps outside her house to urinate or dispose of household refuse. He calls to her by pursing his lips and making a sound such as one might use to summon a kitten. She joins him and has intercourse as rapidly as possible, quite aware that her husband is only a few yards away. They use a standing position, the girl raising one knee and placing her arms about her lover. The moment they have completed the act, hardly a word having been spoken, he races off to his own house while the girl returns to her work as nonchalantly as possible. At this crucial point her husband may come home never suspecting that he has been cuckolded in the few minutes of his absence.

Another kind of liaison requiring still greater boldness occurs within the houses at night. During the rainy season it is occasionally too wet to have sexual relations comfortably outdoors. At such times a man will wait until he knows that his mistress' husband has left the village on a predawn fishing trip or a visit to another tribe. Making certain that his own wife is sleeping soundly, he quietly slips over to his girl friend's house. Entering, he expertly finds his way in the darkness through the tangle of hammock cords at his chest and the clutter of bowls and benches at his feet until at last he comes to his mistress in her hammock. Although she may not have been expecting him she is glad he has come for, as the Mehinaku say, a woman likes sex best of all in her hammock at night with her lover. In this situation the couple makes as little noise as possible for fear of waking those sleeping nearby.

When the girl's husband is present, the lovers may have intercourse on the floor of the house, either in one of the cleared regions facing each door or in the narrow vermin-infested area between the thatch walls and the house poles. Either of these alternatives is said to be an indelicate choice, however, and informants speak deprecatingly of those who employ them.

In utilizing these techniques of concealment, lovers occasionally seem to court danger deliberately. The idea of the game, especially for the younger Mehinaku, is to engage in sex play and flirtatiousness just up to the point of exposure and then to draw back. Hence lovers will take unnecessary risks, such as petting in each other's hammocks and having sexual relations while their spouses are nearby. The ultimate expression of this kind of daring is to have sexual relations with a man's wife in her hammock while her husband is present. To appreciate the boldness required for such an undertaking, the reader must realize that ordinarily husbands and wives sleep within a foot or two of each other. Their hammocks are so close that it is hard to understand why the husband should not be awakened by the slightest movements in the hammock beneath him. Understandably, this kind of liaison does not occur every day.

Let us examine one more instance of sexual activity that seems designed to court danger, the best description of which is contained in an extraordinary myth, "The Tale of the Man Who Lost His Arm."

It was dark, and the shamans were smoking in the center of the village. The plaza was filled with people. One of the men wanted to have sexual relations with his girl friend, but she never seemed to separate herself from her husband. Finally, he went up to the side of her house where she slung her hammock and he whispered through the wall: "*Tswi kwa,*

come here." The girl did not hear, but her husband did. He
responded in a whisper: "Me?" and walked over to the wall.
The lover thrust his arm through the wall since he wanted
to take his girl friend's hand. The husband then grabbed the
arm and pulled and pulled. He put both feet up on one of the
house poles, pulling as hard as he could. The arm came
completely off, and the husband then hurled it onto the plaza.
"What's this?! What's this??" shouted everyone on the plaza.
"It's the arm of a villager! It's the arm of a villager!" they
cried.

"Whose is it? Is it yours? Is it yours? Is it yours?" All the
men raised their right arms to show that it was not theirs:
"No, it's not mine! I have two arms," they all shouted. All
the women rushed to their brothers and husbands: "Do you
have two arms? Do you have two arms?" "Yes, Yes, Yes!"
they all answered.

Finally they found the man who had lost his arm. He had
run into the back door of his house, and he bled to death
in his hammock.

Surprisingly, the sexual activity referred to in the story actually occurs among the Mehinaku. A lover will boldly reach
through the thatch walls of the house in the hope of fondling
his girl friend or holding her hand. Though he may not lose a
limb, he can incur the wrath of a husband who happens to be
around when the arm comes through the wall. Nevertheless,
throwing caution to the winds is a part of the sexual game
which some of the younger men and women enthusiastically
appreciate.

Exchanging Gifts

The bold adventures of lovers are the most dramatic feature of
their relationship and certainly are under the most immediate
pressure because of the low levels of privacy available in the
community. Presents exchanged by lovers (*yamala*), however,
must also be concealed from the cuckolded spouses, since such
gifts are a tangible symbol of their relationship. When a man
returns from a successful fishing trip he will almost invariably
detach a choice fish, one whose flesh is very oily, and have it
delivered to his mistress. He must do this before entering the

village, for the moment he is spotted his return will be announced by all the men of the village, who whoop and call out,
"Ki-ki-ki-ki Kupate!" (Fish!).
Once the community's attention is focused on him all he can
do is to go directly home and turn his fish over to his wife. Publicly delivering the fish to his mistress would not only reveal
their relationship but would indicate they considered each other
husband and wife. He can attempt to circumvent this difficulty
when he enters the village by keeping away from the main paths
and central plaza and delivering the fish to the back door of his
mistress' home. If her husband is home, however, it is advisable
to send the gift with one of the girl's kinsmen. Children are frequently used for errands of this kind, but it is also possible to
recruit an adult, such as the mistress' brother. When the fish is
delivered, the cuckolded husband may believe that the gift has
come from his brother-in-law rather than from his wife's lover.
Gifts that are neither as disposable as food nor as casually
distributed are more difficult to explain. A man may tell his wife
that the spool of cotton thread given him by his mistress was
actually a present from his sister, a plausible though unlikely
explanation. Similarly, a woman with a new basket from her
lover will try to lead her husband to believe that it was made
by her brother or some other close kinsman.

Whether they are exchanging gifts or initiating new affairs,
the Mehinaku value their extramarital relationships as a source
of excitement and a break from the routine of village life. From
the perspective of the outside observer, such affairs may even
seem to be socially useful, for discreetly managed affairs are
seldom disruptive and may actually bind the community together. Extended trips to other tribes and dry season villages
might become permanent arrangements were it not for the fact
that lovers and mistresses regard a long separation as a keen
privation. In order for the underground network of extramarital
relationships to persist, however, affairs must be managed discreetly. No matter how engaged a villager may be in the flirta-
tions and escapades of the sexual game, he must stop and glance
over his shoulder, ever aware of the public nature of Mehinaku
community life.

Communication and the Social Setting

The last few chapters have examined the flow of information in the Mehinaku community. We have been interested in the physical structure of the village, since it forms a pattern that channels information, a pattern that from the perspective of our own society seems surprisingly efficient. Little can occur that does not stand a good chance of being seen, overheard, detected, and discussed. This openness of the Mehinaku community facilitates social relationships, for important news is efficiently broadcast from the center of the village, rituals and collective labor are organized through highly audible public speeches, and good citizens are very conspicuously good citizens as they publicly deliver fish to the men's house or to their neighbors.

In some ways, however, the openness of the community to the flow of information constitutes a pressure to which each individual must adapt. This pressure is most evident in the case of conduct which must be kept hidden, as in the case of theft, sexual affairs, and certain children's games. In managing these activities the villagers take advantage of the cover offered by the back regions surrounding the village, ingeniously hiding their tracks and obscuring their intentions. Lovers and thieves prevaricate about their plans and actions, carry a variety of props and costumes to convince their victims that they have no designs on their wives or property, and prowl about the village under cover of darkness after all honest citizens are abed.

Their task is made easier by the existence of important barriers that offset the relative openness of the village to communication. These barriers include the forests and bushes around the village, the intricate system of hidden paths and ports, the darkness of the houses, the restrictions on movements between and within the houses, the limitations on verbal communications, and the distrust in the gossip system's reliability.

The theoretical point of my argument so far is that the level and flow of information and misinformation constitute an intellectual key to the operation of the community at several levels of analysis. The ground plan, the architecture of the houses, the system of kinship, the rules of etiquette, and the system of verbal communication can be shown to be related in a way that

I believe helps us understand the Mehinaku better. In part 3 of this work, "The Staging of Social Relationships," I hope to develop some of these ideas further, shifting the focus from communication to the communicators: the Mehinaku and their patterns of interaction.

The Staging of Social Relationships

3

A dramatist is interested not only in the physical properties of the theater and the lines of the script but also in the staging of the play. Actors must be in place on time, speak their parts on cue, and get off stage when they do not belong there. Further, to make the drama convincing, they cannot do these things mechanically. Successful actors must have the right presence, projecting a character consistent with the role they perform. Costume is part of presence, for dress and makeup communicate the actors' position in the drama. Among the Mehinaku, body paints and ornaments perform a similar function, both identifying the villagers and signaling their willingness to be engaged in social encounters. In chapter 10 I describe how the Mehinaku prepare for interaction and examine the meaning of the paints and ornaments they use as dress.

Once adorned and ornamented, there are rules that make Mehinaku social encounters an orderly process. Some of these rules are incorporated in a system of initiating and terminating interaction, the "hellos" and "goodbyes" that bound each little social dialogue. As we shall see, these salutations are more than a matter of politeness, for they not only mark the beginning and end of social encounters but also tell the villagers what to expect in the course of interaction.

When the Mehinaku are finally socially engaged, they are not usually bound by the well-known lines that make up specifically defined roles. Unlike actors on a stage, they follow more or less ambiguous guidelines that indicate how good citizens ought to conduct themselves. By variations in their comportment and conduct they present themselves to their comrades as they wish to be seen, as social and generous individuals who merit each other's respect. In chapter 12, "Portraits of Self," I shall examine the content of informal interaction and the kind of characters the villagers strive to portray.

Finally, Mehinaku social life is shaped not only by interaction but also by patterns of avoiding interaction. Villagers who are ambivalent about social situations need defined ways to withdraw and disengage themselves from their fellows. Accordingly, chapters 13 and 14 of this book will describe the institutions that separate the Mehinaku and allow them to hold themselves aloof from social encounters.

Being Well Dressed:
Preparing for Interaction

Now they are really beautiful.

Kuyaparei, pointing to a group of women adorning themselves

The reader who has glanced at some of the accompanying photographs may wonder about the title of this chapter. But if the Mehinaku appear naked to us, it is only because they happen to cover the body in ways different from our own. They are just as preoccupied with dress and appearance as we are and spend perhaps even more time in grooming than most people in Western society. This absorption in dress provides rich material for the anthropologist, for adornment among the Mehinaku is a systematic gestural language that allows villagers to selectively communicate information about their personal moods and positions in the community.

How shall we analyze this language? Terrence Turner (1969), who has written about the system of adornment of the Kaiapó Indians of Brazil, argues that their body paint and ornaments are a symbolic statement about their biological and social world. The lip plug worn by men, for example, is seen as simultaneously a symbol of sexuality (only men who have fathered children may wear one) and oral aggressiveness (men of this age engage in "flamboyant oratory").

I believe that a similar analysis of Mehinaku dress is possible, but I propose to focus less on the psychological meaning of particular ornaments and more on their significance in interaction. From this point of view, Mehinaku adornment has two functions. The first, and perhaps the most important, is to mark off the individual's position within society, that is, to make an emphatic statement about age, sex, wealth, and ritual status. In this sense, Mehinaku adornment resembles uniforms and other patterns of dress that encode social roles in our own society.

The second function is to say something about an individual's mood and character. Here, the meaning of Mehinaku adornment is roughly analogous to our own use of clothes to communicate messages about our personality (conservative, staid, sexy, tough) and our moods (happy, sad, indifferent, contemplative). Since Mehinaku dress is a voluntary enterprise in which individuals deliberately select materials, colors, and ornaments from a limited set of alternatives, it becomes a concise statement about the way individual villagers view themselves in the social world.

Nakedness

Being naked is "being without anything" (*metalutsi*). A second word for nudity, *metalŭte* (literally, "without feathers" or "without earrings"), is especially interesting, since it is also used for a featherless arrow and incorporates the notion of being incomplete. To be naked is to be socially incomplete, and it is fitting only at nonpublic times and places. A villager who is hunting or fishing far from the village may properly wear nothing at all. He may also appear unadorned in his own trash yard since it is a nonpublic region. The only persons who regularly appear in public nearly unclothed are the extremely aged. Close to death, they are to a degree outside the normal social order and free from its restraints. Younger persons who habitually appear naked on the public plaza run the risk of being contemptuously labeled "trash yard men" by their fellow villagers.

Only during the transitional period of rituals of status change such as those of mourning, ear piercing, and the seclusion of adolescents, shamans, and new fathers may the villagers appear wholly unadorned. Nakedness therefore carries an asocial meaning. It is appropriate for places where the villager is not likely to interact with others or on those occasions when he stands between important social positions. The purpose of dress and the significance of nudity thus vary from those of our own culture. Unlike ourselves the Mehinaku attach no shame to being unclothed, for rules of modesty refer to the management of the body rather than the covering of it. Women should hold themselves so that their clitoris and inner labia are not visible; men should avoid erections and keep the glans from showing. Since paint and ornament make little contribution to concealing these parts of the body, it is clear that the Mehinaku do not dress in order to safeguard their sense of modesty. Instead, the purpose of being dressed is to apply that which is social to raw human material.

Getting Dressed

Getting dressed among the Mehinaku is necessarily a social rather than an individual activity. Not only is it proper and fitting to paint up and put on ornaments in the company of others, it is also impossible to execute most of the body paintings and hair designs alone; others must assist. Let us watch a group of men adorning themselves for a ritual. It is a long and painstaking procedure, since the Mehinaku admire well-executed designs and attractive ornaments and have special words of praise for the well-dressed person (*kawushapaitsi*) and of derogation for the slovenly (*mawushapawa*).

The first step in getting dressed is to put on arm and leg bands, lengths of soft cotton rope and bark fiber that are wound repeatedly around the calves, knees, and biceps. Closely identified with the wearer, these "garments" are intended to enhance physical appearance and strength. Winding the cords tightly, especially in adolescence, is believed to produce attractively heavy calves and biceps. Knee bands, in fact, should only be worn by young people. A man who has children but wears knee bands—other than on certain ritual occasions—is laughed at,

Fig. 16. Dressing in front of the men's house. On fine afternoons, the men assemble in front of the men's house to wrestle or to dress up. Wearing the *kajakupéi* design, one of the villagers applies a pattern to his seated companion, who is holding a small ball of red *urucu* pigment. In the background another man combs his hair in preparation for dress, his shell collar and armbands resting on the bench beside him.

as would be a middle-aged man affecting youthful styles in our own society.

The association of leg and arm bands with the individual is strong enough to figure in techniques of witchcraft. Though most witchcraft formulae rely on personal effluvia, such as hair clippings or urine, a witch can also work a deadly spell with a length of cord stolen from the victim's arm and leg bands. The cautious villager keeps these garments in full view whenever he must take them off to bathe in the river.

After winding bands about his legs and arms, the dresser wraps on a pair of bark fiber bands in such a way that they form a shield four to five inches wide above the ankle. These "spats" are clearly useful, helping to protect the wearer against thorns and snake bites. The Mehinaku, however, emphasize their role in good dress and insist that they should be worn by every adult male who participates in a public function.

Belts are the next important garment worn by the men. These include the valuable shell belts traded from one of the Carib-speaking tribes, belts made of large Brazilian beads, and broad cotton belts worn for formal occasions. Young men should only use white cotton belts, but older men with children may dye their belts with *urucu* pigment or a variety of tints obtained at the Indian Post. Recently some of the men have begun to make beadwork belts surprisingly similar to those worn by some North American Indians.

After the Mehinaku have put on their belts and ligatures, they turn their attention to their necklaces made of jaguar claws and shells traded from Carib-speaking tribes. Since not every man has necklaces and since some of the wealthier Mehinaku have several, there is a great deal of borrowing at this point. Children shuttle back and forth between the houses to provide everyone with a proper necklace, a responsibility partly borne by the sponsor of the ritual who will help arrange the loans.

The next step in getting dressed is the ornamentation of the face and the head. The most common decorations are red and yellow feather earrings. These have important symbolic associations and are bestowed upon young men only after an elaborate intertribal ear-piercing ritual in which tribal chiefs are initiated and boys are grouped as *jatsa*, lifetime ceremonial friends who act as pall bearers when one of their membership dies.

The last and the most conspicuous item of dress is the "head clothing" (*etu nãi*), a feather headdress consisting of a round woven form, a band of feather down which ties around the form, and a crown of long feathers tied above the band of down so that it stands vertically erect (see Fenelon and Dias 1968 for photographs and a detailed description). As in the case of necklaces, these items are tokens of wealth and often must be borrowed. On one occasion I recall seeing a man wearing a headdress made up of parts borrowed from three different villagers.

We see that the apparently naked Mehinaku may actually be wearing no less than thirteen separate ornaments—two ankle guards, two knee bands, two arm bands, a belt, a necklace, two earrings, and a three-part headdress—and still he is only partly dressed, for he is not yet painted and oiled.

A Social Pigment

The sine qua non of good dress is the decoration of the hair and body with liberal amounts of the red pigment *urucu* (Portuguese), *Bixa orellana* (Latin), *yucu* (Mehinaku). *Urucu* is an extremely valuable pigment, used not only in the decoration of the human body but also in the painting of wooden benches, masks, and other objects. Its meaning is essentially social, for it symbolizes willingness to engage in interaction. A man who is ashamed, angry, withdrawn, or in ritual isolation never uses *urucu*. A man who has emerged from these states immediately applies it. The Mehinaku are very conscious of this pattern of behavior and are quick to diagnose the mood of their fellow villagers simply by noting whether they are wearing *urucu*. The granddaughter of one of the older men smiled knowingly as he began to decorate himself. "Usually he is a sour-faced old man," she said, "but he's in good spirits now because he just got a new girl friend."

Urucu not only communicates sociability but also enhances the beauty of the wearer. A man who decorates himself with *urucu* is more sexually attractive to women. Pale white skin is ugly, even revolting, but *urucu* attractively reddens the skin while keeping the sun off so that the wearer won't get too dark like the wild Indians (see fig. 26) who live outside the Xingu region—a belief supported by scientific opinion that *urucu* screens out ultraviolet rays (Mors and Rizzini 1966:55). *Urucu* has other virtues. It repels insects and supposedly insures longevity if rubbed on regularly during childhood: all in all, a very useful cosmetic and medicine.

Though *urucu* is a social and personal necessity, not every Mehinaku owns it in quantity, because it requires a great deal of labor to produce. Grown in the Mehinaku gardens, the pods of the *urucu* plant are harvested in large quantities starting in late June and early July. The villagers open the pods in their houses and boil the waxy red seeds in great ceramic pots. A family may be fully occupied harvesting, shelling, and tending the fires for several weeks. The result of their labor is several large balls of pasty red dye, which will last through the year.

Only five of the villagers presently stock *urucu* in large quantity. In a strategic position, these men monopolize an ingredient that is vital for ordinary relationships. Significantly, they are all socially prominent and ritually active individuals who display their good citizenship by providing *urucu* for their fellow villagers as they decorate themselves in front of the men's house. In this conspicuous public setting, where friends and kinsmen pair off to daub each other with the careful red designs that decorate the hair and body, it would be very difficult to overlook the generosity of those who have subsidized the entire show.

Hair Designs

The most intricate painted designs are applied to the hair. The Mehinaku men, like all the Xingu Indians, wear their hair in a straight bowl cut that is nicely adapted to a painted geometric pattern. The repertory of designs, called *teiyu*, is fairly large. I have recorded eleven types, although only a few are regularly used. Some of the designs are representational in that they are titled and it is more or less possible to see the conventions being used. In the "piranha teeth" design (*pyuluma etewe*) depicted in figure 17d, for example, a row of pointed even teeth circle the inner ring of the pattern.

In addition to the hair design's representational meaning, some of the patterns are associated with social roles. I am convinced that the interactional significance of hair painting was once greater than it is at present, the attrition being an example of the process of deculturation taking place among the Xingu tribes. Nevertheless, even today some designs are regarded as more appropriate for certain status holders than others.

The style that retains most significance for interaction is *bajuá* (figure 17a). The word *bajuá* refers to a slicing, stroking, or chopping motion, the kind of movement performed in applying the design. *Bajuá* was first used by the Sun, a great shaman and witch. Accordingly only shamans are supposed to wear this pattern. Let a young nonshaman have the temerity to sport this style and all the shamans will descend upon him with cigars (only shamans may smoke) and derisively say, "You are a shaman? All right, then, here is a cigar: let me see you smoke it!"

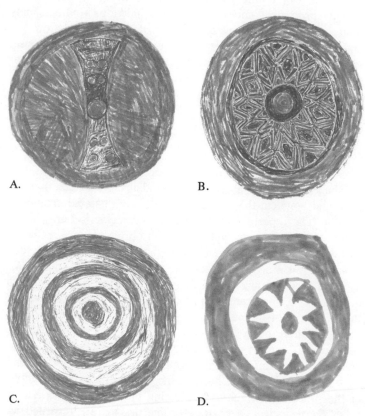

A.

B.

C.

D.

Fig. 17. Examples of hair designs. The pen and ink patterns were drawn by Akanai and include:

A. *Bajuá,* the design used by shamans.
B. *Kulapeiyana,* a motif repeated in the decoration of ceramics, benches, the human body, and houses.
C. *Anapi.*
D. *Pyuluma etewe,* Piranha teeth design.

Under ordinary circumstances the villagers honor the restriction on the use of *bajuá*. During intertribal wrestling matches, however, a few of the young men don this pattern without interference from the shamans. They explain that the wrestlers from other tribes, recognizing the significance of Mehinaku designs, will fear their magical power.

Bajuá is the only hair design associated with the Sun. The remaining patterns were created by the Moon who, unlike the Sun, is a worldly personality associated with mundane activities including practical jokes. Among the Moon's designs are those used by children (*anapi*), by young men recently emerged from seclusion (*kajakupéi*), and by men who are not yet aged (*temepyana*, tapir design; *pyuluma etewe*, piranha tooth design). I have noticed a great deal of variation in the actual use of these designs, however, and I believe they no longer have special interactional significance beyond marking the wearer as a sociable person who is concerned about dressing properly. Such is the decline of the system that some men, on informal occasions, do not even request one pattern over another; they simply are painted up and find out afterwards what they are wearing. It would be a mistake, then, to attribute too much importance to the choice of specific designs other than *bajuá*, the pattern preempted by shamans.

Body Painting

Less intricate than hair decorations, though taking more time to apply, body designs also communicate social status and personal mood. The first step in painting up is to cover the body with oil made from *pequi* fruit, providing a base for other pigments. The villagers hold the oil in high esteem because they believe that it keeps the body supple, preventing broken bones during a wrestling match. After the application of the oil, the area to be painted may be smeared with a contrasting background of charcoal scraped from the handy log stored in the men's house for this purpose. Unlike the material used for blackening, which is rubbed on (*umũka*), the actual design is drawn (*aiyanatapai*) in *urucu* by hand or with a small wooden stylus.

All body designs are representational. Again, like hair paintings, all appear to have had interactional significance at one time, but most such meanings are now defunct. Among these designs is one created by the Sun (*tukupala*, a design representing the lips of a small-mouthed fish), which is ideally limited to shamans. Other patterns created by the Moon were once restricted to young men (*ui*, the snake) and to champion wrestlers (*walamá*, the anaconda). Today these patterns convey so little interactional importance that even Itsa, the most ineffective wrestler in the village, adorns himself with the anaconda design of champions. Only the shamans' design and certain patterns used for rituals continue to retain their significance.

After a Mehinaku has put on his thirteen separate ornaments and painted his hair and body, he may at last be considered fully dressed. The process has been a long one, perhaps two hours counting the frequent breaks for jokes and high jinx in the men's house, but the result is impressive even to outsiders like ourselves. The villager is not only dramatically and esthetically adorned, but his dress is in effect a symbolic statement about his position in society. The knee bands mark his age and whether he is a father. The color of his belt declares how old he is, his earrings identify him as having passed through the ear-piercing ritual, his shell belt, collar, and jaguar claw necklace reveal him as a man of some wealth, and his hair and body designs show him to be a shaman or a participant in a ritual. Collectively, each man's adornment is a summary of his status within the group.

Women's Adornment

But what of female dress? A woman's pattern of dress is far less complex than a man's, incorporates fewer elements, and says less about her social and ritual status. Her basic garment is the belt. There are two kinds, which may be worn simultaneously. The first consists of many loops of beige-colored twine wound about the waist. The width of the belt is a rough indicator of a woman's age, ritual status, and personal mood. If she is sad, ashamed, or in mourning for a husband or lover, she removes strands from her belt. A young woman, recently emerged from adolescent seclusion but not yet a wife or mother, wears the thickest belt of many twine strands. As she goes

Fig. 18. Women's adornment. Ordinarily women are limited to a
minimum of body and facial painting, accompanied only by knee bands,
beads, and the twine *uluri* belt. In the photograph, however, the women
are participating in the ritual of Akajatapá, during which *uluris* are
ceremonially conferred on the young girls of the tribe. On this occasion
they are permitted to wear the men's headdress and *urucu* paint.
Notice the many strands of shell and porcelain beads and the brand new
uluri belts worn for this special ritual occasion.

through the stages of life, she gradually reduces her belt until
she is an *aripi*, an old woman, who wears one thin cord.

   The second kind of belt is perhaps the most distinctive single
garment worn by the Xingu Indians. Called the *uluri*, it was
first recognized by Eduardo Galvão (1953) as exclusive to the
Xingu tribes and a marker of the Xingu culture area. The term

uluri is actually Tupian, and there is no equivalent word in English that will give the reader a clear notion of what it is. The *uluri* consists of a single band of twine worn around the waist. To this band is attached a pocket watch-sized piece of bark in the rough shape of a quadrilateral that sits on the pubis just above the genitals. A long thin cord leads from this bark through the labia of the vagina, through the buttocks, to reappear as a kind of protruding tail in the rear (see fig. 18).

The symbolism of the *uluri* is identical to that of the men's earrings. Just as an intertribal ear-piercing ceremony initiates the male chiefs and associates them with ritual friends, so there is an intertribal ritual in which the women initiate the female chiefs and confer *uluris* upon all the little girls, at the same time associating them with a number of ceremonial friends.

An *uluri*, however, is much more than a mark of maturity. From the men's point of view, it is also a titillating symbol of female sexuality. An old woman should not even wear one, since her vagina has "closed up." A young woman wearing an *uluri*, on the other hand, is regarded as sexually provocative. In fact, the purpose of the garment is to make her beautiful. The cord passing between her legs holds down her clitoris (*itsi kiri*, literally, the vagina's nose) and at the same time focuses attention on the genitalia in a way men find irresistible. Minus the cord (which is primarily worn during rituals), the *uluri* is occasionally left on for sexual relations, enhancing intercourse for both partners.

Although women's belts are the garments that best express their moods and social status, other ornaments and paints are often employed. Like men, women wear necklaces, though never the kind made of jaguar claws. Young women also wear ligatures designed to make their legs beautiful. Girls in seclusion tightly tie the cords around their legs to increase the size and weight of the calf. Yamuni, an eleven-year-old girl currently in puberty seclusion, was quick to point out to me the piano-legged women in the village who had failed to bind themselves as adolescents: "Do you see Kuyalu over there? She's still trying to increase her calf size with leg bands. It will never work. She's an old lady and left seclusion in ancient times!"

Belts, leg bands, and necklaces are the only garments worn by women except during certain rituals. Their body paintings and hair patterns are also few and convey less social meaning than those employed by the men. *Urucu*, for example, is never used to design the hair, the body, or the face; it is merely smeared in a band across the forehead and casually rubbed on the feet, the lower shins, and ankles. A red dye used exclusively by the women (*epitsiri*) and a black paint (*ulutaki*) made from oil and charcoal is applied to the legs and the arms in the three basic female designs. Two of these are geometric, including a polka-dot decoration on the arms and the diamond-shaped "*kulapei*" pattern on the legs, which also appears as a decorative motif in other contexts. The third pattern is the sinuous anaconda design (*walamá*) but without the male connotation of wrestling ability.

As is true of men, a woman's ornaments and paints tell about her mood, her age, her wealth (or at least that of her husband), and even her sexual accessibility. Nevertheless, the men are veritable peacocks in contrast to the women. Not only do they wear more than three times as many ornaments as do the women and have at least five times the number of actively used decorative designs, but the range of social and personal messages expressed in their dress is also more sensitively transmitted. It is worth noting in this context that one of the women's most crucial messages, sexual nubility, is an announcement intended primarily for the men.

A possible explanation of the richness of male attire and the relative poverty of female dress is that adornment among the Mehinaku is a statement about the public relationships between the villagers. The men, in contrast to the women, are continually involved in conduct that is more or less deliberately on display in central village areas for the benefit of the rest of the tribe. They joke, they wrestle, they engage in oratory, they gather for important political decisions—all in full public view. The women, on the other hand, are engaged in domestic affairs in the nonpublic regions behind the houses, avoiding the central plaza unless they have some specific errand there. If the Mehinaku dress is a code that flashes social relationships, we can understand why the signals of male adornment are more complex than female: the men have more to communicate.

The Meaning of Mehinaku Adornment

Adornment is a gestural language that has a rich vocabulary and a complex grammar. Tables 5–7 will help us simplify the presentation of the language of adornment and interpret its message.

One conclusion that we can quickly draw from the data is that significant statuses and personal moods are coded by a distinct pattern of dress: men, women, youths, adults, rich men, poor men, shamans, wrestling champions, chiefs, and persons in seclusion all communicate their status by their choice of ornaments and designs. So too do villagers who are happy, sad, sociable, or withdrawn: their use of adornment proclaims their feelings to the rest of the community. Ceremonial statuses (not shown on the tables) are also richly coded by distinct pigments, designs, and ornaments. The only roles not clearly marked off are those of kinship. Special ornaments and designs would be an awkward way to cue such statuses, since kinship relations overlap: a villager who acts as a father in one encounter may be a son in the next. Short of a society of lightning-change artists, adornment is ill-suited to signaling the rapid-fire changes in perspective demanded by the system of kinship.

In addition to communicating information about status and personal mood, designs and ornaments seem to have a meaning separable from the social roles with which they are associated. This is true because most designs and ornaments are not status and situation specific. Like the morphemes of a language, which can be recombined in many ways, they are associated with a wide range of roles and social contexts. The meaning of any particular design or ornament, then, must be more complex than simply marking a particular role. Black pigment, for example, is used by wrestlers to frighten their opponents, by shamans engaged in therapy, by tribesmen planning to kill a witch, and by workers returning from a collective labor project. It is also one of the principal pigments used to decorate a corpse.

What do these statuses and events have in common, that they are marked with black pigment? "Black is frightening," say the Mehinaku, and makes things "*káukapapai*," worthy of fear and respect. Referring to the list of situations in which charcoal is used as a pigment, we see that most of the activities and roles can be characterized in this way. The corpse, the tribesmen plotting the murder of a witch, the ferocious wrestler, the shaman dealing with spirits that cause disease, all arouse fear. Men returning from a collective labor project also fit this description, for such work parties are usually formed in the name of dangerous spirits. The color black therefore disassociates a man from his ordinary social statuses and identifies him with spirits and superhuman powers.

Most of the remaining pigments and ornaments—such as the garments specific to sex and age, or the jaguar-skin armbands and tattooed lines that identify the tribal chief—convey precisely the opposite message, for they serve to associate the wearer with mundane social relationships. *Urucu* stands as the strongest assertion of this message, for it is the hallmark of the man who is socially engaged with his fellows.

Other ornaments and designs—often the most flamboyant— that seem to have no special function in identifying the actor with his social role may still work this way, by attracting attention to the wearer. Bright feathers on a headdress, earrings, and many hair and body designs seem to be devices that proclaim the individual's sociability and intensify the message conveyed by other aspects of his adornment.

These interpretations suggest that Mehinaku dress is an assertion about the individual's relation to his society. Most ornaments, designs, and colors set him firmly within the framework of the ordinary world and serve to communicate his sociability. Others, like those used by shamans and dancers representing spirits, identify him as transcending the bounds of the ordinary and locate him in the world of superhuman events. Finally, nudity and Brazilian clothing efface the individual's social position and obscure his identity (see table 7).

I have argued that Mehinaku adornment is fundamentally social in nature and is most satisfyingly interpreted as indicating

Table 5

Garment or Ornament

I. "Garments" (*nãi*: belts, bands and other items that surround the wearer)

A. *uwãtã* (Belts)
   1. *uwãtã* (Ordinary cloth belt)

   2. *yamakwipi* (Belt made from shell of land snail by all Carib-speaking tribes) tipa (Stone)

   3. *kajaiba uwãtã* (Bead belt)

   4. *inija* (Uluri belt)

B. *wananãi* (Arm bands)
   1. *wananãi* (Ordinary arm bands)
   2. *tijatapa imapu* (Feather arm bands)

C. *etú nãi* (Headdress)

   1. *etú nãi* (Woven base for headdress)
   2. *kijamapa* (Down feather band)
   3. *hejuãikãi* (Prominent feather crown)

	Comment and Interpretation
ic item of dress for men and women; nen's belt, however, is of twine	To be "beltless" (*mowanatalutsi*) is to be naked. Number of strands in women's belt indicates age, personal mood
-n as belt exclusively by men	A token of wealth, used in ceremonial exchanges
ament on men's shell belt	Ornament carved from stone ax; token of wealth
-n as belt exclusively by men	An inferior belt, worn primarily by trash yard men
-n primarily by sexually nubile nen, though a child may occasionally one during a ritual	A garment exclusively worn by the Xingu Indians
of everyday male dress	Regular use increases size and strength of biceps
e dress	Indicates a ritual occasion or personal happiness and sociability
rn by men for ritual occasions; nen only use during the transvestite *urikumá* ritual	A strong statement of positive personal mood or participation in a ritual
ing men may occasionally use alone	Suggests a jaunty, carefree attitude
rn by young men in seclusion and fathers when they emerge onto plaza iar skin *kijamapa* worn exclusively hief	

(Continued)

Table 5 (Continued)

Garment or Ornament

II. Necklaces (*nete*)

    A. *Yamakwĩpi* (Shell belt worn as necklace)

    B. *kajaiba nete* (Beads)

    C. *itwitsatapi* (Made from water shell-fish; traded from Matipú)

    D. *walupe* (Also made from water shell-fish and traded from Matipú)

    E. *Yanomaka ɨhopa* (jaguar claw necklace)

III. Earrings (*tulũte*)

IV. Leg bands (*kuyapira*)

V. Ankle bands (*itsityalakate*)

ien alone wear as necklaces

ien alone wear as necklaces

n exclusively by men

A token of wealth, indicates wearer is a man of means

n exclusively by men

A token of wealth, indicates wearer is a man of means

n exclusively by men

A token of wealth, indicates wearer is a man of means

n exclusively by men in public tions

Usually a mark of having passed through ear piercing ritual

on litgatures worn by youthful on mal occasions; adults only during ls and to wrestle

Symbol of youthfulness; increases musculature of wearer; not casually used by those who have had children

by men for virtually all activities

Table 6

Oils, Pigments, Designs

I. Pigments (*yana*)
  A. *yucu* (urucu red dye)

  B. *epitsiri* (Women's red dye)

  C. *ulutaki* (A black pigment)

  D. *tipujau* (A black pigment obtained from a tree)
  E. *eje* (Ashes or charcoal)

II. Oils (*imi*)
  A *imi* (Pequi oil)

  B. *mauwayepe* (An oil similar to *imi*)

III. Hair styles and body designs (Partial listing)
  A. Hair styles (*teyu*)
    1. *bajuá* (Stroking design)
    2. *aŋapi*
    3. *temepyana* (Tapir design)
    4. *kajakupéi*
    5. *pyuluma etewe* (Piranha teeth design)
    6. *kuyuwitúi*
    7. *kulapeiyana* (*kulapei* design)

	Interpretation, Comment
¹en on head and body; by women ⁹rehead, shins and feet	Associated with all public secular and ritual occasions; has an association with blood in that in a battle it will "attract" an arrow causing a wound
¹sive use by women for public oc- ⁹ns; "a woman's *urucu*"	Planted, harvested, processed by women; *epitsiri* is "disgusting" to the men who will not use it
¹ by both men and women for facial ¹ns, by women alone as a body	
¹ exclusively by men for facial ¹ns	
¹ixed with oil, used exclusively by	
base for the application of other ¹ents	Makes the body supple, used prior to wrestling matches
¹sive to men; applied with *imi*	
¹ans ¹g men (not yet fathers)	
of status: champion wrestlers and ¹ans	

(Continued)

Table 6 (Continued)

Oils, Pigments, Designs

B. Body designs (*yana*)
1. *ui* (Snake)
2. *tukupala* (Fish)
3. *mahulalopa* (Armadillo design
4. *walama* (Anaconda design)

5. *yanomaka ipute* (Jaguar's tail design; monkey, ant, snake, alligator, etc. tail designs)
6. *kulapei yana* (*kulapei* design)
7. *hipyulāi*

Table 7

The Dress

Black pigment; costumes representing spirits; hair and body paint styles representing shamans

Urucu red pigment; *Uluri* (women's garment); other sex and age classifiers; necklaces and belts that mark the rich and poor; jaguar skin armbands

Nudity; Brazilian clothes; underdress

ıng men only
mans and aged
ımpion wrestlers

mpion wrestlers; also used on
nen's legs
and back of many animals applied
nen's back and thighs

men's legs

ıllel lines tatooed on female chiefs'
, back, shoulders. Only seen today
emale chiefs' upper arms; girls
no longer tatooed

Meaning of Mehinaku Adornment

The Dressed	The Meaning
nans; champion wrestlers; ritual ɔrmers of many kinds; corpses; cipants in collective labor for a ɪ	Transcendence of ordinary relationships
, poor, young, old, chiefs, men, ıen, boys in seclusion, etc.	Identification with ordinary social roles
ɔns undergoing a change of status 's in ear piercing ritual, etc.); ɔns outside the village; persons in ɪte of shame and otherwise unpre- ɪ for normal social encounters, as a sick man	Liminality; being between or outside ordinary relationships

the relationship of the individual to his society. Although I believe this explanation would seem reasonable to the villagers themselves, I must warn the reader that any visual code such as dress has esthetic and psychological components that could be taken as a basis for complementary interpretation. From the dramaturgical perspective, however, dress is a systematic method used by the Mehinaku to tell their fellow actors where they stand with respect to the roles they perform. The ornaments, colors, and decorations supply some of the cues that set the stage for further dramatic action.

We have seen the villagers costumed for interaction. Ornamented with belts, bands, earrings, collars, and feathers, adorned with five basic pigments, the hair and body decorated with one of the many patterns, they stand in the wings ready to face their fellows. What will be the course of interaction? In the next chapter I move the Mehinaku to center stage and examine the simplest and most predictable social encounters: greetings and goodbyes.

"Where are you going?"
"I'm going bathing."
"Well, then go."
Heard many times each day on the path to the river

In "every culture known to history or ethnography" there are regular ways for greeting and taking leave of one's fellows (Murdock 1945: 123). The reason for this universality is that actors can not engage and withdraw haphazardly like billiard balls caroming against each other on a pool table. Interaction, like all social life, is governed by rules, and the way in which the process begins and ends is apparently too vital to leave to chance or individual predilection. The cultural recognition of the significance of properly initiating and terminating an interactional sequence is institutionalized in patterns of greetings and farewells. Among the Mehinaku these patterns furnish us with clues to the relationship of the actors, their definition of the situation, and the course that their interaction will take. Greetings and farewells are not simply a minor part of a system of etiquette but a significant chapter in the ethnography and theory of Mehinaku social relations.

Greetings

Following the Mehinaku classification of greetings, there are four ways of opening interaction with fellow villagers. The method of choice depends on the setting, the relationship, and the definition of the situation. The first method is the most formal and stereotyped, "to greet formally" (*yukapu*). Formal greetings consist of a set pattern of words and gestures. The greeter looks up, raises his eyebrows, smiles, and says, "You are (here)" (*pitsupai*). The response is to nod the head and say, "I am (here)" (*natupai*). This pattern is reserved for Mehinaku who are socially distant from the speaker. A villager who enters his neighbor's house, for example, is likely to be greeted in this fashion. I have noticed that this greeting is sometimes used as a polite veneer that masks a considerable amount of hostility. Ipyana, the alleged Mehinaku witch, was often formally greeted in this fashion by many of his fellow villagers before his execution in 1971.

A second method of opening interaction is simply to "call" the other person (*atakutapu*). Mehinaku call each other under both formal and informal circumstances, the nature of the situation being indicated by the modulation of the voice and the choice of words. The formal method of calling is used on the central plaza to recruit participants in rituals and collective labor projects. The caller steps into the plaza, faces the house of the person he is addressing, and calls in a long drawn-out voice: "My son, Kupatekuma . . . come here!" Invariably this formal pattern begins with a kinship term and then adds a personal name if the term is ambiguous. Calling the name alone is not appropriate in this public setting.

The informal method of calling is less stereotyped and uses different language. It occurs between individuals who are on more or less friendly terms and who share a relationship based on close association. The setting for this kind of interactional opening can be anywhere in the village or around it, though never during a ceremony or other formal occasion. Kuyaparei is being called to the men's bench where his cross-cousins plan to joke with him: "Kuyaparei! Get over here!" (*tswi kwa!*) Kuyaparei responds: "What's up?" (*natsi?*)

Or, a woman inside her house calls her sister-in-law: "Come here, pregnant one!" (*ama kana itsukuyalu*). Kin terms are frequently used in situations similar to these: My son! My sister's child's father! My brother-in-law!, and so on.

A third technique of opening interaction is to ask a question (*aiyapʊ*). This kind of greeting is informal and varies widely in the information requested, the setting in which it appears, and the relationship of the actors. For example, a close relative entering the house may be greeted with, "What's up?" (*natsi?*). Often as not the response is, "Nothing!" (*aitsa wa*). Questions are the most frequently used interactional openers, and we will return to their description and analysis after examining one more class of greetings.

The fourth and last category of greeting is simply "to speak to" (*akaiyakátapʊ*). This type of greeting often uses a special set of words which approach kin terms in their meaning, although they have no genealogical implication. Table 8 summarizes the variables that determine the choice of a particular term.

Table 8   Terms Used in Greeting Kinsmen and In-laws

	Consanguineal relatives (roughly of ego's generation)	Affinal relatives
Male to male	*Hai ja*	*Hai*
Female to female	*Hai ju*	*Hai*

The table shows that the greetings *hai ja, hai ju,* and *hai* code consanguinity, affinity, and sex. In practice they are used in informal contexts and between the speakers of roughly equal status. Thus children do not "*hai ja*" their parents or others who are clearly of the older generation. A listener is most likely to hear these terms where the general atmosphere is one of informal equality, as in the men's house. Interaction between men and women, between persons of different generations, and between parents and children-in-law are opened by using either a kin term or a personal name.

"Greeting," "Calling," "Questioning," and "Speaking" are the approved methods of initiating interaction among the Mehinaku. Each of these opening gambits codes the relationship and the nature of the social situation. The choice of greeting, however, is determined by still another factor: the setting in which the contact occurs.

Some greetings and their stereotyped responses are setting specific, occuring only in certain regions, such as the paths around the village. According to proper etiquette, no one can be passed on a public path without some kind of recognition or display of affinal respect. The only persons who are not expected to greet each other are villagers living in the same household, for as one man put it, "Why bother? You see them all the time anyway." All others, however, must be pleasantly recognized. To fail to do so is to brand oneself as angry or sullen.

Let's listen as the villagers greet Kikyalama as he goes to bathe.

The first person he meets on the path is an older distant kinsman who lives in another house. They do not get along well but conduct themselves courteously in each other's presence. The correct formula for a polite greeting on the way to the bathing area is to ask, "Where are you going?" (*atenãi pyala?*). The man returning to the village always is the one who asks this question first, since his own destination is obvious. And so Kikyalama is questioned:

"Where are you going?"
"I'm going bathing."
"Well, then go."

Neither of the two men has slowed his pace on the path, and each continues on his way. No information has been communicated other than their mutual recognition of the respect that each owes the other.

A bit further down the path Kikyalama passes his cross-cousin, with whom he is obliged by the rules of kinship to tease and joke. His cousin immediately throws his arms about him and demands:

"Where are you going?"
"Nowhere. To bathe."
"Ha! You are going to 'alligator' " (look for women to have sexual relations).

"No, to bathe!"

"You sex fiend!" (*aintyawaka nitséi*).

The next person along the path is one of the oldest women in the village. She is not a close relative of Kikyalama's, but she addresses him as grandson, as she does most of the village men:

"Where are going, grandson?"

"To bathe, old woman" (*aripi*, old woman, not a pejorative term).

"Then go."

"Be careful, grandmother; there is a slippery place on the path. Don't fall and break a bone!"

The last person Kikyalama meets on the way to the stream is his girl friend. He casts a quick glance over his shoulder to make sure that they are unobserved. If she had been with her husband, or if he was nearby, he would have completely ignored her and she him. To do otherwise would have been an affront to her husband, for if they speak to each other at all, it is assumed that the subject is an assignation. Kikyalama hurriedly approaches her:

"I'll wait for you behind your house in the woods."

"Yes!"

Without pausing each continues on, she to the village, he to the river.

All of these exchanges, except for the last, have followed roughly the same form. The person leaving the village is questioned about his destination, he responds in the expected way, and the exchange is capped with a joke, a pleasantry, or a conversational remark. In every instance the dialogue just takes a few moments, and the speakers barely slacken their pace. When the dialogue fails to follow this pattern, it is usually because the speakers are transacting some kind of tangible business, as in the last encounter, rather than merely saluting each other as kinsmen, friends, or in-laws.

Goodbyes

Disengaging from interaction does not require that the actors explicitly recognize each other's social status. The greetings and the course of the interaction have already established these facts, and it only remains for the participants in the encounter to withdraw in some orderly fashion. There are several basic rules, the most important of which is that something must be said. No one can legitimately walk away from a social engagement or out of a house without some kind of leave-taking. The only exceptions to this rule occur between affinal relatives who are honoring an avoidance taboo or close kinsmen who live together. Everyone else must be recognized as he leaves.

The second rule is that the person taking his leave speaks first, unless his intentions are obvious (he is collecting his gear, rolling up his hammock, and saying goodbye to everyone else). Finally, the content of the farewell usually offers some indication of when the person leaving will return. At times this information is built into the structure of the verb:

"I'm going (far off and won't return soon)" (*Niyaneleigu*), or "I'm going (and will be back soon)" (*Niyatekeigu*). The response may simply be, "You are going."

On occasion a leave-taking is a little more elaborate, as when a man gets up to leave the men's house where he has been talking with a friend:

"I'm going (and will return)."
"Don't leave!"
"I'm lazy. I'm getting into my hammock; I'll be back soon."
"Then go."

The Importance of Mehinaku
Greetings and Goodbyes

Mehinaku greetings and farewells are more complicated and convey more information than we might have thought necessary in a small society. After all, there are only seventy-seven people living in an open community and they see each other many times during the course of the day. Why burden ordinary social business with the freight of such stereotyped gestures? Nothing tangible is exchanged in these social engagements, and yet the Mehinaku regard those who ignore them as boors, angry men, and worse. To approach the problem of why the Mehinaku are so punctilious about how social encounters are opened and closed, look at table 9, a summary of some of the data presented above.

Table 9   The Meaning of Mehinaku Greetings

Greetings	The participants and the implication of the greeting or goodbye
No greeting	
1. Avoidance behavior	Parents and children-in-law
2. No avoidance behavior	A. close relatives who live in the same house, suggesting close familiarity. B. potential sexual partners who are maintaining proper appearances.
Greetings	
1. *Hai, Hai ja, Hai ju*	The choice of greeting may reveal whether the speakers are affinal or consanguineal kinsmen, the sex of the speaker and the person spoken to, and the relative age of speakers.
2. Kin term	Kin relationship specified.
3. Personal name	Informal relationship specified; nonaffinal relationship asserted.
4. Formal greeting (*yucapu; "pitsupai"*)	Speakers socially distant, possibly hostile.
5. Ribaldry, sexual joking	Cross-cousins

Goodbyes	
No formal leave-taking	A. Kinsmen who live together B. Mutual hostility
Leave-taking	Suggests polite or friendly relationship

Though greetings and farewells take only a few seconds, the chart shows that a great deal of information is packed into them. The few words of a greeting may state both the speaker's personal feelings towards the villagers addressed as well as the shared social relationship. Information about friendship, hostility, kinship, age, common residence, formality of relationship, and sexual activity is all compressed into a few words.

The richness of greetings in social information is a puzzle, given that this information is available from many other sources and is well known to the Mehinaku. Erving Goffman, in an elegant paper called the "Nature of Deference and Demeanor," suggests that little "rituals" such as greetings and farewells are a vital constituent of the social order:

> The rules of conduct which bind the actor and the recipient together are the bindings of society. But many of the acts which are guided by these rules occur infrequently or take a long time for their consummation. Opportunities to affirm the moral order and the society could therefore be rare. It is here that ceremonial rules play their social function, for many of the acts which are guided by these rules last but a brief moment, involve no substantive outlay, and can be performed in every social interaction (Goffman 1956: 496).

Goffman thus would argue that the Mehinaku reaffirm the order of their society each time they greet and take leave of one another. I would take an even stronger position. In greeting and taking leave of each other the villagers not only affirm the structure of their society but assure their fellows of their location within it. Why do the Mehinaku require such assurances? This is a question that must be held in abeyance, for an answer requires that we consider the extraordinary flexibility in the definition and allocation of Mehinaku social roles, a subject to be considered in detail in part 4 of this book. For the moment, let us move deeper into the process of interaction. We will bring two Mehinaku into social contact. They greet each other in a friendly way. What happens next? What will they say to each other? How will they conduct themselves in each other's presence? The next chapter considers the content of informal interaction.

Look at me. I paint-up nearly every afternoon.
I joke in the men's house. I wrestle and dance.
I'm no "trash yard man."

Shumōi, *explaining the difference between himself*
and his less sociable kinsmen

The analogy between life and theater must
never be taken too literally. In the conven-
tional theater, the actor's lines are specified
so precisely that there is very little room for
improvisation or any other significant departure from the script. In life, however,
relatively few roles are so inflexibly defined
that knowledge of the norms is all that is
required to predict behavior. Among the
Mehinaku only in the acting out of certain
ceremonial and affinal relationships are the
behavioral possibilities so stereotyped that
real-life interaction begins to approach a
staged scene.

Most other conduct, even though it occurs
in a normative framework, is not so limited.
Companions who sit in front of the men's
house, walk along a trail, or fish together
are participating in a very loosely defined
social engagement where there is a great
deal of room for variation. In this chapter
I plan to explore how the Mehinaku conduct themselves when interaction is not

clearly bounded by the constraints of social roles or the guide-lines of well-defined social settings.

A useful concept for understanding encounters of this kind is the notion of the "presentation of self" as developed primarily by Erving Goffman (1959). In every social engagement, Goffman argues, the actors are in an unspoken and often unconscious collusion to maintain the definition of the situation and their position in it. Two businessman who come together to conclude a deal, for example, have a mutual interest in conducting themselves as if each man's competency and integrity were unquestionable. While behind the scenes they may be checking each other's credit rating and character, up front each man offers assurances that the other is honest, trustworthy, efficient, and businesslike. To do otherwise could turn a "high level" commercial transaction into a brawl between street peddlers, doing violence to both the social value of the encounter and the image of the characters engaged in it. Since the result can be bad business and worse etiquette, both parties are constrained to sustain each other's position in the performance and the image of self they choose to present.

The strength of this approach to encounters is that it can take us beyond the role framework. Actors not only perform "selves" that are bound to specific social statuses, such as that of "businessman," but are constantly offering more general presentations that simply identify them as good men. They represent themselves as cooperative, friendly, generous, and trustworthy participants in social engagements. These are the fundamental messages transmitted in the casual and "purposeless" interaction that makes up most of our social day. A description of the basic characters performed in such informal social encounters ought to be a part of the standard ethnography.

We may think of two ways of ferreting out the kind of character a people ascribe to the good citizen. One is to examine the qualities of self that are attributed to such a person. Numerous ethnographies make an effort in this direction, tying a people to a list of adjectives. Ruth Benedict's classic *Patterns of Culture* is an exercise in this kind of description. We are told that the Pueblos of New Mexico are "ceremonious . . . of yielding disposition . . . generous . . . never violent . . . realistic . . . apollonian" (1934).

A second approach is to find out what constitutes a bad citizen. Ethnographies that include such information often fail to explain in sufficient detail just what the bad apples are like. More crucially, the description is usually based on the observer's assessment rather than a people's own concepts of what constitutes the good citizen or the reprobate. It is these native concepts we are after, for they are the guideposts by which each individual directs his conduct and finds his way through the course of informal interaction. Let us examine how the Mehinaku mete out praise and abuse as a means of defining the characters they strive to emulate or reject. The conceptual portraits produced by this method should take us a long way toward understanding social engagements not governed by clearly defined social roles.

The Sociable Man

The basic requirement in Mehinaku social relationships is a willingness to respond to others in a warm and positive manner. The word for this quality is *ketépepei*, a term that also refers to the kind of beauty and balance found in a well-made artifact, such as a basket. An additional linguistic clue to the meaning of *ketépepei* is that it has the same root as the verb "to be happy" (*eketepemunapai*). I gloss *ketépepei* as "sociable" because most of the virtues of the man who is labeled by this term are social ones. He speaks well, he never grows angry, he laughs and smiles often, he has an open and attractive face, he does not avoid others, he is cooperative and generous. These are the qualities that the Mehinaku cite when discussing this kind of individual or when they—as they do more frequently—point out someone who is not sociable.

Conversation and Good Humor

The first quality associated with the sociable man is the ability to "speak well." Whenever two persons are together and their attention is not focused on a particular task, the general rule is that they should enter into conversation. The subjects vary, though they are usually quite commonplace. Men sitting on the bench in front of the men's house may discuss the need for a new men's house, the women's latest ceremonial activity, the likelihood of success on a fishing trip, or the weather—topics that are mulled over again and again among the same participants. The willingness and ability to participate is an attribute of the man who "speaks well." On the other hand, a man who is close-mouthed and sullen is not only socially undesirable but potentially dangerous: "Do you see old 'Rotten Fish' over there?" my friend Kikyalama once asked me. "When he sits on the men's bench he never says anything. He's angry because we had sex with his wife. If he bewitches me or my son I will be furious with him!"

While Mehinaku men keep up the expected conversational patter, they should give evidence of a sense of humor. In ordinary interaction, one jokes a little (*metalawatãi*) in a restrained and inoffensive way. For example, one may tease a child who happens to be standing nearby: "The neck of your penis is small!" (meaning you are immature). This sort of jest gets a sure-fire laugh and at the same time avoids offense since it is not directed at adults. Other humorous sallies involve plays on language. A favorite is to imitate Brazilians or other Xingu tribesmen, some of whom, notably the Trumaí, are said to have the ugliest speech conceivable. On my visit in 1974 some of the villagers were calling each other by the Auití tribe's term for brother-in-law, a word which sounded funny to the Mehinaku ear. A month or so later this fad had died out and everyone was using the Txicão tribe's interrogative (*wa?*) as a new source of amusement.

Joking between men, unless they happen to be cross-cousins, must be practiced with discretion. A few Mehinaku, however, will engage in the broadest kind of humor with virtually everyone. Called *metalawaitsi* (jokers, wise guys), they are a continual source of irritation to the more sober-minded. My friend and informant, Kupate, is a *metalawaitsi*, and though his father has publicly warned him that "wise guys" die young because they arouse the antagonism of witches, he seems irrepressible.

Appreciating Kupate's jokes requires a slapstick sense of humor and a strong stomach. In top form he will throw his arms about a companion and slap at his genitals, or pretending anger he will brandish a machete and then whoop at his victim's discomfiture. At times his conduct becomes a total negation of good deportment. No man, for example, is expected to exhibit his genitals. Yet Kupate will induce an erection, pull back his foreskin, and show off his glans penis. Breaking wind in company is considered a gross act and the offender is subject to being spat upon. Still, every now and then, Kupate will sneak up behind a friend, flatulate, and rush off.

Much of Kupate's humor, like that of other *metalwaitsi*, concerns sexual functions and elimination. Although these jokes are considered funny, furnishing the basis of much of the interaction between cross-cousins, they tend to profane those who are the butt of them. As stated by Erving Goffman (1956), developing an idea first put forward in Durkheim, an individual is a sacred entity, to be approached with ritual displays of respect not very different from the consideration shown any holy object. Far from respecting his comrades, Kupate in effect desecrates them.

Restraining Anger

The ability to speak well and a proper sense of humor are two of the important attributes of the sociable man. A third is the ability to contain negative emotions, especially anger and hostility. A display of anger is a disturbing and even frightening experience for the Mehinaku. The word for being angry (*japʋ-japai*) is applied metaphorically to things that are completely out of control, such as a fire raging in a dry garden or a species of pepper (*japʋjaitsi*) so hot that it leaves any man foolish enough to eat it writhing on the ground in agony. Similarly, thunderstorms, powerful winds, and stinging ants are all *japʋ-japai*. Open anger is associated with unpredictability and violence, characteristics said to be typical of non-Xingu tribes (*wajaiyu*), who are avoided and despised for this reason. Anger is also dangerous to the man who nurses the emotion "in his belly," for he then courts serious illness and becomes undesirable to his wife, friends, and fellow villagers. An angry child is sternly rebuked by his parents and ridiculed as a *japujaitsi* (angry one, "hot pepper").

Although there are occasions when a Mehinaku may legitimately express his anger, such as when discovering his wife *in flagrante*, serious quarrels are rare. In over eighteen months of residence in the Mehinaku village, I never saw any violent expressions of interpersonal hostility except between husbands and wives. Even children feel sufficiently constrained to refrain from real fighting. It is true that the Mehinaku do become angry at times, for there are numerous sources of irritation and antagonism within the society—conflicts aroused by gossip and scandal, jealousies inspired by extramarital affairs, tensions of living in close quarters, fear of witchcraft, and envy over possessions, to name a few. According to the Mehinaku image of the sociable man, however, hostility must not be expressed directly. An unabashed display of anger must be reserved for only the most extreme circumstances.

Generosity

One of the outstanding characteristics of the sociable man is that he is generous. Although there is no word in Mehinaku for "generous" other than "not stingy" (*aitsa kakaianúmapai*), the concept is well-defined by specific acts and obligations and is of great importance to the villagers as a guide to daily conduct. The hallmark of the generous man is that he eats with his kinsmen and friends and shares his food. The man who is stingy with food (*kanahiri*) eats alone. He sneaks back from a fishing trip and enters the village unseen to avoid sharing his catch. When he has to share, he gives up only the poorest fish and keeps the most delectable portions for himself.

Mehinaku women are often regarded as stingy, perhaps because of their key role in the distribution of food. Ijau, though many years dead, is still remembered for her technique of shortchanging her residence mates. After cooking fish stew for the entire household, she would spoon out meager portions onto slabs of manioc bread. Then having made certain that everyone had heard her scraping the pot, she would announce that there was none left. But it turned out that there was a great deal left; the noise of the spoon scraping the bottom of the pot was really the noise of the spoon scraping the side of the pot. The name Ijau is now synonymous with stinginess among the Mehinaku, and I was occasionally called "Ijau" when I refused to share some of my own reserves of food.

A sociable person, unlike Ijau, is not stingy with food. Indeed, he is conspicuously generous with it. On a fishing trip he yields part of his catch to his less successful comrades. On his return he walks through the center of the village so that everyone may see how much he has caught. A short time later he dispatches his children with substantial gifts of fish to kinsmen in other houses. He distributes part of his catch in the men's house and tells the men exactly where he was fishing so that they will be successful the next day.

A generous man is willing to part with valuable possessions. It may be a painful decision since prestige is accorded those who accumulate shell belts, collars, feather headdresses, Brazilian trade goods, and other high status property. A villager nevertheless must be prepared to give away or trade much of his wealth if he is to avoid the stigma of stinginess. He must reward his in-laws with valuable gifts after the birth of a child. He must participate in rituals during which he gives away precious possessions. And, unlike the stingy man who avoids barter sessions on some flimsy pretext, he must always be ready to trade.

One way a villager can remind the community of his generous nature is to grow corn. Planted in September at the beginning of the rainy season, corn reaches maturity by January at the time of a calendrical festival (Amairi) associated with fertility and a short midwinter dry season. In the evening at harvest time a farmer will announce to the entire village that his corn is ripening. The next morning everyone descends on his field and quickly strips away every last ear. The farmer is left with the satisfaction of having been a generous man and the knowledge that his generosity has been unmistakably communicated to the entire community.

Working Hard and Appearing Energetic

A villager not only must share with his comrades, but he must also be hard working. If, for example, he is lounging about the men's house he must be ready to assist anyone who wants help to carry a heavy canoe to the water, lug a newly fallen log from a trail, or prop up a fallen *pequi* tree in a nearby orchard. Unlike the lazy man who conveniently leaves the village "to defecate" when he sees work ahead, the sociable man participates in collective labor with spirit and enthusiasm.

A man's industry may be judged by the frequency of his fishing trips. Fish is the preeminent food for the villagers and, given its role in their diet as the principal source of animal protein, it is not surprising that going fishing is regarded as evidence of good citizenship. Normally, all men fish for their household, but instead of a set schedule or formal system of taking turns, there is a general expectation that one man's contribution today will be reciprocated by another man's tomorrow. During the wet season, however, when fishing becomes frustrating and uncertain, this formal arrangement tends to break down. Relationships among the men in a house become tense as each waits for the other to go first. The war of nerves ends only when someone, driven by annoyance or hunger, finally gives in, packs his gear, and goes off to fish. Such confrontations, however, are rare, largely because the ethic demands that the men work hard and give freely of their services.

No less important than being a hard worker is giving the appearance of being a hard worker. At all times a man should look energetic. In the men's house he is spirited and boisterous. He is the first one up in the morning, blowing on his fire, rousing his children from their hammocks, and marching them down to the stream for cold baths. While other villagers are still asleep, he has already left to clear a distant garden, to hunt monkey along trails miles from the village, or to fish on a hard-to-reach lake. He keeps a rooster or two on a perch near his house to awaken him (and the rest of the village) at four in the morning with their raucous crowing. "Sleep," he loves to explain, "weakens a man and saps his strength. Only a dog or a 'hammock lover' sleeps during the day when he should be fishing, hunting, or clearing land."

Although this work ethic is vigorously promoted by the chief in his evening speeches, it is in reality pursued only by a very few of the younger men. The village is no beehive of productive activity, and it requires little searching to find both the old and the young snoozing in their hammocks or lazing about the men's house. Nevertheless, being vigorous, energetic, and hardworking is one of the "presentations of self" that the Mehinaku deliberately foster; it is part of the portrait of the "good man" by which they guide their conduct and evaluate their fellows.

The Rich and the Poor

Sharing food, work, and possessions are the hallmarks of a good man. Paradoxically, however, the ideal villager not only manages his property and labor generously but profitably as well. He does so because he knows that his wealth is a measure of his worth as an individual and a basis for the respect and esteem of his comrades.

Given our own standards of wealth and poverty, the reader may well wonder just what kind of social distinctions the Mehinaku can draw on the basis of the ownership of material goods. Table 10, which lists every possession of one of the wealthiest men in the village, hardly solves the puzzle. In our society few have less than this "Croesus." Among the Mehinaku, however, the concept of "true or valuable possessions" (*apapálaiyaja*, see chapter 8) helps distinguish two loosely designated but significant economic divisions within the village—the "rich" (*kapapálapai*, having many possessions) and the "poor" (*mapapalawa*, having few possessions). A poor man may have nearly as many possessions as the well-to-do, but he crucially lacks the belts, collars, headdresses, ceramic pots, guns, and other valuables that enrich the wealthy man.

Although a wealthy Mehinaku never brags about his possessions (he usually professes his poverty), the villagers have a fairly accurate idea of the extent of his property. Many of his valued possessions are worn in public and others are easily visible both inside and around his house. The poor man's status is equally conspicuous, revealed by his shabby ornaments, his low status bead belts, and his efforts to borrow headdresses and shell collars for public ceremonies.

Table 10   Inventory of the Possessions of One of the
                               Wealthiest Villagers

---

1. Valuables (*apapalaiyaja*, literally, "true possessions") and other items of considerable worth
   7 shell belts
   4 shell necklaces
   5 stone ornaments for belts
   10 lbs. beads (estimated)
   2 bows
   2 .22 rifles
   1 feather headdress
   1 woven hammock
   1 canoe
   1 dog
   2 large racks for drying manioc
   1 large bamboo barrier for seclusion
   3 gardens

2. Ordinary and lesser possessions (*apapalai,
   apapalaimalú*; literally, possessions, worthless
   possessions)
   35 lbs. salt (estimated) in a large bag; a year's
      supply for personal use and trade
   30 arrows
   3 small suitcases
   2 small aluminum pots
   1 large ball of palm fiber cord
   5 balls of wool (Brazilian manufactured)
   1 large ball of native cotton thread
   50 feet of nylon parachute cord
   3 spools of nylon fishing line and hooks
      Various tools of Brazilian manufacture: pliers,
      machete, ax, plane, chisel drill, pocket knife
   1 flashlight without a bulb or batteries
   1 large box of matches

The rich man is respected because it is supposed that he has
attained his status through hard work. The villagers understand
how valued objects—with the exception of Brazilian trade goods
—are made and judge their worth by the work that has gone
into them. A man examining a feather headdress fully appre-
ciates the skill and labor of the craftsman who put it together.

It follows that all one need do to become wealthy is to apply oneself assiduously. He who will not work is deservedly poor, a lazy fellow without any regard for his appearance minus shell belts and necklaces. I frequently pointed out that a man could be poor because of ill luck, because his parents never taught him to make valued objects, because he was not fortunate enough to have married a skilled Waura ceramicist, or because he was not a shaman who could charge high medical fees. No matter—for all this there were any number of quick retorts. Any man who wants to own valuable property can acquire it through trade. He can cultivate additional gardens, gather salt, or build many canoes and exchange them for belts and necklaces. A man incapable of making a feather headdress or a black bow deserves no one's sympathy. He is a "trash yard man" of the worst sort.

The Skillful and the Knowledgeable

The Mehinaku do not overlook the superb musician, the great raconteur, or the maker of well-balanced arrows. Men may excel in as many ways as there are crafts. A visitor need only ask "Who makes the most beautiful baskets?" to be immediately directed to a select number of villagers who are best in their skill. The best bowmakers, bench carvers, headdress fashioners, flutemakers, and canoe builders are all equally identifiable and accorded respect as *katámapapai* (intelligent, skillful, knowledgeable), a term always applied with a tone of admiration and deference.

In theory, the villagers' skills could all be mastered by one man, but in practice there is considerable variation in knowledge and ability. Just as material wealth is unevenly distributed among the community, so knowledge and skills tend to become the monopoly of a few. Only one of the Mehinaku, for example, knows how to carve the sacred flutes stored in the men's house. Only three are really expert musicians. These monopolies are maintained by the conscious efforts of those who benefit from them as well as by inefficient teaching methods. Methods of teaching are inefficient by our standards because they are limited to a small circle of kin and are primarily imitative. A novice learns by watching an expert, usually his father, perform a task and subsequently repeating what he has seen. There is little questioning or explanation involved in the procedure. Verbal skills such as ritual songs are taught more formally. The singer takes his pupil aside and has him perform the song line by line until he has committed it to memory. Jealous of their knowledge, singers of ritual songs often demand a fee from their apprentices. I was repeatedly urged not to play certain songs I had taped lest someone acquire them without paying the singers.

Less exotic skills also have only a limited distribution in the community. Table 11 documents the men's knowledge of five important craft skills—bench carving, fishtrap making, basket weaving, canoe building and ritual mask making. Although these skills are relatively simple and are economically and socially significant, only five men seem to have mastered them all. On the average, men over forty know 90 percent of the listed skills. Men under forty are familiar with only half the listed skills. Education is a continuing process among the Mehinaku, and the community is far from homogeneous in possession of craft knowledge. The Mehinaku contradict the customary picture of the technologically primitive community in which every man is supposed to be a jack of all trades.

Knowledge of crafts, myths, and tribal lore has an observable effect on informal interaction when it is either grossly deficient or outstanding. Itsa commands so few skills that he seems culturally impoverished. Regarded as a village fool, he is frequently teased in the course of the banter and high jinks that go on in the men's house. Kuya, on the other hand, is a master craftsman and spellbinding raconteur, a man who tells a story so well that no one seems to care whether it is true or not. Respect for his skills is so great that he is accorded deference he would otherwise never receive, for he is far from being an ideal citizen.

Physical Attractiveness

The good man is not only generous, wealthy, skilled, and sociable; he is also attractive. Although ornaments and paints can enhance his looks, the basic measure of attractiveness is physical appearance. For men, the principal requirement of a good appearance is height. Respectfully referred to as *wékepei* (tall, big) and commanding the deference and respect of his comrades, the tall man is an unbeatable wrestler, a successful fisherman, a powerful man of political importance. During an earthly golden age in the mythic past, all the Mehinaku fit that mold. Today such a man is *káukapapai*, a deferential term applied to those worthy of fear and respect. In reality, height, strength, and success as a hunter, wrestler, and politician are not necessarily linked. The Mehinaku stereotype of the ideal man, however, has them intimately connected.

Table 11   Age and Craft Skills

Individual's Estimated Age	Canoe Making	Bench Carving	Mask Carving	Fishtrap Making	Basket Making	Percentage Skills Known
61	+	+	+	+	+	100
55	−	+	+	+	+	80
45	+	+	+	+	+	100
45	+	−	+	+	+	80
45	+	+	+	+	+	100
45	+	+	+	+	+	100
41	+	−	−	+	+	60
41	+	+	+	+	+	100
36	+	+	+	+	−	80
35	+	+	+	+	−	80
31	−	−	+	−	−	20
31	+	+	+	+	+	100
28	−	−	−	+	−	20
28	−	+	+	+	+	80
23	−	−	−	−	+	20
23	−	−	+	−	−	20

+ individual possesses skill
− individual lacks skill

A different portrait emerges of the short man. He is *peritsi*, an abusive term connoting ugliness that is seldom uttered without a sneer or laugh. Scorned by women and rejected by prospective parents-in-law, the *peritsi* is a feeble wrestler, an improvident fisherman, an ineffective leader. He certainly is not *káukapapai* since he lacks those qualities that inspire fear and esteem. Consider Itsa, the village fool, who is one of the shortest men in the community and who is continually teased about his appearance. Itsa has internalized the prevailing attitude toward him by acting the part. When he wrestles, he mimics the style of successful wrestlers while the men laugh and shout mock advice. Often addressed as "Penis," he is teased about the size and shape of his genitals and ribbed about his amorous adventures—for which he must usually bribe the village girls.

Ahira is also considered a *peritsi*. The shortest man in the village, less than five feet tall and shorter than many of the women, he is teased less than Itsa but abused behind his back. Many of the men conduct affairs with his wife and show contemptuously little concern about hiding their indiscretions. They not only make passes at her when her husband is nearby but flirt with her in his presence. To them, a very short man does not merit respect. His size is a justification for taking advantage of him; not only is it safe to abuse him and have relations with his wife, it is also what he deserves.

Judgments based on stature also influence the villagers' allocation of prestigious statuses. Table 12 indicates the close association between a man's height and the number of his mistresses, his wealth, his sponsorship and participation in rituals, and his chiefly status. Most remarkably, the three tallest men in the village have nearly twice as many mistresses as the three shortest men even though their average ages are greater.

To the Mehinaku, height and attractiveness are not simply a matter of genetics and good luck. Being *peritsi* is a moral failing, for the short man could have grown up tall and strong if he had taken the trouble to follow all the rules associated with adolescent seclusion—taking his medicines, winding his biceps and calves with cotton ligatures, and refraining from excessive contact with women. This last restriction is particularly important, because the loss of seminal fluid (*yaki*) saps a man's strength and stunts his growth. In this connection, it is interesting to note that *peritsi* rhymes with *itsi* (penis). In derisive jokes and puns the *peritsi* is mocked as one whose *itsi* is "too hungry" for sex. Lacking the self-discipline required to comply with the rules of adolescent seclusion or to curb his excessive sexual appetite, he grows up ridiculously short and he has no one to blame but himself.

Table 12   Height and Social Participation of the Adult Mehinaku Men

Individual's height in feet and inches from medical records	Esti- mated Age	Num- ber of Mis- tresses	Rich or Poor	Sponsor- ship of important Rituals (#)	Participa- tion in important Rituals (#)	Chief, "C", or Nonchief, "N" or Trash yard man, "T"
5′9¼″	55	6	R	1	1	C
5′5″	23	10	R	1	3	C
5′4½″	35	7	R	1	3	N
5′4¼″	28	7	R	2	1	C
5′4¼″	28	6	?	1	2	N
5′4¼″	45	3	?	0	2	N
5′4¼″	31	3	P	1	0	N
5′3¾″	45	4	?	0	0	N
5′3¾″	45	3	P	1	0	N
5′3¾″	36	2	P	0	0	T
5′3″	41	4	?	0	1	C
5′2¾″	41	2	P	0	1	N
5′¾″	45	3	P	0	0	T
5′1¼″	31	6	P	0	1	N
4′11¾″	23	3	P	0	0	T

The Mehinaku bias for tall men is shared by many other societies, including our own. The sociologist Saul Feldman (1975) reports that "heightism" affects our interpersonal judgments, courtship patterns, job opportunities, and earnings. It should also be pointed out that neither among the Mehinaku nor among ourselves does short stature invariably doom a man to ridicule or failure in sexual or social relations. Atala, though just over five feet tall, has six mistresses. Lapiku, a very short man, was held in awe as a witch before his violent death in 1971. And Kuya, one of the shortest men in the village, is an honored storyteller. Build is only one of the factors in evaluating a man's worth. Let those who cannot achieve the desired physical standards strive to be generous, controlled, well-spoken, skilled, and sociable, and they may yet be well-regarded by their fellows.

Spoiled Identities

The Mehinaku sum up the constituent characteristics of social identity by labeling one another as good men or as failures. The *awujitsi*, or good man, meets all the tests of sociability, generosity, wealth, knowledgeability, and physical attractiveness. At present, however, the village has no one who measures up to this ideal image. "In the days of our grandfathers," as the chief frequently puts the matter in his evening lectures, "there were many truly good men who were generous, hardworking, and sociable. They have all died. The rest of us are not good men; we are bare shadows of our grandfathers, the real *awujitsi*." Although this speech is partly good-old-days rhetoric, it also reflects the fact that it is extremely difficult to be a good man. Some of the requirements are contradictory, simultaneously enjoining a man to accumulate possessions and to give them away. Others are unattainable; not everyone is physically attractive. Given the inflexibility of the critics and the rigor of the standards, it becomes far easier to be a flop than a hit in the theater of Mehinaku social life.

Let us look at several of these failures: the trash yard man, the freeloader, and the witch.

The Trash Yard Man

A visitor walking through the village at almost any hour in the day will encounter many of the adult males in the public areas of the community, chatting, working on crafts, or just observing the daily routine. In Mehinaku, sitting idly with others and watching the passing scene is called "facing" (*upawakatapai*), and it is one of the hallmarks of the sociable man. A rich vocabulary of abuse is applied to the villager who will not "face" his comrades. The *metanaka* (literally "backs" or "back persons"), for example, is always seen from the rear as he flees his more social comrades. Other derisive words and nasty nicknames label the chronically grumpy, sullen, and cold. The significance of the code of sociability and the pejorative terms that back it up becomes clear when we examine one of its most flagrant violators, the *miyeipyenuwanti*, or "trash yard man."

"Trash yard man" is an apt title for one who avoids others, since the trash yards are among the less visible regions of the village. There the trash yard man spends most of his time, working by himself rather than in the men's house.

"Look at old 'Rotten Fish,'" Kikyalama said one day. "He is a *real* trash yard man. He never gets up to bathe at dawn like the rest of us, and he sleeps all day in his hammock. He doesn't own any *urucu* pigment and never paints himself up in front of the men's house. When he isn't sleeping he is moping around the trash yard or the back door of his house. He doesn't even know how to play the sacred flutes. He has no friends and goes fishing by himself. Last month he went on a two-day fish poisoning trip all by himself."

To my knowledge Kikyalama's complaints are essentially just. I have never heard "Rotten Fish" make a joke in public or participate in the banter of the men's house. A dour and close-mouthed individual, he probably knows less than any other villager about crafts and traditional myths and lore.

Trash yard men like "Rotten Fish" are unloved. They are gossiped about and pointed out to children as the kind of people one should not grow up to be. Yet they are tolerated, and their presence in the village is testimony to the Mehinaku's willingness to put up with a diverse range of human types. Nevertheless, considering the contempt in which they are held and the rewards of conforming to the ethic of social participation, how can the existence of marginal characters like "Rotten Fish" and the two other notorious trash yard men be explained?

"Rotten Fish" was orphaned at such an early age that he remembers neither his father nor his mother. Without close kinsmen he was brought up in a family where he was always an outsider. The two other trash yard men have a similar background. As a child one lost close relatives in an epidemic, the other in a witch killing at an equally young age. A child cut off from kinsmen is at an enormous disadvantage in Mehinaku society. He tends to be mistreated by the other children and receives little attention from villagers who could teach him basic crafts and skills. As an adult he is condemned to remain outside a vital network of reciprocal gifts of food and labor and therefore has few opportunities to participate in the practice of generosity. An alienated individual, he can never achieve the image of the enthusiastic, social, and extraverted man admired by the Mehinaku.

The Freeloader

The trash yard man's failing is social: he does not hold up his end of the interactional dialogue that makes everyday life pleasant and spirited. Given the ethic of sociability and a community "traffic pattern" that makes encounters inevitable, his sullenness leaves a trail of resentment that follows him through the day. Nevertheless, as long as his delicts are purely social, the villagers try to receive him with a veneer of their customary good humor. As soon as he begins to shortchange them in the give and take of reciprocal obligations, however, their resentments surface in the form of definite sanctions.

The villagers linguistically recognize several types of freeloaders: those who take advantage of their fellow tribesmen in the areas of production, distribution, or consumption. The lazy man (*miyeikyawairi*) conveniently makes himself scarce when it is time to assist his comrades. He announces he must attend to another errand or slips off when no one is looking. The stingy man (*kakaianumairi*) hoards his possessions and refuses to trade when called upon. Finally, the glutton (*kanahiri*) not only eats more than his share but eats alone, a sure sign of his intention to eat too much. The terms labeling a man "lazy," "stingy," or "gluttonous" are loaded with intense negative feelings. Such men are ungenerous, a serious failing since the economic system depends on generosity, and they are mendacious and furtive as well. The lazy man complains of a sore back when it is time to lift a heavy canoe; the stingy man hides his possessions in the woods to conceal his true wealth; the glutton smuggles fish into the village unseen and then sneaks off to eat by himself. Such abusive terms, as well as the portraits of self they suggest, act as sanctions to encourage generosity throughout the society.

When gossip and abuse are insufficient to bring a miscreant into line, his female residence mates may apply heavier pressure. Each fine evening in the dry season, for example, one of the women prepares a hot drink made from manioc (see fig. 13).

She calls to each of her residence mates to join her: "Kama, come and drink nukaiya!" Stepping out to the back yard, Kama is presented with a gourd dipper brimming with the beverage. He takes his drink and chats awhile with his housemates before leaving. If Kama has been marked as "lazy," "stingy," or "gluttonous," however, he will not be called to join the others. No one will stop him from doing so on his own, but the fact that he has not been invited will rankle.

If he still does not get the message, it will be repeated in another guise. When fish is distributed Kama will get the driest, boniest, and meanest portions. Worse, the women who prepare the fish may wait until he steps out before they decide that the fish is properly cooked and ready to serve. On his return he may find that no one has saved him anything. If he persists in his ways, the pressure will increase. His in-laws will ask his wife to withdraw her sexual and domestic services. She may refuse to go bathing with him, build a fire between her hammock and his, or sleep with her feet on a line with his head. Each of these gestures is a symbolic denial of the marital relationship (see Gregor 1974). Should such sanctions fail to move him, an elder male kinsman may publicly deliver a stern lecture warning him that no woman will ever have anything to do with him unless he reforms and that in addition he risks arousing the rancor of witches.

Kama, who is in fact the most notorious of the Mehinaku freeloaders, has at various times been subject to these measures and yet has not wholly reformed his ways. On my most recent trip to the village (1976) his behavior had become a community concern. Angered by his stinginess and emboldened by his isolated status (Kama has few close kinsmen in the village), practical jokers (*metalawaitsi*) had ripped up portions of his garden and looted his fish traps with such regularity that he had abandoned them. Focusing their attention on Kama's one odd physical feature, an extra-long nose, the jokers had carved his caricature around the village. Trees, charred logs, cleared ground, and termite hills leered at the passerby in a grotesque parody of Kama's malproportioned face.

In a small community like the Mehinaku village these sanctions have tremendous leverage. Kama himself has become somewhat more generous, and certainly no one else so little values his good name and his position in the network of reciprocity that he can be described as incorrigibly lazy, stingy, or gluttonous. On the contrary, the villagers by and large strike the observer as remarkably willing to share their labor, possessions, and food—a pattern that is best explained by the positive ethic of sociability and generosity. The sanctions I have described, and the portraits of self suggested by stinginess, laziness, and gluttony, provide strong additional motivation for striving to become a good citizen, an *awujitsi*.

The Witch

The trash yard man is a villager who has lost his good name. No matter how much effort he may put into being sociable, he brings to each encounter the dead weight of a spoiled identity. The case of the witch, however, is somewhat different. Unlike the trash yard man, he usually is a full participant in the ebb and flow of daily interaction. And yet just beneath the normal courtesy accorded him lie fear, hostility, and often murderous intent.

The villagers believe that human actions are responsible for events we would regard as matters of chance or nature. Children grow into adulthood as a consequence of going into seclusion and taking the proper medicines. Physical attractiveness is no roll of the genetic dice but a result of self-discipline and again, conformity to the rules of seclusion. Health, success in fishing, fertility of orchards, and a happy afterlife at least partly depend on the performance of rituals and self-limitations on sexuality. It follows that life's misfortunes may also be the responsibility of individual Mehinaku. Thunderstorms, invasions of ants, depredations of wild pigs, house-demolishing winds, female sexual aggressiveness, sickness, death, and other mysterious phenomena can all be attributed to witches.

The first witch was the Sun. Plucking a few of his wife's pubic hairs, he fashioned the first *kauki*, or disease-causing objects that are shot into a person's body. The Sun taught his methods to his children and they to theirs, with ever new elaborations and techniques. The process of transmission continues today as parent witches train their sons for the profession. "Making" a witch requires a kind of black seclusion during which a young boy is initiated into witchcraft as well as adulthood. He is scarified as in ordinary seclusion, but the scarifier is made not of fish teeth but of snake's teeth, spider mandibles, or stingers from the ferocious *tocandira* ant. After being thoroughly scraped, venomous compounds and smoke are introduced into the wounds to make the novice's magic powerful. At first, the young witch experiments with his new power by inducing a mild illness in his victims or pestering the village with a modest plague of mosquitoes. In the fullness of time, however, he is capable of killing by a variety of magical techniques such as I have noted in table 13. Listed in rough order of importance in the present (1974) culture of witchcraft, these methods are faddish and change with time. In 1967 virtually all allegations of witchcraft mentioned tiny invisible arrows described as invariably fatal. In 1974 this technique, while still significant, was on the wane as others came into vogue.

Witches resort to deadly magic because of a desire for revenge. The jealous lover, the cuckolded husband, the envious, the robbed, and the slighted are therefore likely targets for accusations of witchcraft. In normal times such accusations may be secretly muttered in the course of malicious gossip. Once a death has occurred, however, they become the basis for action. The deceased's relatives may publicly denounce the witch; they may shoot volleys of arrows and bullets through the roof of his house; or they may attempt to kill him magically using the "grilling" method described in chapter 4. On occasion they murder the witch, especially if he is an individual who has no kinsmen to defend or avenge him. The last thirty years have seen four such killings, a rate undoubtedly inflated by the fears aroused by epidemics of measles and influenza.

A witch killing is a grisly affair, the details of which are told and retold by the villagers. The victim's last words, his dying shrieks, his groans as he is clubbed or shot are as much a part of Mehinaku oral history as the description of the activities of a great chief. In 1972, for example, Keje told me how he had killed a witch named Tipana several years before.

I didn't want to kill Tipana, but all my kinsmen told me I
had to, and I *was* angry. My stepfather asked some of the
villagers if we could go ahead, and word of our intentions got
back to Tipana. He was afraid to leave his house. One day
he went to the Post and we were on the trail to ambush him
He tried to run, but I grabbed him from behind. The others

Table 13   Witches and Some of Their Methods

1. *ipyanawekehe* (literally, *ipyana*, "wood master")
   The *ipyanawekehe* is the witch par excellence. Using slivers of *ipyana*
   wood (a dark, heavy wood, probably of the genus *Tecoma*), he shoots
   his victims with magic darts or, more commonly at present, "ties
   them" with cord by wrapping some thread tightly around a wooden
   splinter. The term *ipyana* is used generally to refer to all kinds of
   witchcraft and *ipyanawekehe* loosely designates a witch using any
   of the techniques listed below.

2. *itsítyawekehe* (literally, "tie master")
   The "tying witch" casts his spells by stealing his victim's armbands
   and tightly tying them up. The victim sickens and eventually dies.
   The *itsítyawekehe* may also be a sorcerer who practices revenge witchcraft for paying clients (see chapter 5)

3. *ejáiwekehe* (literally, "blood master")
   The "blood witch" kills by introducing poisonous animal blood into
   his victim's food.

4. *majajáiwekehe* (translation unknown)
   A ball of waxy *majajái* is shot at the victim with a tiny slingshot.
   His face turns red, his hair falls out, he gradually dies.

5. *eíyuwekehe* (literally, mosquito master")
   The "mosquito witch" torments the entire community by generating
   mosquitoes from wax pellets that he surreptitiously seeds about the
   village.

6. *ejekekíwekehe* (literally, "breath master")
   The "breath master" is only marginally a witch, since blowing can
   cure as well as harm. Just as a fire can be started by blowing on it,
   so a man can be restored to health by puffs of breath. Malevolent
   witches, however, can kill their victims by blowing in their direction.

7. *kurítsiwekehe* (literally, "love wax master")
   The *kurítsiwekehe* makes women sexually aggressive by secretly
   applying *kuritsi* wax to their bodies. He is tolerated as long as he
   confines his magic to this one technique.

held back. I shouted, "Are you women? Kill him!" They clubbed him on the head with sticks and machetes until he fell down groaning. We buried him nearby. No one dares go along the trail to the Post, for his soul (*ĩyeweku*, literally, shadow) still roams about, moaning and shrieking in pain.

This description is typical of others for, like Tipana, the victims of witch killings are usually men who are socially estranged and lack the protection of male kin. As in this case, the victim is ambushed and outnumbered, unable to protect himself against his assailants. The unusual element of Tipana's slaying was the effort to seek some consensus in the village before the killing took place. Wide agreement is not usually sought because communication networks are far too open to conceal preliminary deals. Unlike other tribal societies where a killing may be a community-approved execution (compare Hoebel's [1970: 89] account of the execution of Eskimo recidivist murderers), the Mehinaku witch killing is the action of a tight handful of aggrieved individuals.

Despite the killings, the accusations, and the belief that misfortune is caused by magic, there are few, if any, practitioners of witchcraft present in the community. Some of the villagers may have tried out a few of the simpler techniques to work off a grudge, but no evidence suggests that the institution is as elaborate or entrenched as the Mehinaku would have it. The evil intentions attributed to witches and their fanciful methods seem to be a projection of the villagers' own hostility and fear. The best evidence for this point, the sociology of allegations of witchcraft, will also take us into the effect of witchcraft beliefs on informal encounters.

Table 14 lists accusations of witchcraft by approximately half the adults in the tribe. All the suspects named are men because the villagers believe that only males can be witches. The thirteen persons questioned offered eighty-nine allegations of witchcraft, nearly seven accusations per individual. Every Mehinaku male was regarded as a witch by at least one informant, and two men were named as witches by every informant. As the table shows, accusations of witchcraft are most often directed against persons who are neither relatives nor residence mates of the informant. Unlike other South American tribes (such as the

Mundurucú as reported by Murphy 1960), the Mehinaku have no tendency to accuse shamans of witchcraft nor do they link a shaman's and a witch's magic.

Table 14   Accusations of Witchcraft by Thirteen Mehinaku Adults

Accusation, Assertion of Innocence, or Denial of Knowledge	Relationship of Informant and Suspect		Residence of Informant and Suspect		
	Kinsmen	Not Kinsmen	Coresidents, or Coresidents Prior to Marriage	Not Coresidents	Totals
Suspect Guilty of Witchcraft	9	80	6	83	89
Suspect Innocent	52	25	37	40	77
Informant Unsure of Suspect's Innocence	8	20	8	20	28

Village life is not as grim as the data in table 14 suggests. Though each man believes his neighbor is capable of bewitching him, this does not mean he will actually do so. The witch may be out of practice, his magic may be weak, he may even be a friend. The chief puts the matter in this fashion: "Yes, I think Yuta is a little bit of a witch. But it has been a long time since he made anyone sick, and I know he never would hurt me. He is my friend." The truly dangerous witches apparently number only one or two individuals, their identity depending on who is asked and changing as new tales are churned out by the ever-active gossip mill.

Although the villagers are not continually fearful, reminders of their uneasiness are always visible. During a recent visit, the doors to my house were tied shut at night to keep out prowling witches. A cautious householder patched up the holes in the thatch wall near his hammock so that he would not be shot with magic arrows. An older woman constructed an alarm system of old pot lids to alert her to nocturnal intruders. One of my companions took special pains to keep his clothes, arm bands, hair clippings, chewed fishbones, and other effluvia well away from neighbors he distrusted.

Casual interaction is also marked by anxiety about witchcraft. I have already noted how Ipyana was treated with deference and formality by villagers fearful of his power (chapter 11). Other suspected witches receive courteous or seemingly friendly treatment for the same reason. Kikyalama explains his special greeting and a big smile for Yuma: "He nearly killed my son last year because he was jealous of my new gun. If I were not afraid of him, I would not treat him so sociably." And Metawa, a compulsive practical joker, never dares to pull a prank on a suspected witch. His interactional style is far more muted and respectful in the presence of a villager he fears: "Did you see me with Yuta? I never play around with him. I pay him respect. Whenever we wrestle I let him win. I make absolutely sure he does not find out when I have sexual relations with his wife." If Metawa's and Kikyalama's restraint is typical, then one of the effects of belief in witches is to give community life a veneer of courtesy and affability it otherwise might not have. Each villager is motivated to be sociable not only by the carrot of community acceptance but also by the stick of witchcraft.

Portraits of Self

A villager's identity is largely comprised of the roles he acts within the community. His position as a kinsman, chief, or shaman, for example, affects the way others form judgments about him and interact with him. Cutting across a man's social positions, however, are the attributes of self I have described in this chapter. All of a man's roles will be affected by his sociability, his generosity, his riches, his knowledge, and his physical attractiveness. In the course of casual social engagements not clearly governed by well-defined social roles, these characteristics may become crucial. Taken together they help to determine who a man is within the community. They identify him to his fellows and allow them to evaluate his moral worth, to predict his conduct, and to respond to his overtures.

The theater of Mehinaku social life, unlike the legitimate stage, is a theater of improvisation. Actors do not bring scripts to their informal engagements, merely rough guidelines of how they ought to act. A scene may occasionally surprise us with an unexpected turn or a trick ending. Nonetheless, the portraits of self I have described impose a regularity on such encounters, providing a basis for understanding the course of informal interaction and the motives of the participants. They are, in effect, the unwritten lines that give direction, purpose, and predictability to everyday life.

Withdrawal and Disengagement

I'm going for a stroll. I'll be back later.

Kuyaparei, to his wife

In my description of Mehinaku interaction, I have been concerned with how the villagers prepare for interaction, how they greet each other, and how they present themselves once they are engaged in informal social situations. A full description of interaction, however, requires attention to the values and institutions that separate people and disengage them from social contact. Patterned methods of withdrawal and disengagement are in fact prerequisites for a society. If individuals are to come together in an orderly way, there must be times when they stay apart. The shape of interactional patterns in a society is determined by rules of separation as well as rules of engagement.

The ability to break off and withdraw from social engagements appears to be intertwined with personality and the emotional perception of one's fellows. Constant engagement is de-selfing and a possible threat to the differentiation of the ego. The psychological realization of one's self as a unique entity requires some means of social separation. It is only during moments of isolation that we can integrate and reflect on our experiences and return to new encounters with a sense of our own history and an awareness of ourselves as individuals.

Although withdrawal and disengagement help to determine the total pattern and rate of interaction, the topic has attracted little ethnographic attention. Anthropologists have usually focused on the bizarre examples of institutions that facilitate social separation, as in the case of patterns of affinal avoidance. In this chapter I plan to examine some of the problems posed by the frequent interaction that arise out of daily living and the techniques by which the Mehinaku manage to hold themselves aloof from social contact.

There are relatively few shelters from social engagement available within the Mehinaku community, and strong sanctions prevent a villager from making too much use of them. The reader can get a rough idea of the extent of the Mehinaku's exposure to one another by reconsidering the social events that can occur on the short walk to the bathing area described in chapter 11. In a brief ten-minute walk a young man had to act virtually his entire repertory of social characters—the respectful son-in-law, the sober brother-in-law, the concerned grandchild, the joking cross-cousin, and the desirous lover. Even on a very personal errand, a villager is continually open to social engagement.

Shumõɪ is on his way out of the village. As he leaves his house, his wife questions him: "Shumõɪ, where are you going?" He answers with the apparent indifference of a husband: "Nowhere, just to defecate." "Oh." As he passes a neighboring house, his uncle spots him through a tiny window in the thatch wall: "Nephew!" (the voice emerges through the wall) "Where are you going?" "To defecate." "Then go." Finally, on the path he meets his cross-cousin who is returning to the village with firewood: "Hai ja! Where are you going? Are you alligatoring the girls again?" "No, you vagina lover, I'm just carrying my egg" (that is, going to defecate). "Ha! Go ahead then!" And so it goes. A walk through the village is a journey through Mehinaku social structure, an unending series of social encounters from which there is no apparent escape.

Although I have no statistical information on precisely how often the Mehinaku are engaged with each other, the actual rate of interaction is less important than the fact that the Mehinaku sometimes find exposure to social contact abrasive and unwanted. The source of this attitude is that many of the persons with whom the villagers must interact are feared as witches, thieves, and gossips. To these fears must be added all the disagreements and antagonisms that are probably inevitable in any small human community. The Mehinaku therefore regard much of the courteous interaction that occurs in the men's house and on the public paths as something of a conscious presentation for the sake of social appearances. Repeated day after day, such presentations become habitual but, according to some of my informants, are nonetheless burdensome.

Several of the Mehinaku trash yard men seem to have given up the burden entirely. "Rotten Fish" not only avoids social contact as often as he can, but when greeted by others, responds with an unsmiling dour expression. Although only a few villagers conduct themselves like "Rotten Fish," many others are sullen from time to time. On such occasions their bad temper and rudeness generate waves of irritation and hostility among those who must deal with them. Admittedly sullenness and irritability are human universals, but the openness of the Mehinaku community to social engagement and the ethic that encourages men to initiate social encounters makes such moods unusually abrasive. There are devices, however, which enable the villagers to disengage themselves from unwanted social involvements.

Spatial Methods of Disengagement

The man who wants to avoid his comrades simply packs his bags and leaves the tribe. His destination is either another tribe, the Indian Post, a dry season village, or just the forest, where he can wander about.

Visits to Other Tribes

The Mehinaku, like other Xinguanos, are inveterate travelers. As Robert Carneiro rightly notes, "A common sight in the Upper Xingu is a traveling family: the man with his bow and

arrows in his hand, the woman with a gourd or basketful of
flour on her head, and their children carrying a few odds and
ends" (1957: 242). Although there are many motives for these
trips, some are clearly attributable to disaffection with local
village life. There is no better antidote to the pressures or the
occasional slow pace of community activities, for example, than
a trip to another tribe. Normally these visits are short and informal, ending after the visitor has participated in his hosts' rituals
or arranged to trade a shell belt or ceramic pot. On occasion,
however, the intertribal visit is a method of leaving the home
community on a permanent or semipermanent basis. One of the
few Xinguanos to embrace this strategy is Kua. Regarded as a
malevolent gossip, he is almost always seething with anger over
some slight or other. After the death of both his parents in a
measles epidemic, he went to live with an American missionary
along the Batovi River, where he spent almost all of his grow-
ing-up years.

After the missionary left the Xingu region, Kua (now with
the new name of Carlos) returned to his community but found
himself unable to get along with the villagers. He felt persecuted
by the men whose wives and mistresses became his girl friends
and by the chief who, so he believed, begrudged him the fact
that he was also of a chiefly line. Stories kept circulating through
the village that he was a magician skilled in love magic and in
the production of stinging ants.

Kua has told me of his feelings:

> When I greet everyone on the path and smile, don't think
> that I am happy here. At night, after the fires have died down
> and everyone is sleeping, I cry in my hammock. I know
> what everyone says about me, but I will not confront them.
> I am a great chief. When I am dying everyone will come to
> me in my hammock and I will say: "Look what you and your
> malicious gossip have done." And then *they* will be sad.

Kua's problems have driven him from one village to another
in the course of which he has mastered all of the Upper Xingu
languages but Trumaí. Leaving a trail of stories behind him
alleging that he beat children and practiced witchcraft, he was
never able to find a welcome in any tribe. He is now considering

giving up his own people and going to live for good at the Batovi Post of the Indian service.

Despite Kua's unhappy experience, the Xingu tribes are not always unreceptive to long-term visitors. As we shall see in chapter 18, the Xinguanos' formal pattern of hospitality ensures that virtually any visitor can count on a friendly reception. An unwanted guest finds that this welcome quickly wears thin, but in some cases he can integrate himself in his host's community on a long-term basis. In the course of most of my field work, for example, there was at least one family from another Xingu tribe living with their Mehinaku kinsmen. The motives for these extended stays were usually based on accusations or fear of witchcraft in the visitors' home village. At present (1976), two Mehinaku are living outside their own community and are unlikely to return. Ukalu, for example, lives among the Waura partly because the Mehinaku still recall the disgraceful years in which she incestuously cohabited with her father. Mutu lives a marginal existence shuttling between several of the neighboring tribes, ever fearful that he will be slain as a witch if he returns to the Mehinaku village.

The Indian Post

A man who moves from house to house is a bad sort, a man on his way out of the community. A man who shifts from village to village is said to be just like the man who can not get along with his residence mates. He, however, is not just on the way out of his home community; he is on the way out of the traditional social world. His destination is a life of exile along the margins of Brazilian civilization. He may, for example, go to work as a temporary laborer earning only his keep at one of the ranches now located along the boundaries of the Xingu reservation. None of the Mehinaku other than Kua have considered this alternative, for leaving the reservation is social suicide, a renunciation of one's entire previous life.

A less extreme and more common refuge from social pressures can be found at the Indian Post, Posto Leonardo Villas Boas, an agency of Brazil's Indian Foundation (Fundação Nacional do Indio). At present the Post consists of an air strip, a small clinic and dispensary, a guest house, and several homes for the Foundation's employees. In addition, each of the Xingu tribes has built a house at the Post to use during their visits to receive medical aid, to trade with the crews of air force planes, and to learn the latest news about the white man. The tribal houses continue to serve these functions as well as an unanticipated one: sheltering villagers marked as witches who cannot return to their own homes. At home they would be killed as soon as the next epidemic provided their accusers with a motive. Ipyana, for example, had lived for a considerable time at the Post before his death at the hands of some of the Mehinaku in 1971. He occasionally returned to the village, but there he remained in fear of his life. So afraid was he of an ambush that each time he went on an errand he carried his small son on his shoulders to discourage and shame would-be assailants. Whenever anyone in the village became ill during his stay, he promptly rolled up his hammock, shouldered his fishing gear and rifle, and left for the Post.

Ipyana would probably be alive today had he stayed at Posto Leonardo. To date the Xinguanos have had the temerity to kill only one witch at the Post ("the white man's village") and then only under extraordinary circumstances. Three alleged witches remain there, including one Mehinaku, all living rather marginal lives away from the ceremonial and social activities that make village life exciting and worthwhile. Most of them have exhausted their welcome in all the Xingu tribes, and spend much of their time hanging about the Post buildings, cadging gifts from visitors, and (when hunger and their families drive them to it) going on short fishing trips. Their presence is an embarrassment for the Post personnel, who are appalled at witch killings but who also respect the autonomy and traditions of the Xingu tribes. The dilemma is compounded by the Xinguanos' fear of the witches, sometimes leading them to put off going to the clinic when they badly need medical treatment. From the point of view of the accused witches, however, the Post offers an opportunity that had never previously existed. If village life becomes intolerable, if one is hated and feared by his comrades, there is at least an alternative; a final sanctuary for the outcasts of Xingu village society.

The Dry Season Village

A less radical alternative to permanent departure from the home community is to establish a dry season village (*uleinejepu*). At present two Mehinaku families and their dependent relatives regularly leave the community to cut new gardens near their dry season villages, each of which consists of a shabbily constructed house in a clearing near the Culiseu River. During the months that a family spends in the dry season village, the men clear new fields and the women harvest the old ones, building up a large surplus of manioc flour for the coming rainy season. Shortly before the first rains, the villagers return home with their flour.

One of the questions that puzzled me when I began my research was Why do the Mehinaku bother to make dry season villages? The gardener can plant his manioc in the ample land still surrounding the main village and spare himself the arduous task of transporting the flour home over a long distance. A partial explanation of the pattern is related to warfare. In the 1950s the Mehinaku were the victims of a series of raids by the Carib-speaking Txicão. At one point, fearing for their lives, the tribe broke into its constituent house groups and moved to a number of dry season villages hidden away in the forest. Having a second home and a garden ready to harvest was a form of survival insurance in the days when the Xingu peoples were preyed upon by "wild Indians" from beyond their borders.

How can we, however, account for the persistence of dry season villages today? I believe that one of their attractions is that they offer the Mehinaku a legitimate way of leaving the village for a prolonged period. When community tensions mount, that is the time to move to a dry season village. My friend Shumõi explained one man's departure: "Whenever he gets mad at the men for having sexual relations with his wife, that's when he decides to go to his dry season village." Shumõi, who is himself planning to clear a dry season garden site, says that he is doing so to get away from village gossip. At the dry season village there are no accusations of witchcraft, no invidious gossip, no intrigues between adulterous lovers, nor any of the other potentially abrasive situations that mar life back home.

Wandering

The dry season village and relocating in another tribe help the Mehinaku to withdraw from unwanted social contact. Still another shelter from unwanted engagements is the pattern of "strolling" or "wandering" (*etunauwakátapai*, derived from the verb *etúnapai*, to walk).

Wandering is such an entrenched institution among the Xingu tribes that the observer who is accustomed to it must make a deliberate effort to see its significance. Exclusively a male activity, it is usually done alone, although on occasion two men may go out together. Often the wanderer has some vague purpose in mind. I have strolled through the forest with Mehinaku who were ostensibly looking for root medicines, reeds suitable for flutes, or birds with feathers for decorating headdresses. Invariably they carried guns just in case they ran across a jaguar, a monkey, or an edible bird. Sometimes we would go out to the gardens in the hope of finding a ripe pineapple or a tree full of edible locusts. Once we went on a half-hearted jaguar hunt in which neither of my companions seemed to have much interest in tracking down the animal (fortunately!). Although it was usually not what we were seeking, we almost always brought back something useful: a fledgling bird to give to the children as a pet, edible wild fruit, or at least bark fiber for making ankle bands.

Although these strolls allow the Mehinaku to scan their environment and its potential resources, I am convinced that there is something else that sends them out on such excursions. The trips are far too frequent (a man is apt to be off wandering every two or three days for two to three hours at a time) to explain them as merely subsistence activities. At least some of the "walk abouts" have to be understood in the light of what is happening in the village. My impression is that the men go strolling under two conditions, the first of which is stress. Men who quarrel with their wives are especially likely to go wandering. The second condition is boredom. Whenever there is very little happening in the village, men will go for a stroll. The forests and streams are potentially exciting places where men may have chance meetings with animals and even spirits. In short, wandering through the woods enables the Mehinaku to make short-term adjustments to unsatisfactory patterns of interaction. When relationships become particularly difficult or uninteresting, a stroll though the forest provides welcome relief.

Symbolic Methods of Disengagement

The techniques of withdrawal I have just described are primarily spatial. A man simply rolls up his hammock, shoulders his rifle, and leaves the village. There are communities, however, where it is possible to secure privacy simply with gestures or other conventionalized signals. Consider the elegant method of social disengagement used by the Yagua, as described by Paul Fejos:

> Although an entire Yagua community lives and sleeps in one large house devoid of partitions or screens, its members, nevertheless, are able to obtain perfect privacy whenever they wish it simply by turning their faces toward the wall of the house. Whenever a man, woman, or child faces the wall, the others regard that individual as if he were no longer present. No one in the house will look upon, or observe, one who is in private facing the wall, no matter how urgently he may wish to talk to him. I observed this custom for the first time at the Ant settlement when I entered the house to question the chief. As the chief was unable to answer some of my questions, I asked him to call over the shaman who was sitting nearby on his hammock facing the wall. The chief declined to call him and seemed astonished at my ignorance in wishing to disturb a person who was in private and therefore not "at home." We waited for almost an hour until the shaman turned toward the center of the house and only then did the chief call him over. At first I thought that this rule applied only to the shaman, but later I discovered that all members of the clan, even children, possessed this privilege (Fejos 1943: 87).

The Mehinaku, however, have not developed any comparable method of symbolically isolating themselves except when they are emotionally unprepared for interaction, as when a villager feels shame.

The relationship of interactional withdrawal to the personal feeling of shame (*iaipiripyai*) is a healthy reminder to us that, unlike actors on the legitimate stage, the real life actors in the

Mehinaku community are fully engaged in their roles. They not only appear as kinsmen, shamans, and chiefs, they are kinsmen, shamans, and chiefs. A corollary is that interaction for them, unlike theatrical interaction, is psychologically real. They are not simply concerned with how their performance looks but how it is personally experienced. When the Mehinaku discuss their experience they employ a small number of descriptive words that summarize a complex pattern of emotions and attitudes, including "sociability," "respect," and "shame." One or more of these terms applies to every Mehinaku relationship, labeling a continuum of attitudes that we would call openness at one end, and withdrawal and disengagement at the other. We are already well-acquainted with the importance of sociability, a term suggesting a cheerful receptiveness to others, enjoyment of interaction, and warmth of disposition. Respect suggests the less spontaneous feelings associated with deference and is appropriate for the unequal or opposed relationships of in-laws and tribal chiefs. Shame is the extreme end of the continuum, a feeling associated with disengagement and retreat.

Shame

The Mehinaku feel shame in a wide variety of circumstances. Shumõi tells me that he feels shame in predictable situations, such as when he visits another tribe, when he speaks a foreign language, when he enters someone else's house, and when he speaks as a chief on the plaza at night. On the other hand, Ulawalu, an attractive adolescent girl, feels shame in virtually any public situation, such as appearing on the main plaza.

The experience of shame appears to be associated with misconduct, uncertainty about what is expected, or inability to carry off a role performance. A visit to another tribe, for example, is an uncomfortable experience, given the ambivalent relationship of the Xingu villages, the lack of familiarity with the language, and the proximity of many persons with whom there is no established basis for interaction. Entering another person's house, usually considered a violation of privacy, places the visitor in a socially anomalous position. So far as public oratory is concerned, Shumõi is unused to speaking on the plaza, feels unprepared for his chiefly role, and experiences shame when he tries to carry it off. Ulawalu's chronic sense of shame in public situations has a similar source. Only recently emerged from adolescent seclusion, she is now of sexual interest to many men who had previously been indifferent to her. She is exposed to a great deal of sexual joking from her cross-cousins. Conscious of the glances and laughter of the men seated on the bench in front of the men's house, she suspects that some of them will remark about her obvious comeliness and gossip about her affairs. Unprepared for this kind of attention and unused to her new role as a woman, she is understandably in a state of shame.

Whatever the source of shame, the villager who experiences it separates himself from his comrades. "When you are ashamed it hurts to be seen," the Mehinaku say, so the shamed man keeps out of the public eye. He may spend the day wandering through the forest or working in his garden. On his return he sits for hours on a bench staring out of a small hole he has made in the thatch wall of the house. When he goes to the river, he will use the alternate bathing areas and hidden paths that lead from the back door of each house. At night he ties his hammock between two trees in the forest to pass the night far from his family and neighbors. On his return to his house in the morning, he takes to his hammock again, lying on his side with his knees pulled up to his chest. He is said to be "curled up" with shame, just as a caterpillar curls up when held in the hand. If a kinsman or friend makes an effort to humor him out of his withdrawal, he places both hands over his eyes to communicate his unwillingness to be engaged.

Only the grossest mismanagement of affinal taboos or the exposure of serious misconduct would lead a villager to retreat so far. Less grave sources of shame, however, also make him avoid his fellows. To communicate his isolated status, he may discard feather ornaments and body paints or go about naked, without even a shell belt. Like a man in seclusion he keeps off the plaza in daylight hours, avoids the companionship of the men's house, and keeps to himself when his housemates assemble to drink tapioca (*nukaiya*) in the early evening. In these ways the shamed person physically and symbolically establishes a private world for himself. Ordinarily he will not have to live in this world for very long, for he gradually allows his friends and kin to woo him back to his normal routine. When he at last begins to feel a whole social person, he rubs his body with red *urucu* body paint and reenters the public life of the community.

Shame is thus an antisocial emotion, the antithesis of sociability. The shamed man strips himself of the paints, costumes, and other accoutrements of interaction and retreats from his comrades. In acute form, the emotion forces him into a presocial state, his eyes hidden from the "painful gaze" of his comrades, his body curled up into a fetal position, wrapped unseen in his hammock.

Disengagement and the Dramaturgical Perspective

The dramatist does not always bring his characters onto the scene; at times he must make sure they are kept well in the wings and hidden from the audience. In real life the divisions between actors and audience or stage and green room can not always be neatly drawn. Nonetheless, the members of a small community like the Mehinaku must take care not to clutter up the action when they are ill-prepared to participate in it. Chronic public sullenness like that of "Rotten Fish" or anger like that of Kua is intolerable when the script calls for courtesy and good humor. For them and for others who are not up to participating in the drama, there are techniques of disengagement—visits to other tribes, wandering in the forest, and respites in the dry season village. If they choose to remain in the community and are still badly prepared for their performance, they may feel shame. From our perspective this emotion is the personal experience of a dramaturgical imperative: the play cannot be staged by amateurs just learning their lines or even by experienced actors who muff their cues. Shame drives such performers into the wings as effectively as the yank of the classic shepherd's crook.

Leaving the community and exhibiting signs of shame may well be employed as techniques of disengagement by all peoples. The Mehinaku have other methods of social withdrawal that undoubtedly are equally widely distributed, such as the short periods of avoiding others associated with sullenness or "feeling blue." A man who is sad withdraws from the public life of the community. Being sad (*amakanatúapai*) literally means to "place oneself in one's hammock" and, like the shamed man, the sad man spends much of his day sleeping, thereby avoiding his companions.

Sadness, shame, and the other techniques we have examined, are all informal and noninstitutionalized methods of separating oneself from one's community. There is an additional method of social disengagement which goes well beyond any of these simple techniques. This is the Mehinaku's ethnographically extraordinary custom of seclusion, an institution that I shall describe in detail in the next chapter.

"Mamá! Can I go out now?"
"Someone will kill you."
Temepehu, *warning her son to stay in seclusion.*

One day in November 1971, Kikyalama erected a high barrier of palmwood staves across one end of his house, walling off his twelve-year-old son Amairi behind it. There the boy was to live by himself, separated from his family, friends, and kinsmen for almost three years. Like other Mehinaku, young and old, Amairi had entered seclusion.

Of all the customs the Mehinaku employ to set themselves apart from their fellows, the most elaborate and highly institutionalized is that of seclusion. Varying in duration from one month to three years, seclusion is a period of isolation during which a villager lives behind a partition set up in his house for the purpose. He incurs limitations on his movements about the village, his adornment, his speech, and his eating habits. His demeanor, his diet, and his consumption of special medicines symbolize his new status and mark him off from the rest of the community. Whether lounging behind his partition or skulking around the village after dark, no one can fail to recognize the secluded man.

Beginning at birth, the Mehinaku enter seclusion at key points in their social careers. A rapid inspection of table 15 indicates that seclusion is associated with changes of status related to age, kinship, and ceremonial position. On the average males will spend more time in seclusion than females since females need not be secluded for a prolonged period after the birth of the first child. Depending on whether he becomes a shaman, how often he has been widowed, and other events in the course of his social career, a man could spend up to eight years of his life in seclusion.

As we have already noted, the spatial and social setting of the Mehinaku community hardly provides fertile ground for institutions that separate and disengage social actors. The gen-

Table 15	Periods of Seclusion
Birth	A child is secluded together with his parents for a period of several months to one year.
Adolescence	An adolescent girl is continuously secluded for approximately three years beginning at her first menses.
	A boy is secluded for about three years beginning at age twelve or younger, but his period of isolation is broken at intervals during which he rejoins community life for several months at a time.
Parenthood	New fathers are continuously secluded for a period of about a year on the birth of their first child. Mothers are secluded after the birth of all their children until their postpartum bleeding stops, about six weeks.
Mourning	Husbands or wives are ritually shorn upon the death of their spouse. They remain in uninterrupted seclusion for up to a year, until their hair has grown back to its normal length.
Becoming a shaman	A novice shaman is secluded for about three months to "learn how to smoke" and communicate with the spirits.
Ear Piercing	Boys are secluded from one to three months after their ritual ear piercing at seven to twelve years of age.

eral ethic of sociability demands public interaction and prohibits disengagement and aloofness. Running directly contrary to this tendency, seclusion establishes a semipermanent backstage enclave guarded by both physical and symbolic limitations on communication and engagement. How can we account for the existence of such an institution within the Mehinaku community? One of the purposes of this chapter will be to suggest an answer to this question. But let us first look more closely at the practice itself by following young Amairi through his term of adolescent seclusion.

The Seclusion of Amairi

Before entering adolescent seclusion, Amairi understood its significance as a gateway to adulthood. He knew that it was intended to make him grow up into a man. For some time he had been playing at seclusion by setting up his own small barrier of tattered blankets and sleeping behind it. Though he honored none of the customary food taboos, took none of the seclusion medicines, and played with his friends at will, he spent more time indoors than in the past and his skin became appreciably lighter.

During this period, however, Amairi was conducting an intermittent affair with Ulawalu, one of the younger girls of the village. When his father heard about this romance, he explained to me that it was high time the boy was seriously secluded: "That will keep him away from her; I don't want him to grow up stunted."

The following day Kikyalama built a high barrier of palm wood staves inside his house behind which Amairi set up his hammock (see fig. 10). The boy then opened a small window in the thatch wall so that he would have light to work on handicrafts and see his way about in the gloom. He also thrust a long tube through the wall of the house so that he could urinate without having to go outside. Once these preparations were completed his father lectured him, "Don't you play around in here, or the Master of the Medicines will get you. Never have sexual relations with Uluwalu, unless you want to get paralyzed by the medicine spirit! Don't sleep late or go out before dusk.

Make baskets and arrows; think about wrestling. Do this and you will be a champion!"

Once behind the barrier, Amairi came under the protection and discipline of "the Master of the Medicine" (Ataiyuwekehe; *atái*, a growth-promoting medicine), a spirit who lived alongside him and who would assure the potency of the root medicines taken during seclusion. If Amairi were to fail to honor the rules of isolation, the spirit stood ready to punish him with paralysis and even death. This threat is not an idle one, for according to medical personnel who have worked in the area, the roots used to make the broths contain a toxin that can be fatal, especially if the root is collected during the dry season when the poison is

Fig. 19. A boy in seclusion. To provide light for craft work and to keep track of the day's events, a person in seclusion makes a small window through the thatch wall of the house. During the least stringent periods of seclusion, an adolescent boy will carry on an occasional whispered conversation with a friend through the window or even permit himself to be photographed by a visitor to the community.

highly concentrated. Fortunately for Amairi and other boys in seclusion, they are taught to vomit the broth immediately after they have swallowed it.

The assistance of the Medicine Spirit and his brews are the principal agencies for helping Amairi to become a man, but there are other techniques such as scarification. Nearly every concerned father has a scarifier, a gourd closely set with dogfish teeth, called a *piya*. An instrument of many uses, such as treating illness and disciplining children, its primary function is to increase muscular strength. Amairi's grandfather and father regularly appeared behind the seclusion barrier to scarify the muscles of the boy's arms, chest, back, calves, and thighs. On occasion the long parallel cuts opened by the scarifier became infected, once leading to what seemed to be septicemia, but Amairi endured it all, certain that the treatments were increasing his strength. Each time he was scraped, the wounds swelled and stretched as they filled with blood and lymphatic fluid, making him feel that his muscles were ballooning in size and growing in power.

The pain of the *piya* scarifier had to be borne with dignity, for becoming a man is a painful process. In fact, the most efficacious medicine taken by all boys in puberty isolation is called *káu*, a word referring to pain and also applied to painful foods like hot pepper. Most young men accept the discomfort because they believe it is good for them and because they know that the period of seclusion is a particularly hazardous one. Not only is the capricious medicine spirit in constant attendance but the danger from all other sources of misfortune—whether village witches, spirits armed with magic arrows, or contamination from menstrual blood—is believed to be particularly acute. Accordingly the restrictions that Amairi honored were extremely rigid: during the entire day he had to confine himself behind his partition, sitting on a bench in front of the window. Late one afternoon when his father discovered him lounging in his hammock rather than seated on his bench working on handicrafts, he reprimanded him: "Worthless little boy! Do you want to grow up stunted and unattractive? No woman will ever have anything to do with you. Look at that runt Itsa; he was just like you in seclusion, lying all day in his hammock."

In the early evening Amairi was allowed to leave his house to defecate, but only after he had carefully draped an old blanket over his head in the manner of an Arab sheik. When no one was in sight, he slipped out the back door and headed for the scrub forest behind the house, his father repeatedly warning him not to go too far lest a jaguar attack him since he was highly vulnerable to accident.

In effect, the rules of seclusion stripped Amairi of his customary freedom and social contacts. True, he was occasionally able to see his younger brothers and parents, but their visits were short and not especially interesting. Besides myself, the only other person who regularly visited him was a young virgin assigned to bring water for his daily bath. In speaking to these visitors he was obliged to use a half whisper; further, he was cautioned never to show any strong emotion such as anger or amusement.

To appreciate the radical changes in life style experienced by Amairi, we must keep in mind that formerly he had been free to roam about the village and its environs, and now he was hemmed into an area of less than seventy-five square feet. Formerly he fished, hunted, played "jaguar" on the path to the bathing area, met his girl friend, and joked with the boys and men; now he was cut off from every one of these activities and all of his friends. He was, however, getting something in return for these sacrifices. Where before he had lived in a world peopled with ordinary persons and events, now he was the center of a small, extraordinary world peopled by himself and the Medicine Spirit, who though unseen was always present. Where he had once been a boy, now he was on the road to adulthood.

How does a twelve-year-old cope with this sudden and wrenching loss of freedom? Amairi's first reaction to seclusion was pride. For several days he closely followed all the rules and diligently spent his time weaving a large basket. Periodically his father came behind the isolation barrier to supervise him and remind him of the importance of seclusion and the necessity of obeying all the restrictions. Soon, however, his new status and the novelty of isolation ceased to involve him fully. After his initial enthusiasm, he became petulant and morose. During the rest of the first week, he spent hours staring out of his small window and lying in his hammock whenever he thought his parents were not watching.

Alternately, his mood became slightly hysterical. When I came to talk with him, he was uncharacteristically unable to sustain a focused discussion and would lapse into foolish jokes about feces and oversized genitals. A great deal of time was passed in sadistic efforts to shoot vermin. Armed with a small bow, he patrolled his seclusion area hunting mice and two-inch-long cockroaches (depressingly easy to find). Impaling these creatures on an arrow, he would allow them to wriggle about for a while before tossing them into the fire or out the window.

Kikyalama realized that his son was not happy in seclusion. "He hears the other boys shouting outside and wants to join them," he told me. Periodically Kikyalama lectured Amairi on the importance of seclusion and the necessity of the rules. And, perhaps like all parents, he could not help reminding him that things were tougher in his day:

> No more of this playing around. In seclusion you sit and work quietly. You think about wrestling so that you will grow strong. When I was in seclusion it was much harder. My father went to hunt monkey and birds for me, but he just had a bow and arrow. Tomorrow I'll take my rifle and shoot some for you so you will have something to eat besides manioc.

After about a week Amairi appeared to settle down somewhat; his activities became more regular and the hysterical joking and vermin hunting ceased. He reluctantly admitted that he was not enjoying himself, but at least he seemed to be adjusting to his low-key life behind the barrier.

In 1972, I made an effort to find out exactly what Amairi did in seclusion by recording his behavior during several hundred randomly selected intervals over a period of several months. Table 16 represents a profile of Amairi's activities during a fifty-six-day period of observation, long after he had made his initial adjustment to the restrictions of seclusion.

An interesting figure in this table is the percentage of time Amairi devoted to doing nothing or next to nothing. More than a quarter of his time was spent doing little more than staring

Table 16   Activities in Seclusion
(305 random observations over a period of fifty-six days)

Activity	Percentage of Observations
Personal needs, including bathing, preparation and consumption of food, personal adornment	15
Crafts, including basketry, arrow making, manufacture of belts, ornaments, combs, etc.; arranging of possessions, drawing	49
Interaction, with parents, water girl, sister, smaller brothers, unrelated children	9
Withdrawal, including sleeping during the day, day-dreaming in the hammock, staring out of the window, sitting on the bench and doing nothing	27

out the window or lying in his hammock and, according to Amairi, daydreaming.

Less than 9 percent of Amairi's time was spent in interaction with his family and others. This figure, however, is far too high for the more rigorous phases of Amairi's isolation when he was taking medicines, for during this period I found him interacting with others less than 2 percent of the time. Despite these low rates of interaction Amairi was not totally cut off from his society. Not only did he occasionally speak to his relatives, but he also remained very much involved in the affairs of his household. I became aware of this involvement when I lived on the opposite side of his seclusion partition and frequently heard him giggling or making soft comments to himself over what was being said in another part of the house. On occasion I caught him staring out of a small break in the barrier to see what was going on. Though Amairi was not interactionally present to his housemates, he was aware of their presence and influenced by their activities and speech. In no sense is seclusion anything like the total isolation of solitary confinement.

Amairi's activities in seclusion did not occur randomly but followed a regular pattern. For a few days he would involve himself in a project, such as working on a basket or a bead belt. But once the project was completed, he would do little but lounge about in his hammock and stare vacantly out the window until the Spirit (or his father!) moved him to get started on something else. This cycle of activities is most clearly revealed by my random observations of Amairi's behavior during a ten-day period in December 1971, when he was taking medicines and closely observing the restrictions of seclusion. Thus during the eleven random visits I made between December 4 and December 8, 1971, I found him each time actively engaged in handicrafts. But then in the period between December 9 and December 13, all activity seemed to cease and he spent his time for the most part resting in his hammock. This rhythm of activity alternating with passivity seems to have persisted during the entire course of my observations, the cycle varying in length between two and five days.

I have written about Amairi's seclusion as though it kept him from all public appearances. Seclusion, however, includes two phases: one in which the adolescent takes medicines, closely honors the various restrictions and remains behind his barrier, and a second less rigorous stage in which he emerges into the light of day for the purpose of wrestling with his mates. The phases are unnamed, though some of the villagers distinguish between the "master or taker of medicines" (ataiyuwekehe, the first phase) and the somewhat ambiguously labeled "house stayer" (pãiyukwá, the second phase).

Amairi had been in seclusion for about five months when his father and grandfather decided that it was time for him "to learn to wrestle:" Although several months had already passed since the boy had last taken medicines, it is well known that the Spirit's powerful brews remain in the stomach for a long time, making it dangerous to try to wrestle before they are entirely gone. In April 1972 Amairi made his first public appearance. He covered his body with oil to make himself supple, bound his arms and knees tightly to increase his strength, and put on the feather headdress that marked him as an adolescent in seclusion. Leaving his house early, he sat down on the bench in front of the men's house and awaited an opponent. Other villagers came out to join him. But Amairi would wrestle only with close kinsmen and other boys in seclusion. He knew that as a boy in isolation he was especially vulnerable to witches or to physical contact with men who had recently had sexual relations. Between bouts he sat apart from the others, maintaining the circumspect air appropriate to a young man in seclusion. No matter how strong the temptation, he refrained from joining in the banter of the men's house and the teasing of the little boys who playfully wrestled nearby their parents and older brothers.

Shortly after beginning to wrestle, Amairi became more casual about allowing himsef to be seen by others. He bathed in the house outside the seclusion barrier, came to talk to me and to lounge in my hammock, and spent more time out of doors. He said that since he had been seen wrestling, and since he had stopped taking medicines, he was much freer to move about. Still, he had to cover himself with clothing during his movements about the village and keep to the back paths so that he would be seen as little as possible. Going down to the river, for example, he followed an alternate path, the *atiyuwekehe napu,* "master of the medicine's path."

Eventually, Amairi told me, he would be permitted to go fishing by himself and make a garden. Important symbols of adult status, Amairi had constantly urged them upon his parents. Like parents everywhere, however, they were inclined to resist his demands to be treated as grown-up. When he pleaded with his mother for permission to go fishing alone, for example, she curtly replied, "Someone might kill you!" A witch was likely to get him while he was still so young and in seclusion.

Amairi was still limited in the number of people with whom he could interact, yet he took this constraint much less seriously than in the past. At night he came out of his house to sit on the plaza and joke with the other boys. When public bartering sessions were held in his house he traded through intermediaries, passing his purchases and payments across the seclusion barrier. He frequently teased younger boys who came too close to his partitioned area, poking them with headless arrows and cursing them whenever their play became irritating: "Shut up, 'Head Louse'! Get away, 'Tiny Penis'!"

The transition between phases of seclusion was also marked by changes in dietary rules. Until this point he was only allowed to eat "tasteless" foods like manioc bread and unspiced fish. Once he emerged to wrestle, food restrictions were lifted. To start, he was given a small amount of hot sweet tapioca porridge prepared by a virgin. He took only a sip of this food, to let the sweetness reach him gradually. Other foods and spices, such as pepper and salt, were introduced in the same careful fashion. Finally he was permitted to enjoy a more ordinary diet.

When I saw Amairi in January 1974, he had totally emerged from seclusion, after being sickened by one of the root medicines. According to his father, however, his term of isolation was far from over and he was due to reenter within a few months. Other parents commonly move their children in and out of isolation in accordance with their growth, health, and adaptability to seclusion. One father whose son was needed on a salt-making expedition, for example, simply told him he could leave isolation for a few months. Similarly, another decided that his son was maturing too rapidly and had the boy leave for a while to slow down the process of growth. Finally, fathers whose children engage in sexual relations or otherwise fail to honor the restrictions of seclusion may simply tear down the barriers and unceremoniously evict their boys into public life.

The Symbolism and Meaning of Seclusion

All periods of seclusion, whether for paternity, shamanism, or adolescence, make use of a similar set of symbols to mark the status of the villager in isolation, as is shown in table 17. Food taboos radically alter his diet and provide a code which marks transitions between seclusion and normal life. The categories of food relevant to the system are listed in table 18, along with a number of examples of each type.

The basic diet prescribed for persons in seclusion is usually drawn from bland and tasteless (*mana*) items. A few foods within this category, however, are also tabooed in order to protect the health of the individual in isolation. Fish, for example, must never be eaten by secluded persons who are bleeding or symbolically associated with blood. Basso (1973: 70) has described this prohibition among the Kalapalo, but it is even more

Table 17   Symbols of Seclusion

Symbol	Everyday Village Life	Periods of Seclusion
1. Food	Foods of all classes, textures, and modes of preparation are permissible	Food in certain classes prescribed or prohibited; food of certain textures and methods of preparation forbidden
2. Ornamentation	*Urucu* red pigment used as a symbol of social accessibility	*Urucu* prohibited
3. Demeanor	Sociable, outgoing demeanor (*ketepepei*)	Interaction with others severely curtailed; muted demeanor

elaborately developed by the Mehinaku. Fish is prohibited to menstruating women, young men who have just had their ears pierced, and husbands awaiting the cessation of their wives' post partum flow of blood. The Mehinaku say that the bones of fish will prevent the bleeding (which is usually considered dangerous and even disgusting) from coming to a quick halt. "Painful foods" (pepper, salt) are believed to have a similar effect, and are scrupulously avoided.

Fish is opposed to other "tasteless" bony foods, such as monkey and birds, in the sense that all three foods are never tabooed

Table 18   Classes of Food Relevant to Seclusion Taboos

1. Sweet foods (*puya*), including fruits, honey, boiled manioc porridge (*nukaiya*)

2. Painful foods (*kaki*), including salt and pepper

3. Fermented and rotted foods (*ahala*), including fermented *pequi* fruit

4. Bland, tasteless foods (*mana*), including the most common foods eaten: water, manioc bread and porridge, fish, birds, monkey, locusts, etc.

simultaneously. When one set is permitted, the other is prohibited, as shown in table 19. I am aware of no specific explanation for this opposition of bony foods, but it clearly functions to leave at least one important source of protein in the secluded individual's diet, as well as dramatizing the socially important transition between "bleeding" and "nonbleeding" stages in seclusion.

Table 19   The Prohibition of Fish, Monkey, and
Bird Meat in Seclusion

Seclusion	Fish	Monkey and Bird
1. Female adolescent seclusion		
A. During menstruation	Forbidden	Permitted
B. Before and after menstruation	Permitted	Forbidden
2. Father's seclusion (*couvade*)		
A. During mother's *post partum* bleeding	Forbidden	Permitted
B. After mother's *post partum* bleeding	Permitted	Forbidden

Other categories of food also have specific associations during seclusion. Sweet foods (*puya*) and painful foods (*kaki*), for example, have opposite meanings. Painful foods, such as pepper and salt, are associated with potent effects, being used as medicines for a sore throat or a wound. Sweet foods, on the other hand, are associated with heightened sensitivity rather than powerful effects. Honey, for example, is eaten by the secluded shaman who wants to make his lips sensitive to the presence of intrusive disease objects which he can then suck out of his patient's body. Appropriately, he also takes pepper (painful food) to make his lips and throat powerful.

During every other period of seclusion (with the exception of mourning and the initiation of shamans), painful and sweet foods are tabooed for at least a part of the period of isolation. These foods, the Mehinaku say, do not "mix" with the medicines that the isolated individual must take. The medicines, the villagers claim, would be confused by the addition of such distinctive foods such as those which are sweet and painful.

Two basic ideas lie behind the various taboos and restrictions associated with Mehinaku seclusion. The first is that the changes in growth and health that we view as natural, they regard as largely following from procedures for which they themselves are responsible. Boys mature sexually, grow strong, and become good wrestlers and fishermen because the Mehinaku follow certain rules. Boys who have had their ears pierced, girls who menstruate for the first time, and mothers who have newborn children stop bleeding because they take medicines and honor the other rules associated with seclusion. Girls mature and grow strong and beautiful because they were secluded upon their first menstruation.

A second idea is that the individual in seclusion is in jeopardy from forces over which he has little control. The Medicine Spirit lives in association with every boy and girl in puberty isolation, and he is capricious. He not only punishes a child who fails to follow the rules, but occasionally may paralyze a person who honors all the prohibitions. An individual who escapes this fate still feels that he is at the crossroads of his life. His size, strength, attractiveness, and skills will depend on his correct behavior and attitude during seclusion. Just thinking about wrestling will help to make him a more powerful wrestler. At night there is no respite, for even dreams can have a profound influence on the rest of his life. Amairi, once again, sums up the pressures, dangers, and pay-offs of seclusion:

> Look at how I live. I sit on my bench all day working. I eat only stewed fish without pepper and salt. I swallow and vomit medicines my father gets for me. Little boys tease me from outside. But I can't leave the house. Witches would shoot me with magic arrows if I did. I must stay in seclusion. That is the way to become a man.

Seclusion: Disengagement and Withdrawal

Among the Mehinaku the institution of seclusion concerns itself with growth, health, and changes in status. The restrictions of diet, demeanor, and ornamentation are expressions of these concerns and methods of achieving certain desired ends. This view of seclusion, however, is primarily an insider's understanding of the institution, the kind of explanation that a Mehinaku himself might offer. What are the functions of seclusion for individuals and the greater society? Dramaturgically, the central fact of seclusion is that actors are artificially screened from public view for years at a time. I therefore believe the best way to understand the institution is to consider how it reduces the flow of information and the play of interaction within the village-theater.

How does seclusion affect interaction and communication? For the villager who is isolated the answer is obvious. He is effectively cut off from most of his kinsmen, his comrades, and village public life. In almost every one of my observations, the secluded individual was present behind his partition. Instances of engagement with others were rare. Isolation follows the secluded individual even when he violates the rules and leaves his shelter, for he is socially separated from his fellows though in their presence. They do not greet him on the paths or engage him in any other way.

One new father in seclusion, for example, carelessly allowed himself to be seen around the public plaza. Feeling ambivalent about this obvious violation of seclusion restrictions, he dressed in old clothes and carried an umbrella to hide himself. During intertribal wrestling matches he sat on the men's bench to watch the action, his outlandish garb signaling to the villagers that though physically present he was to be treated as if he was interactionally absent. In fact, he was studiously ignored by both the Mehinaku and their guests.

Some of the villagers have told me that they enjoy the reduced social contacts and the temporary holiday from village tensions that seclusion offers. Explaining the practice by individual motivation, however, fails to account for the fact that seclusion occurs at unpredictable times during an individual's social career, such as the death of a spouse, paternity, or the onset of puberty. Even if seclusion could be initiated at will, it is too long and too unrelieved to meet the needs of most people. A little isolation every day might seem like a good thing, but three years is obviously too much. The difficulties that some of the Mehinaku have in adapting to seclusion further suggests that isolation is not an unmixed blessing.

We may be able to offer a more satisfactory explanation of isolation practices among the Mehinaku by extending our attention from the individual in seclusion to those who remain outside. There are, so to speak, two sides to every wall. If the individual in seclusion is cut off from his fellows, they are also cut off from him. In this sense the barriers and the restrictions of seclusion have an effect on all the Mehinaku, not just on those in isolation.

Let's first consider the matter of the partition. Ordinarily Mehinaku houses are undivided. Indeed, to build a barrier and hide behind it away from one's fellows is a mark of an undesirable man—a "trash yard man" at best, at worst a witch. I know of only one villager who attempted to wall himself off from his community for any length of time. He was executed as a witch shortly after a measles epidemic during the early 1960s, and his death was neither mourned nor regretted.

In 1972, I had a good opportunity to see the informal sanctions imposed on a Mehinaku who though not in seclusion tried to live behind a partition. Kehe, one of the younger men, had abandoned his wife and gone off to live with a woman in another tribe. One night he secretly returned under the cover of darkness and slipped into an abandoned house which had a seclusion partition blocking off one end. Ashamed to be seen, he slung his hammock behind the barrier. Within twenty-four hours the entire village was gossiping about him. Kehe, people said, must be in puberty seclusion. His wife was quickly labeled his "mother," who had to bring him water for bathing as would any parent who had a child in seclusion. Finally, after one of Kehe's older kinsmen appeared and read him a lecture on his shameful conduct, he gave way to public pressure and left his seclusion barrier.

Obviously no Mehinaku can casually wall himself off from his neighbors without evoking a public reaction. Nevertheless there are some situations in which seclusion is an acceptable response to personal and family problems. A man whose kinsman is in seclusion, for example, may choose to live with him behind the partition, honoring none of the restrictions but taking advantage of the increased privacy offered by the barrier. Consider figure 20 which shows how Kikyalama constructed and changed the seclusion partitions for his son over a period of about six months. His justification for each new pattern was invariably that it was best for his children, but it was also clearly related to his own needs. The arrangement that produced the most privacy corresponded to periods of greatest friction within the household, especially between Kikyalama and his father-in-law.

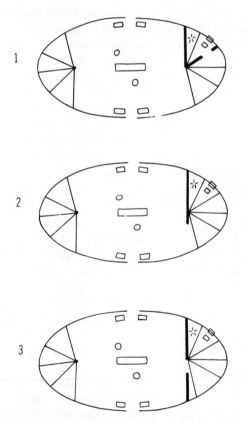

Fig. 20. Variations in seclusion partitions. Over a period of three months, Kikyulama adjusted the seclusion partitions both in response to his children's needs and to his interest in obtaining a degree of privacy within the house.

Kikyalama's experience shows that seclusion provides relief from interaction and surveillance for others besides those living behind the partition. In 1967, when my wife and I were living in the house of the chief, a barrier was constructed halfway across one side of the residence to accommodate a boy in adolescent seclusion. Immediately the house became quieter and interaction between people on each side was less frequent. The boisterous remarks shouted back and forth across the house at night died down. Each side of the house, it seemed, was now a separate residence.

If those who live within the house of a person in seclusion enjoy reduced social exposure, so to a lesser extent does everyone else in the tribe. If a villager cannot see or make contact with those who are in seclusion, he is also free from their surveillance and contact. We must remember that there are only seventy-seven people in the entire village, over half of whom are children. Just one or two adults in seclusion can make a real difference in the amount of social contact. It is possible to make a rough calculation of the reduction in contact and exposure associated with Mehinaku seclusion practices. The rules of seclusion call for each Mehinaku to spend about five years in isolation. Some Mehinaku are more lax than others, however, and not everyone is secluded when he is supposed to be. "Trash yard men" are derisively pointed out as examples of what happens to those who leave seclusion prematurely. Chiefs and other high status individuals, however, are especially scrupulous about honoring seclusion taboos. Taking these considerations into account, I estimate that each Mehinaku spends an average of three years in seclusion. Assuming an average life span of fifty years, we can expect that about 6 percent of the population will be in isolation at any one time. It follows that seclusion should reduce rates of social engagement by about 6 percent for all the villagers even when they themselves are not in isolation.

Another way that seclusion regulates interaction is through the changes it induces in residence. With the exception of the movements that follow marriage, the Mehinaku do not usually move from one house to another. To do so is an admission of social failure. A divorce, a quarrel, or some other serious dispute is usually behind each move. People say that a man who chronically moves from house to house is a malcontent, one who slanders the good name of his former residence mates.

Seclusion, however, can provide a justification for shifts in residence owing to the vulnerability of the individuals in isolation. A young man in puberty seclusion is in continual danger not only from witches but also from menstruating women. The presence of a large number of sexually active women is painfully disgusting (*kamayũpapapi*) to him and he may spit on the ground if they should come into his house, both to express and relieve his revulsion. When Amairi entered isolation, for example, his father was concerned that one of the women living close to his seclusion partition would unexpectedly have her period while he was taking medicines. Since the menstrual blood could "get into the medicine" and place the boy in serious jeopardy, his father prevailed upon the woman and her husband to move out of the house temporarily. To this end they built a small outbuilding (*mehehe*) behind the main house.

Though this woman was now out of the house, Amairi faced still another hazard: his own mother's menstrual discharge. Less threatening, to be sure, than that of an unrelated woman, it was nevertheless a sufficient motive for Kikyalama to build a second outbuilding behind his house to accommodate his son whenever it became necessary.

Later, Kikyalama decided that it was too dangerous to leave Amairi in the outbuilding. A witch might sneak up to the side of the house and kill him with an invisible arrow as he knelt by the light of his fire. Kikyalama and his wife moved into the outbuilding themselves, sending Amairi back to the main house to stay with his grandparents. When this arrangement looked as though it were becoming permanent, Kikyalama's father-in-law made a speech on the plaza in which he suggested that his daughter and son-in-law were neglecting their family and should return to their own home. The couple did so, but after a short time they were out again. The move was justified as being for their son's welfare, but it also seemed connected with their relationships within the larger household as well as their evident pleasure in living by themselves.

We can see that wholesale changes in residence accompanied one boy's seclusion. Two houses were built, one of them quite possibly a permanent, one-family residence, and four adults shifted residence permanently or temporarily. Seclusion, then, offers opportunities to change residence without the opprobrium usually associated with such moves.

The Balance of Engagement and Withdrawal

The Mehinaku tell us that seclusion insures physical growth and maturity. From our perspective, however, seclusion is a dramaturgical device that limits interaction and the flow of information within the village-theater. Surrounding the individual with physical and symbolic barriers that separate him from his fellows, seclusion serves to increase not only his privacy but that of the outside community as well. In so doing seclusion provides a kind of backstage area in a theater where normally each actor has full access to his fellows.

An important question remains. Surely the Mehinaku could have come up with a less awkward and artificial solution to the problem of disengagement and social distance. Why not build permanent partitions within the houses or live in many separate houses? I believe such a solution would subvert village cohesion. Unlike other preliterate societies, community stability and unity are not structured by out-group antagonism or rules of exogamy. Pacification of the Xingu region, the presence of the white man, and the coalescence of tribes around the Indian Post have somewhat blunted tribal consciousness and identity. Villagers simultaneously claiming membership in two tribes can simply pull up stakes and go to live with their kinsmen in another village whenever the spirit moves them. Even "pure" Mehinaku have longstanding ties with distant kin in other tribes which allow them to make similar moves when the pressure of village life requires it. The danger of separate residences is that when a man changes his home, he is considered to be on the way out of the community and perhaps even the social world of the Xinguanos. Kuyaparei, in talking about one of the village trash yard men, puts it like this: "Last month he lived in Iyepe's house. Yesterday he was at Imi's. Today he is joining us. Soon he will go to live with some other tribe; and then he'll go off to become a *kajaiba* (white man)."

Although the relative openness of the Xingu tribes allows the Mehinaku to live with their neighbors, the integrity of the home village is also important. During crop blights and epidemics a willingness to cooperate and stick together may be crucial. My point is that one-family houses, or even permanently partitioned residences, could be a threat to community integrity. Within the community today, it is almost invariably the man in the "other house" who is suspected of the most invidious gossip and witchcraft. The man whose hammock swings close to yours, however, is trustworthy. Conceivably he may be a witch too, but it is known that witches are not dangerous to their residence mates. Witches and their accusors came from different houses in all the cases of witch killings that I have been able to document. Increase the number of houses in which the Mehinaku live and you may also increase the suspicion and the ill-will which separates the villagers from their fellows. Among the Mehinaku as among ourselves, good walls can make bad neighbors.

Although I have argued that disengagement and privacy are prerequisites of Mehinaku (and all) social life, it is apparent that the opposite is also true. The Mehinaku must never become too disengaged or too ignorant of each other's activities and intentions. In a community such as theirs, we find a narrow optimum range between what constitutes too little and too much interaction and exposure. The institution of seclusion may be regarded as a way of maintaining this range by providing an acceptable shelter from engagement and exposure and at the same time preventing this shelter from becoming a permanent and centrifugal way of life.

(On following page). Wearing gourd calabashes, three masked dancers imitate the grotesque movements of the spirit Yakweikwityumá. Like the dancers, Yakweikwityumá and the other spirits in the Mehinaku pantheon resemble ordinary persons when they are stripped of their ghastly apparel. More frequently, however, the spirits make themselves known to the villagers in full costume, for they, too, are performers in the drama of Mehinaku life. *Reproduced from a watercolor painting by the Xinguano (Trumai) artist, Amatiwana.*

4

Thus far I have described Mehinaku society as if it were a kind of social drama. The village is the setting for this drama, forming a great theater in the round where actors and audience communicate and move in and out of play. I have paid little attention to the script, except for a discussion of some of the entrance and exit lines and the "images of self" that the actors present to their audiences. Some parts of the script, however, are more formally written and require fairly extensive treatment. These parts are the roles that the Mehinaku perform. This portion of my report describes Mehinaku role structure and attempts to relate the formal demands of the role with the theatrical problems involved in staging it. A good way to begin is with the point of view of the Mehinaku themselves. How do they view the roles they act and their relationship to them? Chapter 15 explores this question.

The Mehinaku Concept of Social Roles

He's a lot my brother-in-law and a little my cousin.

The chief, speaking of his wife's first cousin

Robert Murphy, in the *Dialectics of Social Life*, has remarked that all men are students of society: "One of the most useful lessons in the study of society is that Everyman is an anthropologist or sociologist of sorts . . . a student of society, however untalented or limited in perspective, and not merely a victim of custom" (1971: 6). All men, by virtue of their need to predict the behavior of their fellows, must reflect upon their society and their position within it. Although the Mehinaku are not given to self-conscious social philosophy, their language, their institutions, and their evaluations of their fellows amount to an implicit theory of the relationship of men to their society. This is a theory to which we must attend, for it helps explain much of the remarkable flexibility and personal creativity that goes into the system of social roles among the Mehinaku.

Men and Social Roles

The Mehinaku have a language by which they are able to describe their relationship to their society. One of the morphemes in this language is *wekehe*, a term used to designate a wide variety of relationships and associations. The simplest kinds of associations marked by this word are those of property and there the term simply means "owner." Hence, individuals are identified as owners of canoes, gardens, headdresses, and so forth, simply by placing the morpheme *wekehe* after the noun, as in Kuyaparei is the *itsa wekehe*, or the canoe owner.

Similarly, persons who possess special skills are also identified as *wekehe*. A shaman who cures with a song is called an *apái* (song) *yekehe* (*wekehe*). In this sense, I gloss *wekehe* as "master." Villagers also may be identified as masters of the bow (great hunters and fishermen), masters of witchcraft (witches), masters of the word (public speakers), masters of myth (story tellers), and masters of wrestling (champions). Virtually every social role, with the exception of those of age, sex, kinship, and the chieftainship, may be linguistically stated in the same way. The fact that the term *wekehe* appears to have an equivalent among both speakers of Carib (*oto*; see Basso 1973: 154) and Tupi (the suffix *-át*; see Zarur 1975: 41) strongly suggests that a similar system of labeling roles prevails among most of the Xinguano tribes.

The significance of these linguistic markers becomes clear when we look at ceremonial roles. The Mehinaku have a pantheon of spirits who can associate themselves with an individual in a variety of ways. Once this association is complete, the individual becomes a spirit *wekehe* who is responsible for the performance of a series of rituals given in the spirit's name. In the course of the rituals, the *wekehe* chooses other villagers (*petewekehe*) who are charged with initiating and directing the ceremonies. To clarify the roles of *wekehe* and *petewekehe*, Shumõı kindly offered me the following analogy: "You have seen the planes land at the Post? Well, the spirit *wekehe* is like the owner of the plane, and the *petewekehe* is like the pilot." In short, both pilot and owner have a relationship to an entity (the plane) which also has an existence of its own apart from either of them. In the case of Mehinaku ritual life, this entity is a spirit, approached through a complex set of ritual obligations and conduct.

The fact that one word, *wekehe*, is used to mark very different roles, including those of witch, hunter, farmer, shaman, and sponsor of rituals, suggests a conception of social statuses. A role is seen as a relationship that a person has to a skill, a possession, or a supernatural being. A person is not subsumed by his social position, for there must be a man to relate to the spirit, the object, or the skill. The Mehinaku are thereby suggesting that men are different and separate from the roles they act, that behind each social mask there is a man.

Relationships and Roles

A second word that the Mehinaku use when they talk about their position in society is *ehewe*, or "relationship." Thus, when a villager is uncertain about the roles that bind one man to another, he may well ask "What is your relationship to him?" (*Atsa pitya héwepei jahã?*). Unless a relationship is simply denied, the answer will almost always be couched in the form of a kinship term or an indication of formal friendship, such as "*Nutanuléi, jahã*" (He is my cross-cousin.). What strikes us is that, like sociologists, the Mehinaku have an abstract vocabulary for talking about social relationships quite apart from individuals or specific roles.

Crucial to understanding Mehinaku society is the villagers' idea that relationships are a matter of degree rather than "all or nothing." Individuals are associated with objects, skills, spiritual beings, and each other to an extent. If the association is close, any ambiguity about the relationship may be clarified by appending the morpheme *waja* (true, genuine, very much) to the social position. Hence a villager may be referred to as a true bowman (*ĩtai wekehewaja*), true brother-in-law (*upuhunei-waja*), true witch (*ipyana wekehewaja*), and so on.

When the association between the person and the status is less complete, then the diminutive *hatãi*, "a little bit," may be added to the title. A villager may be very much a brother-in-law, a genuine bowman, a full-fledged witch, or a little bit of a chief. Even consanguineal and affinal relationships are quantified in this fashion. A villager can have a "little bit of a wife," a "real son," or a "little cross-cousin."

Each of these distinctions has important behavioral implications that will concern us further on. For the moment, however, it is enough to note that there is a separation between men and their social roles, and that this distance is measurable and may be cited as a significant feature of the relationship.

Attitudes Toward Social Relationships

The distinction that the Mehinaku make between people and their social roles also comes up in their attitude toward their relationships. Some social roles, they quite frankly say, are burdensome. Ritual and affinal obligations are often shouldered only after considerable reluctance and occasionally they are altogether refused. A villager may list the duties of being a brother-in-law, complain that he already has too many brothers-in-law, and then refuse to fill this obligation for a new in-law. His refusal suggests that the Mehinaku are quite capable of sitting back and objectively adding up the usefulness and desirability of certain relationships. In short, they can take distance from their roles and assess their value.

The way the Mehinaku praise and criticize each other offers us further insight into their view of social relationships. They could see each other primarily as incumbents of specific statuses: a woman could be lauded as a good wife or as a responsible mother; a man could be damned as a bad father, a lazy son-in-law, or a miserable chief. And it is true that such comments are frequently heard among the Mehinaku, but perhaps not as often as another kind of evaluation that looks past the social actor and sees the person as an individual. A man is criticized for being angry, sullen, stingy, flippant, gossipy, malicious, or antisocial. He is praised for his generosity, his emotional control, or his sociability.

Personal judgments such as these are usually expressed differently from the language of social roles. When the Mehinaku discuss the psychological proclivities of individuals, they append the affix *airi* (or one of its morphophonemic equivalents), which I gloss "one who is," to a given trait. The *kakaianumairi*, for example, is the "one who is stingy," the *eketepemʊnairi* is the "one who is happy," the *japʊjaitsi* is the "one who is angry," and the *miyeikyawairi* the "one who is lazy." Since these terms do not connote definite obligations and privileges, they, like other words taking the affix *airi*, are primarily the evaluation of men rather than named social statuses. Recognition of men both as social actors and individual personalities is thus built into the language.

Attitudes towards relationships and judgments of others add up to a theory of human motivation. The behavior of people cannot be wholly explained because they are the incumbents of certain social statuses; they also have a predisposition to act in certain ways. The basis for the predisposition varies. Sometimes it is supposed to be inherited and sometimes it is supposed to have been learned. In any case the belief represents, again, an explicit awareness that behind the social mask there is a person.

The Social Contract: Relationships Are Made by Men and May Be Changed by Them

The most revealing evidence of the Mehinaku attitude towards social relationships is not linguistic but behavioral. The Mehinaku view roles not as given and immutable but as subject to change through manipulation and new understandings. Mutability of relationships affects both the rules of allocation of social roles and the behavioral prescriptions of the roles themselves. Changes in relationships can occur during a process of role bargaining associated with marriage, sexual affairs, and intertribal contact during which the villagers can agree to "be" certain kinds of relatives and can even more or less define for themselves the nature of their mutual obligations. There are, of course, definite limits to such changes, for social life is never left entirely to the whim of individuals.

The element of creativity inherent in role bargaining is also characteristic of the villagers' ritual life, for there is substantial evidence that much of their religious system is deliberately authored. Inspired individuals are left free to compose new songs, choreograph new dances, devise new musical instruments, and discover new demons. Rather than destroying spontaneity and initiative, social roles and religious practices have given the Mehinaku remarkable freedom to improvise and create new material for the continuing drama of community life.

We will document the openness of Mehinaku kinship and ritual life to the contributions of individuals later. Let us now briefly examine two institutions, those of sex roles and naming practices, that provide especially clear evidence of the dialectic of society and the individual characteristic of Mehinaku culture.

The Origins of Men's and Women's Roles

No roles are so basic or so immutable as those of the sexes. In our own society the differences between men and women are among the first social distinctions that children make, and by age three their gender identity is so firmly fixed that it can be reversed only at considerable psychic cost. The ethnographic record suggests that other societies also give great weight to sex roles, for everywhere boys and girls are socialized differently and enter adulthood prepared to follow different social careers. The Mehinaku are by no means exempt from this pattern, but in one important respect their attitudes towards gender are unusual: they do not regard the roles of men and women as natural, god-given, or inevitable, but they regard them like other institutions as man-made and on occasion subject to change.

In support of this point, I cite both the conduct of men and women and Mehinaku myth and ritual. The villagers, for example, tolerate sexual deviance. Girls who experiment in lesbian affairs or men who participate in homosexual encounters are regarded as extremely foolish, but no one would directly interfere. Some forty years ago one of the village men donned women's garments and paint, performed women's tasks, and took an occasional male lover. Humorously called "the strong woman" by the villagers because of his prodigious capacity for women's work, he lived as a women until his death from natural causes in the 1940s. Only jokes and light teasing marked the fact that his conduct was bizarre by normal Mehinaku standards.

In myth and ritual, we find more evidence of the mutability of gender. During two ceremonies men shed "menstrual" blood by scarifying their bodies and piercing their ears and in many rituals they pair off as "husbands" and "wives" to represent male and female spirits. For their part, the women tell myths of a community of women who took on the ways of men. In two

transvestite rituals (Yamurikumá, and the *uluri*-giving ceremony, Akajatapá) the women wear men's paint and headdresses,
wrestle women from neighboring tribes, and collectively perform men's tasks, such as building a house, making a canoe, or
cutting a path through the forest. Although these rituals of role-
reversal serve by contrast to dramatize normal relationships
rather than subvert them, their occurrence suggests that the
villagers see the conduct of the sexes as potentially modifiable.
It is not that men and women by their nature are incapable of
performing each other's roles, since on occasion they do just
that.

For further insight into the villlagers' own perception of gender, let us look at an important myth that describes the origin
of the difference between the sexes:

> In ancient times the women occupied the men's houses and
> played the sacred flutes inside. We men took care of the
> children, processed manioc flour, wove hammocks, and spent
> our time in the residences while the women cleared fields,
> fished, and hunted monkey. In those days the children even
> nursed at our breasts. A man who dared enter the women's
> house during their ceremonies would be gang-raped by all
> the women of the village on the central plaza.
>
> One day the chief called us together and showed us how to
> make bullroarers to frighten the women. As soon as the
> women heard the terrible drone they dropped the sacred flutes
> and ran into the houses to hide. We grabbed the flutes and
> took over the men's houses. Today if a woman comes in here
> and sees our flutes we rape her. Today the women nurse
> babies, process manioc flour, and weave hammocks, while
> *we* hunt, fish, and farm.

This myth, a commentary on the relations between the sexes,
tells us that men and women act as they do today only by virtue
of an ancient political event: the insurrection of the men. Add
the implications of this tale to those of other rituals and practices, and we see that the differences between the sexes are not
simply the natural facts of life. These differences are at least
partly the choice and intentions of individuals. Like other Mehinaku institutions, the roles of men and women never wholly
succeed in effacing the person behind the social mask but inevitably reflect his presence and interests.

Names

The crossroads of social and personal identity, a name at once differentiates its bearer from his fellows and identifies him socially. Among the villagers a name places a man squarely in the network of community relationships and yet, in typical Mehinaku fashion, takes ample recognition of the individual who is far more than just a social actor.

Mehinaku names are often the names of objects, spirits, animals, landmarks, and events, such as "Great Canoe Spirit," "Lake," "Corn Woman," "Tocandira Ant," and "Sunset." The names of the villagers recapitulate the names of their grandparents of the same sex, so that each villager has two names simultaneously. Since a person may never mention the name of an in-law, mothers and fathers must call their child by their own parent's name; to do otherwise would be to name a parent-in-law.

As the child goes through the life cycle, he accumulates additional names, which, like other changes in personal status, are formally announced in the course of major calendrical and religious ceremonies. When a child learns to walk, for example, he acquires his first set of "real names" (until this time he has had a nickname), those of his grandparents at their infancy. The name, however, "must wait for a festival" when it is formally proclaimed to the villagers. Thereafter new names are substituted for old ones as the individual passes through the ear-piercing ceremony, marries, has children, and advances to old age.

To receive a name (*pekaweintsa*, literally, "to trade objects of equal value"), a man's grandfather tells the new name to a "speaker of the name," a mature relative well-accustomed to public oratory. In exchange for a number of small gifts, several other villagers "take" (*etuka*) the person to be named by the arm and remain in contact with him during the naming ritual—a symbolic act used in many Mehinaku rituals that expresses the liminal status of the individual. Let us listen in 1972 as Akusa, the "speaker of the name," dramatically raises his arms over his nephew to proclaim the boy's new identity to the community: "Listen, listen all of you to my foolish speech. Now, no

longer say the name Kama. His name is Ayui! Say his grandfather's name, Ayui!" As the new name is pronounced the namer
moves his arms up and down above the named as if forcing the
name into his body, simultaneously adding *"kununu, kununu,
kununu"* (I push, I throttle).

A Mehinaku name is a signal that encodes a great deal of
social information. Most broadly, a name declares a villager's
membership in the tribe and identifies him with the history and
traditions of his grandparents' generation. A name squarely
places him in the network of kinship, providing his fellows with
the outlines of a three-generation genealogy. And finally, a name
declares his age, sex, passage through the life cycle, and participation in public rituals. Like greetings or patterns of dress, the
naming system is supremely social in nature, apparently obscuring the personality behind a barrage of structural information. And yet, in actual practice, names often reflect each villager's individuality.

Let us look once again at the method of choosing names.
Although in theory the system is inflexible, in reality there is
considerable freedom. Each grandparent, for example, has two
names—one from each of their grandparents—either of which
may be passed along to younger generations. Once a choice is
made, the newly-named villager himself has two names, only
one of which normally becomes widely current in the community and well-known to outsiders. Still more flexibility is introduced if his grandparents die in early maturity, a contingency
handled by turning to their siblings or cousins as name donors.

Taking advantage of the openness of the naming system, the
villagers maximize their individuality, avoiding names that du-
plicate those in current use and selecting names that project a
positive self-image. Thanks to his father's flexible reading of
genealogies, for example, Maiyuwekai bears the name of a great
chief whom he one day hopes to emulate. Similarly, Walama-
kuma (literally, "Anaconda Spirit") hopes to be a champion
wrestler—an interest reflected in his choice of this name, for in
Mehinaku mythology the anaconda is the champion above all
others. On the other hand, some names carry implications that
most villagers would prefer to avoid. Huyukai, for example

(literally, "soft dung") is not overly fond of his name even though it is in no sense derogatory. Respecting his wishes, the villagers and outsiders call him by his second name, Akusa.

The recognition of the villager's individuality is also built into the naming ceremony, which is only occasionally a stereotyped and unvarying process. The namer usually takes time out to remind the community of the personal characteristics of the named: "Listen, listen all you women, hear my grandchild's foolish name; my grandchild who just received her *uluri* . . . Your name is Kamanairu! Kamanairu, you will rob another woman's husband!"

As the villagers laugh and the comely Kamanairu smiles in embarrassment, other members of the community receive their names. A child is identified as "that very small one," while her older brother is described as a provident fisherman. One young man, much to the amusement of the village, receives a Brazilian name because of his fondness for visiting the Indian Post. And so it goes, each individual receiving not only a new name but also recognition of the qualities that set him off from his fellows. We see then that although names are an escutcheon of social identity, like many other Mehinaku institutions, they also provide a basis for the display of that which is individual and personal to their bearers.

Self and Society

Although the Mehinaku opposition of self and society seems similar to our own folk view of men and relationships, we should not assume that we are dealing with a universal. Godfrey Lienhardt, for example, in *Divinity and Experience*, argues that the African Dinka do not possess the same sense of individuality that we do. Attributing what we would call personal motives to the action of spirits, they apparently have no theory of a separate self that exists behind the social mask (1961: 149–150).

More recently, Fredrick Gearing, in *Face of the Fox*, claims that the Fox Indians also lack a sense of self apart from the social positions that they occupy. Gearing's discussion is more qualified than Lienhardt's, but he believes that the Fox conceive of themselves and others primarily as occupants of socially given statuses:

> To the Fox "the very idea of personality is cumbersome and awkward, or even meaningless. . . . A Fox . . . sees another most concretely and precisely when he views him as an incumbent in a social slot. . . ." (1970: 137–138)

Although I am not wholly persuaded by the ethnography that supports Lienhardt's and Gearing's conclusions, I do believe that the Mehinaku recognize the distinction between men and their roles more explicitly than many other peoples. Linguistically, roles are described as an association between men and things, spirits, skills, and other men. This association is highly flexible and both its definition and mode of allocation are subject to negotiation. The Mehinaku can take distance from their roles, evaluating them according to their own self-interest. Finally, they are inclined to understand each other's behavior in psychological as opposed to social terms. In short, the dialectic between the man and the social mask is a real one to the Mehinaku, and they take recognition of this separation of self from society on the level of their language, their culture, their conduct, and the expression of their feelings.

As we now turn to an examination of relationships that are based on kinship, tribal affiliation, and ritual, we will want to keep in mind the villagers' talent for social flexibility. Roles do not swallow men up or hammer them down but leave them free to make creative modifications based on mutual interest and agreement. Perhaps the best case in point is that of kinship, described in the following two chapters.

*Make children . . . they will get fish for you
when they grow up and you are old.*
The chief, in a public speech

Anthropologists have been increasingly concerned with defining the meaning of institutions from the point of view of the people
who live them. The Mehinaku, however,
have no ready definition of kinship. We must
infer the cultural basis of the institution
from the language of kinship, the metaphors
the villagers use to express relatedness, and
the explanations they offer of why some persons are relatives and others are not.

The Mehinaku's principal method of explaining why two persons are related is the
biological fact of procreation. Villagers are
related to their parents because they were
"made" (*utumapai*) by them. They are related to their siblings because they are of
"the same navel," that is, made by the same
parent. Cousins and more distant relatives
are kinsmen because they had parents or
grandparents who were siblings. Two dis-
tantly related individuals who cannot precisely trace the genealogical connections that
link them will say "our grandfathers were
of one group" (*tipa*). The word *tipa* refers
to a group or cluster of things that have a

similar appearance or origin, such as feathers from the same bird. The basis for the similarity of the grandparents in the quoted phrase is that they were closely related or "made" by the same parents in the act of sexual relations.

How do sexual relations establish a connection between relatives? According to the villagers, a foetus is built up in the course of repeated acts of sex. A man's semen (*yaki*) contains a "seed" (*ite*; the same word is also used for genitals). In the act of intercourse the man "plants" this seed in the body of the woman. The child that is born may be referred to as the man's "seedling" (*panala*). Fathering a child, however, does not occur in a single act of sexual relations as we might expect, given the image of planting a seed. Instead, procreation requires repeated acts of sexual relations, during which the father and any other men who may be having intercourse with the mother "make" the infant together. This process occurs only very gradually, the head of the baby being formed first, then its arms, trunk, and legs—the order, my informants point out, in which a newborn baby normally appears during parturition.

A woman's role in procreation is far less active than the man's. She contributes neither substance nor nourishment to the developing fetus, simply sheltering it. According to the Mehinaku, she "wombs" (*itsichuitsa*; womb, stomach, or lower abdomen) the child. Although this function is not as creative as that of the male, Mehinaku institutions and the conduct of relatives reflect a bilateral concept of kinship.

Table 20   A Continuum of Possible Relationships
Between Kinsmen and Nonkinsmen

1. "True" kinsman (of own generation)	*Epene* or *epenewaja*
2. "A little bit" of a kinsman (of own generation)	*Epenehatāi*
3. Fictive kinsman (of own generation)	*Penerí*
4. Nonrelatives ("just people")	*Neuneihete*

Following the model of biological kinship presented above, the universe of humans should logically be divisible into two groups. The first would consist of a kindred of persons who considered themselves related because they have an ancestor in common; the second would consist of persons who were completely unrelated. In fact, the Mehinaku do make this distinction, labeling some persons as relatives and others as "just people" (*neuneihete*). Between these categories, however, the Mehinaku recognize a gradation of people who, though related, are something less than full kinsmen (see table 20).

Epenewaja or simply *epene* is used to refer to persons who consider themselves closely related. Normally this term is reserved for persons who are demonstrably biological relatives; at times, however, it is applied to persons who like each other and exchange food and labor as if they were true kin.

Epenehatāi are a "little bit kinsmen" who are thought to have had a common ancestor but whose connection is too remote to be significant. Kinsmen like these include almost all villagers who are not recognized as true kinsmen.

The third class of kin (*penerí*) is regarded as fictive, involving no genealogical connection at all, however remote. Such kinsmen agree to establish relationships that they themselves regard as "a little lie." These relatives (*penerí*) are said to "kid each other" when they invoke the relationship, which occurs most frequently between members of different tribes. The fictive tie, however, not only establishes bonds between the kinsmen but also between their children who eventually regard themselves as "a little bit" related by virtue of their parents' relationship.

The final category is that of "just people," with whom a Mehinaku recognizes no kinship relationship at all. Ordinarily, it includes no or very few villagers but most of the members of other Xingu tribes.

There are two ways in which bilateral kinship systems curtail the number of persons related to a particular individual. One is to set an arbitrary limit on the extent of ties, such as to third cousins or to the descendants of an ancestor a given number of generations back. A second method is to leave the problem of defining the outer limits of the kin group to each individual's discretion. This is the solution that the Mehinaku have chosen and, although each ego-centered kindred includes a minimal core of relatives (at least first cousins), the boundaries beyond that point are shaped by the quality of the relationship as well as by genealogical distance. Let us examine the process of "peeling" kindreds, since it is basic to the system.

The most painstaking of the Mehinaku genealogists, the chief, recalls the names of 62 consanguineal relatives, living and deceased. His kindred is wide in scope because, unlike most of the villagers, he recalls the names and relationships of his grandparent's siblings. As table 21 demonstrates, the average Mehinaku kindred is considerably smaller, including only one-quarter of the tribe as "true kin." Given that the tribe is small and essentially endogamous, this figure is surprising. How can the villagers fail to keep better records of the genealogical ties that associate them? The Mehinaku appear to practice a kind of genealogical amnesia (Geertz and Geertz 1964) that rapidly retires information about their ancestors into obscurity.

Table 21   The Depth and Scope of Mehinaku Kindreds

Average size	
living kin	19.2
living and deceased kin	30.2
Average depth	1.7 (slightly less than grandparents' generation)
Maximum depth	3 (great grandparents' generation)
Average scope	1.2 (slightly beyond first cousins)
Maximum scope	3d cousins
Generation including most relatives	0 (ego's generation)

Compiled from a list of every adult's "true kin." Deceased persons are included in the figures only if the informant knew their names.

The shallow genealogies seem to result partly from epidemics, several villagers having no memory of their parents at all. Depopulation, however, is not a complete answer, for genealogical lore often is not transmitted from generation to generation even when a villager's parents are alive. Extensive information about Mehinaku genealogy is known only to the elders of the community. Although they can be induced to produce it for a persistent anthropologist, they simply do not pass it along to the younger generation.

A number of institutions discourage them from doing so. The first is a taboo on mentioning the names of affinal relatives, a serious limitation on the transmission of genealogical information. The second taboo prevents mentioning the names of the dead, affinal or not. Strictly applied to people who have died within a few years, it is also extended in an informal way to the entire subject of ancestors. It is not good to talk too much about dead people. These taboos probably account for the indifference to genealogy expressed by many of the younger villagers, who were only able to give me relatively scanty information about their ancestors. Pressed for an explanation of why they did not know more, they would look at me in puzzlement (sometimes in irritation), and say: "Why don't I know the name of my mother's father's brother? He died a long time ago. Go ask an old man. I'm not from mythical times!" On many occasions, however, a more suggestive answer was offered: "I don't know his name because he died a long time ago and *I never saw him*." The last phrase is significant. Genealogical lore is accumulated primarily by living through a number of generations of birth and death rather than by being told by one's parents.

The effect of this pattern of learning or failing to learn genealogy is that the richest histories are found only among the oldest members of the community. With each generation there is increasing impoverishment of information. On the basis of comparing genealogies provided by fathers and sons, I have calculated a decay rate of 60 percent: each generation knows only 60 percent of the genealogy of the generation that preceded it.

Relations Among True Kinsmen

Genealogical amnesia helps us understand that true kinsmen cannot always state the genealogical links that connect them. A glance at the chief's genealogy, for example, would show that one relationship is merely putative. The chief nonetheless feels that he and this relative are true kin. On the other hand, one of the chief's genealogically traceable relatives is explicitly excluded from his list of true kin, despite my best efforts to convince him that this individual should be included according to the logic of the villagers' biological concept of kinship. In actual practice, being a kinsman is more than being "wombed" and "planted" by the same ancestors. The relationship is justified in that way, but it also involves social considerations, of which one of the most important is the sharing of food.

True Kinsmen Share Food

True kinsmen "eat each other's food." Sharing is the most frequently cited behavioral criterion of a true relationship, a justification for either intimate or distant conduct. "I don't eat *his* food," is Kuyaparei's immediate explanation for being unrelated to the chief. As a practical field method, listing the participants in a network of food exchange is a good method of identifying clusters of kinsmen. Although food is shared beyond these limits, such sharing is conditioned by other clearly discernible obligations—those associated with friendship, sexual affairs, common residence, hospitality, or rituals.

Sharing food has obvious economic and social value in a society like that of the Mehinaku. Manioc is usually available in abundance but it is a poor food nutritionally. Like bread, manioc alone never makes a complete meal but should be eaten with fish, monkey, fowl, or a hot pepper sauce. Of these, fish is the most prized and giving it away is a clear symbol of generosity.

I was able to understand how the Mehinaku felt about the sharing of fish after I had lived in the community for a while. Toward late afternoon everyone, including the anthropologist, begins to get hungry and does little but stare down the main roads waiting for the men to return from fishing. At last, when the first fisherman appears, the men whoop and the women rush to the doorways to see who is coming and how much fish he has caught. The fisherman enters his house and lies down in his hammock while his wife prepares a fire for manioc bread and fish stew. She is referred to as the "mistress of the stew" (*wakula weketu*), and personally distributes cooked fish to everyone within her house. She then sends portions to both her own and

her husband's true kin who reside in other houses. To neglect
a relative regularly is to invite gossip, retaliation, and possibly
loss of the sharing relationship.

Obligations of True Kinsmen

Among the Mehinaku the network of food sharing is a visible
link between kinsmen. There are additional ties, of which the
most significant is common residence. As the Mehinaku explain
it, each cluster of kinsmen is associated with a particular household because their grandfathers established the house together.
The oldest of the coresidential kinsmen is considered the "house
owner" (*pãi wekehe*), although he cannot buy or sell his house,
collect rent, or evict his coresidents. Figure 21 demonstrates
how kinship and residence are related, all the residence mates
in the diagram being close relatives with the exception of persons who have married in and their kin.

As among other Xingu tribes (see Basso 1973, Carneiro
1957), postmarital residence is very flexible. Ideally, a young
man lives with his wife's parents until he has had several children, at which time he returns to his own home permanently.
In practice, however, decisions about residence reflect the pref-
erences of the couple and their parents, so that the actual residence pattern is regular only in that husbands and wives live
with one set of parents or the other.

All residence mates incur obligations by virtue of living together. Jointly they keep the surrounding grounds free of weeds
and other fire hazards, patch the roof when it leaks, sweep the
interior, shore up rotten poles, and otherwise maintain the
house. Further, the householders form a consumption unit, since
food is routinely distributed to everyone present. Nevertheless,
the organizational basis of a household is kinship, not simply
the fact of common residence. A husband who lives with his
bride's kin continues to participate in the maintenance of his
parent's home, shares food with his own relatives, and sits with
his back to his natal house every night in the smoker's circle.
We will explore the ambivalent role of a villager living with
his inlaws but for the moment it is sufficient to note that houses
are primarily kinship institutions and living together is an activity of kinsmen.

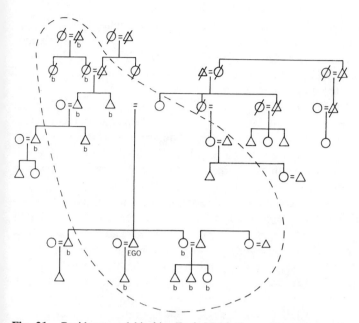

Fig. 21. Residence and kinship. Each Mehinaku residence is associated
with a core of kinsmen who build the house and form its nucleus. In
the diagram the dotted line encloses all of ego's related residence mates.
Members of his kindred who were born in his house are marked with
a "*b*". These data illustrate that: (1) The core of related individuals
constitutes the majority of the household. All but five of the residents
of this house are members of ego's kindred. (2) There is no regularly
followed rule of postmarital residence. (3) Persons who marry into the
residence may bring others along with them. Ego's mother, for example,
brought her sister and her sister's children into the household and
they are now permanent residents.

Kinship is also the principal basis of cooperation in everyday
subsistence. Closely related kinsmen make their gardens near
one another, borrow each other's tools, go fishing and monkey
hunting together, and cooperate in making canoes and houses
and in other projects that require heavy labor. It is evident that
the villagers engage in such activities with others as well, but
they do them more often with close kinsmen than with anyone
else. To measure the importance of kinship in forming work
relationships, I recorded the composition of two hundred two-
man task teams (usually fishermen) over a six-month period

in 1967. These teams consisted of true kinsmen nearly 60 percent of the time. Common residence apparently was a less significant factor than kinship in pairing off workers, since men chose unrelated residence mates as work partners less than half as often as kin selected from other households.

Kinsmen bear a special obligation to support each other in times of adversity. A sick man, for example, who faces bankrupting payments to the village shamans is invariably helped to meet his debts by his close relatives. Should he die, they will mourn his death with great intensity and clamor for revenge if they suspect witchcraft.

Kinsmen are emotionally supportive and sensitive to each other's moods and problems. I recall one occasion when one of the younger women was so crushed by her parents-in-law's hostility and her husband's indifference that she ran out of her house and sat weeping in the bushes. Her cousin went out to her, talked to her quietly, and finally led her by the hand back into the house. He later said to me: "She is my cousin! She doesn't get along well here because her father-in-law is a surly old 'trash yard man.' I told her to do the best she can, because she is pregnant and has no other choice; I told her I would be here to help her."

This discussion of true kinship has indicated the general tone of relations between relatives as contrasted with relationships with other Mehinaku. Although these generalizations mark the distinctions between true kin and others, they do not do full justice to the complexity of relationships among true kinsmen. Let us begin to fill in this overly broad treatment by looking at one of the most important groups of true relatives in Mehinaku society, the family.

Parents, Children and the Family

At first glance the nuclear family among the Mehinaku appears minimally developed. There is no word in the language for "family," nor are there rituals in which the family participates as a social unit. Further, although family members live together, they live in a large unpartitioned house where their identity as

a special group seems to disappear among other kinsmen who
share the same dwelling.

Nevertheless the family is a significant and discrete grouping
among the Mehinaku. Families live on close terms but they are
in fact socially separate. Each family suspends its hammocks
in its own part of the house, stores its property on its own
shelves, and utilizes a separate hearth, set of pots, and water
supply. Family "apartments" may be as little as two or three
feet apart but their boundaries are fully respected by all the
adult residents of the house. The well-mannered villager keeps
close to the main house poles as he moves through the house
so that he does not intrude and so that his neighbor's hammock
cords are disturbed as little as possible (see House Plan, figure
10). Since families not only live together but eat together and
travel together, we can see that, superficial appearances aside,
they are in no sense submerged by the larger residential unit or
the network of kinsmen.

Parents and Children

The integrity of the Mehinaku family is assured by the special
relationship between parents and children. Let me cite the authority of the chief who in June 1972 addressed his people on
the advantages of children:

> There are no children here! All the Xingu tribes have
> many, but we have none. Make children, my sisters! Our
> houses are not lively and filled with many people. If a house
> is filled with people and there is a death, we are not des-
> perately sad. But when the house is nearly empty and the
> owner dies, the house is burned and the kin group dies too.
> I don't want to live alone! I would be sad in my house all
> alone.

The Mehinaku have a pervasive fear that they and their culture
will soon die out; children and their energetic presence offer
promise of a more optimistic future. The chief continues:

> All my sisters, you have long labia. Make children- My
> son, Kupatekuma, make more children. Like a copulating
> frog thrust your semen deep inside. Look at yourself, all
> alone, without kinsmen. Make children and they will help you

later. They will get fish for you when they grow up and you are old!

An incentive for having children, then, is support in old age. As men age, they increasingly rely on their children for fish and other food. Although no old person will go hungry in Mehinaku society, his social standing will be higher if he has children who help him out and justify his inactivity.

Another incentive is that children are considered to embody the favorable characteristics of their parents, who sometimes refer to their offspring as "my former self" (*nuwẽi*). The chief's son, for example, is a champion wrestler as the chief formerly was. He proudly regards the boy as recapitulating his life and social career. Similarly, a father who is a good fisherman can expect a son who is a fine fisherman. A mother who was beautiful when she was a child will look forward to a daughter who is also attractive. Other children are equally "chips off the old block," for it is natural that young people will resemble their parents of the same sex. Parents have children to preserve their prized qualities and skills for the admiration of posterity.

The Couvade and Other Precautions

Striking evidence of parents' special relationship to their children occurs during an infant's first year. At this time the child's identity is closely associated with that of its parents. Without a name of his own he is addressed by teknonymous terms or personally coined nicknames, such as "fat belly," "laughter," or funny-sounding foreign words. Regarded as especially vulnerable, the baby is kept out of the public regions of the community, for were he seen by anyone who recently had sexual relations he might sicken and die. His soul (*ĩyeweku*, literally, shadow) is not yet firmly fixed and could easily be taken away by a spirit.

To protect his child a new father honors a couvade, one of the most elaborate, restrictive, and lengthy on record. The moment the baby is born, the father is referred to by a special term, "infant's father" (*háuka ɪnɪja*) and enters an initial period of seclusion along with the child and the mother, during which time he is regarded as being "like" the mother. Not only does he stay indoors with her and take the same medicines, he also eats the foods appropriate to a woman with a post partum blood flow. He must faithfully follow these procedures, for their objective is to prevent the mother from hemorrhaging and to terminate her flow of blood.

After the post-partum blood ceases, the mother bathes and is once again a full participant in community life although her movements are somewhat curtailed by her child, who must remain out of the public eye. For his part, the father remains behind the seclusion barrier and will spend another six to ten months in isolation. During this period of seclusion, the restrictions imposed on him are primarily in the interest of the child rather than the mother. Were he, for example, to violate the food taboos and other restrictions (see chapter 14), the child would sicken and die.

Although fathers go into seclusion only upon the birth of their first child, they are still obliged to follow many other precautions on the birth of subsequent children. A list of these precautions, all of which are intended to preserve the child's health and well-being, offer a clue to the nature of the relationship of parents and children (see table 22). The activities of a father of young children are strictly limited. His sexual life is supposed to be nonexistent, his subsistence work is severely restricted, certain foods are to be avoided, and participation in certain rituals is prohibited. Ideally all these restrictions last until the child (either a boy or a girl) is given his first real name and a hair cut and is painted with *urucu* pigment—events that occur toward the end of the first year after he has begun to walk. No longer is he a baby that just "lies about, gurgling and crawling on the ground."

The point of the restrictions is that a father's activities are related to his child's well-being in a direct and literal way. The first eight prohibitions prevent the father from handling heavy things such as silos, house poles, fence rails, and animals. No matter that only the father comes into contact with them, they must be avoided for their weight is too great to be borne by the child.

Restrictions nine to eleven keep the father from handling materials that could be dangerous to the child, things like thatch, spiny bark, and basket material. Prohibitions twelve to fourteen prevent the father from coming into contact with chemical substances that could burn or poison the child. The last three restrictions refer to a variety of other activities that are also risky because their effect can be transmitted to the infant.

Table 22   Restrictions Honored by Fathers During Their Infants' First Year

Restrictions honored by father	Specific motive for restriction
1. Can't kill large animals	The animal or fish is too heavy and ferocious for the child.
2. Can't catch large fish; they must be thrown back.	
3. Can't chop down big trees or make a new garden.	The child could be killed since the trees are too heavy for him.
4. Can't plant a garden or get clay for pots.	The child could be killed since the earth and clay are too heavy.
5. Can't dig a hole for large house poles (small ones are all right).	
6. Can't do heavy work on a house.	The wood is too heavy.
7. Can't build a fence.	The rails and posts are too heavy.
8. Can't make a *pequi* silo.	Silo is too heavy.
9. Can't get thatch for house roof.	The thatch is too sharp.
10. Can't get wood for making flutes.	Spiny hairs on bark can "get" and hurt the child.
11. Can't make a basket.	The material draws and cuts too much.
12. Can't make salt.	It burns and hurts too much.
13. Can't make black wood bows; other bows are permissible.	The hard wood (*muyapi* genus *Tecoma*) is poisonous and used by witches.
14. Can't make *urucu* pigment.	It can burn the eyes.
15. Can't make a headdress.	As the feathers are tied in place, the child will be prevented from urinating.
16. Can't be associated with the spirit of the bull roarer (Matapu) or eat his food.	The spirit will seize the child's soul.
17. Must avoid sexual relations.	The child's belly fills with semen and it becomes sick.

It is doubtful that any villager actually follows all of these prohibitions. To do so would make it very difficult to function as a farmer, a fisherman, or a hunter. Nevertheless, a father can not shirk his moral responsibility for whatever happens to his infant. If his child becomes sick, the village shamans are likely to attribute the illness to the father's negligence. Using sleight of hand, a shaman will appear to remove a semen-like fluid from the infant's stomach, proving that the father had sexual relations in violation of the taboo. A second shaman will remove a piece of thatch and a third, a bit of basket straw, announcing their diagnosis and the father's culpability to everyone present. The father usually attempts to "undo" his error and if his child is very sick, his efforts can be dramatic. I have seen thatch ripped off a roof by a father desperately trying to make his child well. When that failed, he threw down a long fence that he had spent several days building to keep pigs out of his garden.

If a child dies or is permanently injured, a father can do nothing but live with his misdeed. One of the young men in the village, for example, lost the sight of one eye as an infant because of an infection. According to the village shamans, however, he was blinded because his father made *urucu* pigment. Even after twenty-five years, the father's irresponsibility is still remembered.

The net effect of these customs is to associate parents closely with children. Children are both precious and vulnerable. The source of their vulnerability is in their parents' relationship to objects, foods, tasks, and people. By honoring the restrictions that protect their offspring, parents recognize their full responsibility for the welfare of their children.

Infancy and Childhood

Though the moral and symbolic association of parents and children is most visible during a child's first year, it hardly ends after that time. Throughout their life, children will be identified with their parents and their conduct and appearance will be explained as deriving from them. Understandably, then, parents are concerned about their children and anxious for them to do well. Practically, this concern takes the form of teaching the children basic skills, criticizing their misconduct, looking out for their social and economic interests, and providing emotional support. When the children are young, they are adored, fondled, and praised. I have often seen fathers gurgling at their one-year-olds, holding them up in the air, and making little jokes with their wives about their affectionate nicknames.

Weaning is a gradual and gentle process, beginning before the birth of a younger sibling, at about age two-and-one-half. Boys and girls of four and five years, however, may be offered the breast on rare occasions. I have heard that some women place hot pepper juice on their nipples to discourage children who persist in nursing, but this is an exception to the more typical gentle pattern.

Another potentially traumatic break with the mother is also handled with sensitivity. A toddler normally sleeps with his mother until the birth of her next child. Because of a long post partum sex taboo and continual nursing, this event may not occur until the first child is nearly three years old. Before that time the mother gently trains her child to sleep in a separate hammock. Each evening after he has fallen asleep, she carefully transfers him to his own hammock. If he wakes crying in the night, she takes him back with her until he has fallen asleep again and patiently repeats the process. Toilet training, that bane of the American middle class, is simply managed. There are no diapers, no clothes to soil, and no parquet floor to worry about. An accident is a casual affair: the mother simply wipes the child clean with some leaves and instructs him to go outside the next time.

Other People's Children

The special nature of close family relationships contrasts with the pronounced ambivalence some villagers feel towards other people's children. Consider what it is like to live closely under the same roof with numerous infants and toddlers. Babies do not respect the unwalled "apartments" and freely move about, disturbing residence mates with their crying and mischievousness. Some villagers freely express their irritation. Tewe, for example, was especially unhappy when a mother moved into our household with her two small daughters. Whenever they cried and their mother was not present, he mimicked their tears and told them to shut up. "No one," he explained to me, "likes to live in a house where there are a large number of children. They not only keep you awake with their tears and noise, but they eat a lot of fish." The chief summed up the villagers feelings about other people's children in a speech:

> Children are very difficult. Even a good woman who is never angry gets mad at other people's children. Children get in your things, they make practical jokes, they are angry and cry. They are a nuisance and hard to take care of. I don't take the hand of that little fat-bellied one (a child living in his house) when he gets into my things. His father has to do that! Children defecate on you—it is very smelly. And they never pay you back for all that defecation and crying!

Though young children are not always indulged outside the nuclear family, they appear to live in a child's paradise, at least from the point of view of a parent coming from an urban environment. Boys and girls are never cooped up in a house or a room, never told to keep off the furniture or away from the electrical outlets, never dressed and undressed, diapered and undiapered, or told to watch out for the traffic. They lead as free a life as possible for small children, and it may well be that the creativity they exhibit in social relationships and artistic expression as adults is related to this early period of acceptance and freedom.

Childhood Training for Responsibility

As children grow older, their parents begin to treat them less indulgently and more as "their former selves" (*nuwēi*) upon whom they would like to work some improvements. Girls begin to help their mothers at an early age. By the time a girl is seven or eight, she is taking care of younger siblings, fetching water from the river, and helping process manioc flour. Initially, little boys have a somewhat easier time. On occasion their fathers take them fishing but until they are about ten, they are as much a liability as an asset. Men's work, in contrast to much of women's labor, often requires sudden spurts of energy, close timing, and considerable skill. Little boys are largely left to their own devices, spending most of their time playing games in the woods, wrestling on the central plaza, making bows and arrows, and shooting small fish in the bathing area. Despite their relatively free life, however, boys as well as girls are severely criticized if they show signs of laziness. Let a boy sleep late, lounge about the house, or hesitate to accompany his father on a fishing expedition, and he is chastised as a "little girl," a "lover of infant's games," or a "louse egg." He is warned that when he grows up he will be small (*peritsi*), unattractive, and undesirable to women.

If the boy persists in misconduct, he risks the penalty of scarification. The Mehinaku seldom hit their children, but they do use fish-tooth scrapers (*piya*) as disciplinary devices (as well as for increasing strength—see chapter 14). With a sudden move, a parent will grab a child by the wrist, drag him to a corner, slosh a dipper full of water on his legs and vigorously scarify his calves and thighs. Children scream in anger and rage, and for some it is a terrifying experience. I am not convinced that it is an effective deterrent to misbehavior, however, since parents seem to apply it more in response to their own emotions than to their child's actual conduct. One mother, for example, pulls out the scarifier whenever she is feeling angry and her daughter has offered her some slight pretext.

Though parents are punitive on occasion, they are genuinely proud of their children. They seldom voice their pride directly, however, for it is bad form to boast about one's children. In fact, the only way a parent can legitimately call public attention to his child is through a kind of ritualized criticism. At the ear-piercing ceremony for initiating chiefs, fathers publicly denigrate their sons, insisting that their boys are stingy, given to slandering others, and incapable of becoming good chiefs. During an intertribal wrestling match, a mother or grandmother will emerge from her house and run up to a boy engaged in a bout: "You little girl," she shouts, "you will never be a wrestling champion. You are just a shadow of a real wrestler. Look at you!" The boy continues to wrestle as if he had not heard her, neither he nor anyone else taking her obviously false criticism seriously. The net effect of her harangue is to single the boy out for special attention and admiration.

Siblings and Cousins

The most significant terminological and behavioral division within a villager's network of kinship is the distinction between "cross" and "parallel" relatives. A glance at the kin term chart and the text below shows that kinsmen linked by relatives of the same sex to ego are usually labeled by kinship terms that

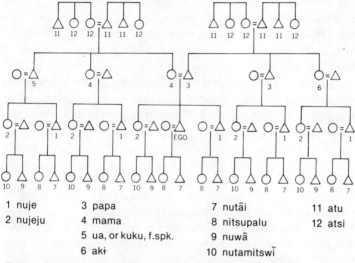

1 nuje	3 papa	7 nutāi	11 atu
2 nujeju	4 mama	8 nitsupalu	12 atsi
	5 ua, or kuku, f.spk.	9 nuwā	
	6 akɨ	10 nutamitswĩ	

Ego's grandchildren and their cousins are addressed as weku

Fig. 22. Mehinaku consanguineal kinship terminology, simplified. *Nuje* and *Nujeju* (terms 1 and 2) are used on ego's generation to address younger kinsmen. Additional terms, *teté* and *uyú* are terms of address for older and younger relatives of either sex. Men may address older female kin as *nutukakalu*, and older male kin as *nutapʋje*. Women use *nutapʋju* and *nutukaká* to address older female and male kin. All these terms are applied to all kinsmen of ego's generation, following the Hawaiian pattern. One term, however, (*nutanuléi*, masculine, and *nutanuleju*, feminine) is used to refer to (but usually not to address) cross-cousins.

In usage all the terms indicate not only genealogical connectedness but qualities of social relationships as well. The pattern is further complicated by the existence of terms that assert a kinship relationship but are ambiguous as to the exact genealogical tie (see chapter 11). These modifications of the formal system permit the Mehinaku to specify relationships with varying degrees of precision and ambiguity, a distinct advantage given the flexibility of kinship relations.

are also used within the nuclear family. Kinsmen who trace their relationship through relatives of the opposite sex, however, may be described by a different nomenclature.

Called by the same terms, siblings and parallel cousins have a relationship that reflects mutual respect. When they are young they play together a great deal, but as they grow older their relationship becomes more formal. They may not joke sexually nor have sexual relations with each other's wives. They have free access to one another's personal possessions, although they are expected to return what they have borrowed. They should also assist each other in fishing, processing manioc, and other tasks.

The roles of siblings and parallel cousins of the opposite sex are somewhat distant because there are very few economic or ceremonial projects in which they can cooperate and many subjects which they are not supposed to discuss—witchcraft and sex, for example. Nevertheless, a woman may send her cousin manioc cakes and fish stew as a gesture of relatedness, and he will reciprocate with gifts of uncooked fish.

Actually there is important variation in the relationship of siblings and first cousins that this sketch obscures. True siblings ("of the same navel") are regarded as having a more important and more intense relationship than first cousins. Again, the relative age of siblings and cousins is significant for behavior, discipline, and access to valued things. Within the nuclear family the younger sibling is called *jeri*, the older, *tapuri*. Younger siblings are less likely than their older brothers and sisters to be initiated as chiefs or given valued gifts by their parents. One man was able to explain simply why he was not initiated as a chief: "I was the worthless younger one."

There is some disagreement among the villagers about the proper relationship between cross-cousins. Most people say that all first cousins are "real kin, too close to marry." They further comment that a cousin's husband becomes one's brother-in-law, as does a sister's husband, and that a marriage is therefore inappropriate. According to some Mehinaku, however, a true mother's brother's or father's sister's daughter is "a little bit" marriageable. Accordingly, it is "somewhat" permissible to have sexual relations with the girl just as long as the affair is kept hidden.

The system is conceptually if not behaviorally consistent. True kinship and sexuality simply do not go together, and young men who maintain affairs with their true cross-cousins do it "so that others do not find out." The method they use for masking their relationship plays on the ambiguity inherent in the system. The reader will have already noticed that all relatives of ego's generation—no matter how distant—may be addressed by the same kinship term as true brothers and sisters though there is a referential term that designates cross-cousins and potential in-laws. When a man wishes to conceal a liaison with a true kinswoman, he never refers to her as his cross-cousin (*nutanuleju*) because that would give away the relationship. Instead, he is careful to refer to her as "sister" or to avoid the use of kin terms.

Kinship terminology becomes a crucial element in courtship, since it can signal a person's intentions or put off an unwanted overture. I recall that Kama was very much interested in a young and recently nubile village girl. "Wow, she's pretty; I want to have sex with her!" he told me. One day her husband and parents were out of the village and she was alone. Kama insisted I accompany him to her house to give him a pretext for his visit. We stayed a while, idly talked about a heron that the girl's father had caught as a pet, and then left. To my surprise Kama appeared defeated. "What went wrong?" I asked. "She called me by a kin term," he replied.

Relationship by Marriage

The Mehinaku have no term for "affinal kinship." Words exist for "all my brothers-in-law" and "all my fathers-in-law," but "all my relatives by marriage" requires a sentence or two of explanation. My justification for treating affinal relationships as a distinct category of kinship rests on the special recognition they receive in behavior and attitude: in all cases, relationships by marriage are marked by qualities of conduct that are culturally recognized under the terms "joking and teasing" (*amana-piritsapu, autapátapai*), "respect" (*amunapátapai*), and "shame" (*iaipíripyai*). In the Mehinaku language "joking," "respect," and "shame" have opposite meanings and connotations, but as we shall see, all the relationships characterized by these terms are nonetheless similar in that they incorporate elements of opposition, social distance, and separation.

Jokes Between Cross Cousins

The most dramatic example of opposition between affinal relatives is the relationship of classificatory cross-cousins. Cross-cousins are in our terms blood relatives, but the Mehinaku system assigns affinal characteristics to consanguines who are potentially in-laws. Classificatory cross-cousins, for example, are potential spouses or brothers- and sisters-in-law who are obliged to maintain a joking relationship before marriage. I am in a good position to describe the repertoire of pranks and practical jokes, since I have a number of fictive cross-cousins and I was all too often their victim. On one occasion I recall looking for *pequi* fruit with one of my "cousins." *Pequi* is about the size and weight of a baseball and when it falls from the tree it hits the ground with a heavy thud. As we walked through the orchard, *pequi* would occasionally hit the ground nearby. I would collect the fruit and pass it back to my "cousin," who put it inside his net sack. Each time we went through this procedure, he was barely able to contain his mirth. Suddenly I realized that, although I had retrieved a good number of *pequi*, his bag contained only two or three. All the fruit I had harvested had been the same *pequi*. He had repeatedly thrown them into the trees while I dutifully ran and fetched like a dog after a stick.

Most jokes between cross-cousins are less well-planned and the humor is even broader. Yuka is lounging in front of the men's house. Pitsa, his cross-cousin, comes up to him, tickles his ribs, throws his arms about him, bats his genitals, and says: "Your penis is immensely long! It must be hungry for sex; I saw your penis' food (his mistress) by the bathing area—hurry down there before she leaves!" The hallmark of the cross-cousin relationship, sexual jokes of this sort, would be profaning and unacceptable between any other class of relatives.

High jinx between cross-cousins often seems to incorporate a degree of antagonism that can become both dramatic and

Fig. 23. Joking with a cross-cousin. While Kamulei decorates a mask, Paraguai sneaks up behind him in an attempt to engage him in a game of "guess who." Among the Mehinaku it is never very difficult to figure out who the prankster might be, for he is invariably a cross-cousin.

Notice in the picture the feather earrings adorning Paraguai, and the background typical of the Mehinaku trash yards.

blatant. In the *Jawarí* spear-throwing ritual, cross-cousins belonging to different tribes hurl wax-tipped spears at each other. Although the spears do not penetrate the skin, they leave nasty bruises and may, the villagers say, break a bone. Even when antagonism between cross-cousins is more muted, there always remains an element of distance. Obligatory joking, like any other kind of stereotyped behavior, places a mask between oneself and one's fellows. Despite the pranks, the jokes, and the apparent good fellowship, cross-cousins seldom become very close friends.

Marriage and Respect

As soon as a marriage unites cross-cousins, the pranks and high jinx cease. Getting married is a serious business, affecting not only the spouses who are party to the relationship but their parents and kinsmen as well. As among other Xingu tribes (see especially Basso's description of the Kalapalo, 1973), there are two modes of marriage. The first and most prestigious is marriage to a newly adolescent girl still in seclusion. Called "bringing up one's bride," the girl moves into her fiancé's house to live behind a seclusion barrier until the day of her marriage when she formally emerges. Such a girl is regarded as being "new" (*autsapairi*) and the marriage involves heavy payments ("*epetei*," the same term used for a commercial transaction) and displays of respect to her relatives. Secondary marriages are far less demanding, the marriage being officiated by one of the bride's kinsmen who carries the groom's hammock to her house. Taking note of the marriages, the men imitate the cries of a newborn baby: "Wa-wa-wa-wa!" thereby insuring the wife's fertility.

Etiquette and codes of respect also proclaim the marriage to the community, commemorating the new relationship between persons who were previously distant kin. Husband and wife, for example, must bathe together at least once a day, share utensils, use appropriate kin terms, sleep in adjacent hammocks, and participate in other stereotyped scenes that present their relationship to the rest of the community (see Gregor 1974 for a detailed dramaturgical analysis of Mehinaku marriage).

Equally crucial to the dramatization of the marital tie are the displays of respect that husbands and wives owe each other's kinsmen. Respect relationships among the Mehinaku are seemingly balanced, in that the taboos on the use of names and physical contact are honored both by parents and their children's spouses. In reality, however, there is a strong and weak side to every in-law relationship, insuring that the reciprocal of respect is shame (*iaipiripyai*). A young man who has recently acquired a wife therefore not only respects (*amυnapatapai*) his spouse's brothers and parents but is chronically ashamed in their presence. He occupies the position of a debtor, owing them payment and labor. The justification for his subordinate status is that his wife's parents have gone through the pain of childbirth and the endless irritation of child rearing, all in the interest of their daughter's husband-to-be. Upon him are bestowed not only the bride and her services but also the rights to her children. For all this he must make restitution.

His role is particularly onerous if he has moved into his spouse's household. Often sharing the same half of the house as his parents-in-law and ever under their watchful eye, the so-called *inyerí* (*inswí*, feminine, in-married spouse) walks a narrow line. As I suggested earlier, many of the regulations governing his conduct can be seen as rules which limit contact between him and his wife's parents and thereby facilitate the transition from one residence to another. He steps away from the doorways when his parents-in-law pass through, and he is careful to avoid their cooking area and hammocks. He looks down and to the side in their presence so that their eyes seldom meet. He never touches his parents-in-law; he does not even hold the same object simultaneously. If he wishes to pass something to his father-in-law, he first places it on the ground.

A young husband's work load is far greater than it was in his natal home. He is expected to fish for his in-laws almost every day and in his spare time construct a canoe or clear a new garden. During the cool months of the dry season, he will return home in the evening with a huge load of firewood, not only for himself and his wife but for her parents as well.

It is difficult for us to appreciate the distance and sense of shame associated with son-in-law–parent-in-law interaction since there is no relationship quite like it in our own society. One measure of the strain, however, is that the respect and avoidance associated with the role must be kept permanently in mind. A Mehinaku continually keeps a sharp eye out for his in-laws to avoid violating any of the taboos against contact or proximity. Villagers deliberately schedule their day to reduce the chances of meeting a spouse's parents. Tewe, for example, will never go to the port on the Culiseu river on the same day as his father-in-law.

The avoidance taboo involves not only encounters with in-laws but the use of their name. The prohibition would be simple to honor were it not for the fact that each adult has a good many in-laws and each in-law has several names. To further complicate the picture, Mehinaku names are also the names of animals, household objects, and natural events, so that a villager has to be on guard even in talk that has nothing to do with his in-laws.

The Mehinaku circumvent the taboo by means of a convention of referring to a name without actually mentioning it. For example, since species of fish and other fauna are used for personal names, the Mehinaku (as table 23 indicates) have worked out a number of circumlocutions that avoid referring to the species by their names.

Following table 23, a Mehinaku whose father-in-law is called Yapu (sting ray) must eliminate the *yapu* from his vocabulary; instead he says "has arrow" whenever he wants to talk about

Table 23   Circumlocutions Used to Avoid the Names
                      of Affinal Relatives

Names of affinal relative	Mehinaku term	Descriptive phrase used to avoid the name
Sting ray	Yapu	has arrow
Piau (Portuguese)	Walaku	dark face
Tukunaré (Portuguese)	Ieitsapa	big mouth
Pintado (Portuguese)	Tulupi	painted, spotted
Pirarara (Portuguese)	Yuma	red one
Monkey (Cebus)	Pahɨ	Kaiyʋh (Kuikuru for monkey)
Turtle	Epyu	strong back

this creature. This evasion is important, because to use the name is a Mehinaku's way of showing he has broken off with his in-law. Accordingly, accidentally saying a tabooed name is an occasion for acute embarrassment.

It is apparent that the Mehinaku owe their parents-in-law burdensome obligations. Not only must they work for them, give them expensive gifts, and avoid social contact, but they must also reschedule their daily activities and alter their vocabulary. There are compensations, however, for those who honor the regulations. In-laws hurry to support each other. If a man's possessions are stolen, for example, his brothers-in-law are the first and the most vociferous in proclaiming their anger at the thief. We also note that the rules of affinal kinship become far less stringent after the birth of children. Mother and daughter-in-law, constantly brought together by household activities, ultimately develop a warm association and take pleasure in each other's company. Brothers-in-law often come to enjoy a cordial relationship, counting on one another as fishing companions and work partners. When the villagers can do so, they deliberately emphasize the supportive and reciprocal aspects of their relationship over the distancing and formal ones.

One strategy is to sidestep the whole problem by marrying a girl whose parents have already died. The epidemics of measles and influenza that ravaged the Upper Xingu during the 1950s have provided many partners for such "in-lawless" marriages. Distant kin often take over some of the functions of parents-in-law in such cases, but they are never very demanding.

A second technique of handling the in-law problem is to balance it out. An ideal form of marriage is the union of two pairs of brothers and sisters. Here there is no strong or weak side to the in-law relationship but rather a perfect balance in which the brothers- and sisters-in-law are free from some of the tension normally associated with their roles.

At best, however, affinal kinship is regarded as burdensome, and it is not surprising that the institution is marked by covert antagonism which finds expression in invidious gossip and surreptitious insults. One son-in-law accuses his wife's father of witchcraft and theft. Behind the old man's back, he contemptuously violates the naming taboo and derogatorily refers to him as "grandfather." For his part, the father-in-law takes every opportunity to denigrate his daughter's husband. Nevertheless, the code of shame and respect associated with in-law relationships makes it unlikely that this tension will erupt into open hostility.

A clearly institutionalized expression of the antagonism between affines occurs in mourning practices. Frequently, a bereaved husband or his kinsmen are suspected of witchcraft, especially if the deceased wife was treated badly or gave her husband cause for jealousy. At the time of death, the husband expresses intense grief and enters a period of mourning seclusion that can last up to a year. The seclusion begins when his hair is shorn by a relative of his dead spouse, who is responsible for the supervision of the entire period of mourning. Because of the Mehinaku belief that virtually all deaths, except those of young children, are caused or abetted by witches, the haircutter may be full of rage. If he has the slightest suspicion that the widower was responsible for the death, he will brutally shave the husband's head using a nicked razor. Not only does this act express his feelings but the amount of hair he removes determines the time the husband will spend in mourner's isolation, for he may come out of seclusion only after his hair has grown back to a normal length. Shaving the head as close as possible insures that the mourner will be out of circulation for at least a year, much to the satisfaction of the deceased wife's kin.

The antagonism between affinal relatives is also expressed in jokes and myths about young men and their mothers-in-law. These stories are surprising, because the son-in-law–mother-in-law relationship is not tense. Although she is a remote and distant figure, the object of many avoidances and taboos, she never directly initiates demands for labor and gifts. Since the father-in-law is the source of these demands, one might expect that he would be the chief focus of hostile jokes. In most stories such as the myth of the bat (*alua*), however, the mother-in-law is the central figure who draws all the lightning.

Bat was asked by the vultures to provide feather headdresses for all their young men. Previously having noticed that his mother-in-law had huge labia, he said to himself, "There are the headdresses I need." He lured his mother-in-law to a dry season village on the pretext that the rest of the tribe would also be there. Finding the village deserted, they hung their hammocks at the opposite ends of the house, as was appropriate for mother-and son-in-law. Later in the evening, however, a night hawk screamed. Frightened by the sound, the mother-in-law asked Bat to come closer. Other animals cried in the night and soon Bat's hammock was right next to hers.

Finally, when the jaguar roared, she asked Bat to get into her hammock. Bat did and had sexual relations with her. He then took a knife and cut out her labia, a huge volume of tissue which he carried away in many baskets to the village of the vultures. The labia was given to various birds, including the vultures, the turkey, the ducks and others, to become their crowns and throat folds.

Typical of many stories I have collected, the mother-in-law is punished for sexual activities and interest in her daughter's husband. The very idea of such contact is repulsive to the Mehinaku, perhaps even more so than incestuous relationships within the nuclear family, which are regarded as merely absurd. It is possible that aggressive myths and jokes about the mother-in-law are an expression of sexual wishes rechanneled as aggression, an emotion that can be admitted and accepted far more readily than sexual interest.

Kinship among the Mehinaku is regarded as a biological link between persons who are of common parentage. The links are the basis of fundamental institutions such as the family, and are the justification for food sharing, emotional support, mutual help, and coresidence. In-law relationships, in contrast to blood ties, are expressed in conduct ranging from ribaldry and joking to extreme deference and respect. My presentation so far, however, has primarily described the ideal pattern rather than actual conduct. In the next chapter, we shall see that the system is very flexible and responsive to individual needs.

17

Writing Your Own Ticket: Manipulating Kinship

*She is my sister because **I** want her husband as my brother-in-law.*

Keje, explaining why he has established a sibling-like relationship with a distant cousin

The Mehinaku system of kinship is "Dravidian" (Dumont 1953) in that classificatory cross-cousins and their parents act as in-laws or potential in-laws while other kin are consanguines. Although among the Mehinaku the nature of the system is partially obscured by the fact that first cousins are unmarriageable, the Dravidian model is a reasonable description of their rules of kinship. This same system has been described by anthropologists working among other Xingu tribes, particularly Galvão (1953), Carneiro (1957), and in greatest detail, by Basso (1973). In one very significant respect, however, the Mehinaku appear to be different from other Xingu peoples: the rules of the kinship system are applied very flexibly, so flexibly that at times it appears the Mehinaku can "write their own ticket" for defining their position within the relationship system.

The flexibility of kinship relations hinges principally on the distinction between "true" and more distant kin. Relationships between true kin are fixed and not subject to manipulation. In speaking of these relationships, a villager will point to his navel and say, "We are kinsmen *here*; we *must* behave as we do." Relationships between more distant kin, however, are far more mutable in character. The basis of this mutability is the system of "double relationships" (*mıpyama ehewe*).

Double Relationships

I first became aware of the pattern of double relationships when I asked each villager to list all of the kin terms by which he referred to every one of his fellows, a technique used by Arnold Rose (1960) in Australia. To my surprise, some of the Mehinaku offered more than one kinship term for the same person. A kinsman could be simultaneously a father's brother (*papá*) and a mother's brother (*uá*) or even a father's brother (*papá*) and a brother (*nujé*). It took me a long time to understand precisely what this apparent confusion of terminology meant, but the results were worth the effort. Double relationships are one of the more remarkable features of Mehinaku kinship and a good clue to their system of defining and allocating social roles.

Double relationships arise from the Mehinaku method of extending kinship beyond the small circle of true kin. The reader will recall that on the average, each villager's true kinsmen include about one-quarter of the community. The remainder of the tribe consists of people who are "a little bit" (*ahatāi*) kinsmen or "distant" (*mawákapai*) kinsmen, and it is among these relatives that "double relationships" occur. A villager's kinship term for these distant relatives is based on his parents' position within the network of relationships. The fact that the system is bilateral and that the position of both parents is given equal weight gives rise to double relationships. Let's look at the system from the perspective of Kuyaparei's eight-year-old son, Waku.

Waku is a prime candidate for errand boy whenever his parents have a message or food to deliver to their neighbors. Typically, Kuyaparei will direct him to take some fish hooks over to one of his classificatory brothers. Instead of saying, "Take this to my brother," however, Kuyaparei changes the kin term to reflect Waku's point of view: "Take these fish hooks to your *papá* (father's brother, father).

Later in the day, however, Waku's mother sends him with a message to the same individual, also her classificatory brother. She says "Go tell your *uá* (mother's brother) that Kuyaparei has gone to check his fish traps." Waku is thereby learning two kinship terms for the same person. His father's and his mother's classificatory brother is simultaneously *papá* and *uá*.

Virtually all of the Mehinaku can justify similar double relationships for at least some of the villagers who are not true kinsmen. Often the combinations of kin terms are apparently odder than the two above. On occasion, for example, a Mehinaku may address one of his fellows both as *papá* (father) and *teté* (older brother), thus confusing generations. The confusion, of course, is wholly in the mind of the outside observer and never seems to bother the Mehinaku at all. The reason is that kinship terms used between persons who are not true kinsmen, or who are "just a little bit" related, may be salutations rather than serious efforts to assert genealogical connectedness or to invoke a specific relationship. Under these circumstances it does not much matter which of the alternate terms is chosen. In either case, the use of the term affirms a correct social relationship between fellow tribesmen even if it does not specify a precise role.

There are times, however, when double relationships are a problem. Consider the case of a young man reaching adolescence. Before this time he has played with the other youngsters in the village with little regard for their relationship to him. Certainly he has never preoccupied himself with whether they are his cross-cousins or parallel cousins. At adolescence, however, the distinction suddenly is critical. Cross-cousins are targets for extramarital affairs and ribald jokes. Parallel cousins are more like true siblings, among whom such conduct is forbidden. How is a young Mehinaku to decide who is a cross-cousin and who is not?

Resolving Some of the Ambiguity

The Mehinaku define a cross-cousin (*utanuléi*) as the child of parents who are called father's sister (*aki*) and mother's brother (*uá*). In practice, however, there are very few such unambiguous cases. More often only one of the parents is clearly a mother's brother or father's sister, while the other is a classificatory father, mother, or even a sibling. The number of alternate possibilities is further increased by the pattern of double relationships. In this confusion a young man can expect little guidance from his parents. They have already established their network of marital and extramarital relationships so that they can afford to take a tough line on what constitutes incest for their children.

The course that most young villagers follow is to approach any attractive girl for whom the slightest case can be made for a cross-cousin relationship. Needless to say, this approach is potentially a shameful experience, and a young man waits until the girl is bathing alone or is outside the village on some errand. He takes her by the wrist and proposes sexual relations. According to Ipyu, a sexually active young man who has a great deal of experience in such matters, girls will sometimes respond, "No! I am like your true sister. When I get married my husband and you will be brothers-in-law." Ipyu says that he will sometimes argue with the girl to show her how they can legitimately be considered cross-cousins. If she nevertheless continues to turn him down he is humiliated, but at least he will not misread the nature of their relationship again. Similarly, if she accepts him as a lover, any element of ambiguity about the character of their relationship is effectively eliminated.

Ipyu's approach suggests that sexual attraction is one way to resolve the ambiguity inherent in overlapping relationships. Pretty girls and sexually receptive girls are in fact much more likely to become "cross-cousins" than girls who are unattractive and unreceptive. Admittedly, many of the liaisons that develop from such affairs are at least marginally in violation of the incest taboo, but fear of incest does not unduly alarm the villagers. There is no term for incest in the Mehinaku language other than *atalaitsuapai*, a word that simply means "to misuse." A man who eats sand, wrongly accuses a kinsman of witchcraft, or has sexual relations with his parallel cousin is equally *ataláistsuapai*: the principal meaning of the word is far broader than "incest." In addition, the villagers regard most forms of incest as ridiculous rather than horrifying. The notorious Yuta openly cohabited with his daughter before his death in the early 1960s, but nasty gossip and furtive jokes were the villagers' only response.

Outside the circle of true kin, where the boundaries of the incest taboo are difficult to delineate, the sanctions against sexual relations are minimal and the chances of justifying an affair are high. Ipyu, for example, has been mildly criticized for conducting an extramarital affair with his *mama* (mother and mother's sister). He pointed out in his own defense that by reckoning his relationship to the girl through his mother rather than his father, he could more or less claim that she was his cross-cousin. And in fact, he refers to the girl's father as his *uá* (mother's brother) rather than his *atú* (grandfather) in order to slip the girl into the right kinship category. In the girl's father's presence, however, I notice that he no longer uses any kinship term at all, since his claim that this man is a mother's brother is pretty thin.

By altering the terms by which he refers to his girl friend's father, Ipyu has been forced by the logic of the system to modify the way in which he treats his girl's younger brothers. He acts towards them as if they were his cross-cousins, engaging in a great deal of horseplay and practical joking. As they are all younger than Ipyu, he is able to manipulate his relationship with them more directly than he can with their father.

Ipyu's extramarital affair not only alters his relationships to his girl friend and her family but also affects the kinship position of future generations. The basis of this effect is a device for extending paternity called relationships of the "same foot," an institution that is not only ethnographically unusual but helps in establishing well-defined kinship roles.

Relationships of the "Same Foot"

The reader will recall that the Mehinaku theory of paternity holds that children are produced through many acts of sexual relations; once is not enough. Several men who have sexual relations with the same women will produce a child jointly. Ipyu says, with no little humor, that such pregnancies are like a *wanaki*, or collective labor project. When the child is born, every man who regularly had sexual relations with the mother may be regarded as the father. The institution of multiple paternity affects the kinship system by widening the set of individuals who can be considered close kinsmen. The recognition of paternity, however, depends primarily on the woman involved because she is in a strategic position to manipulate the situation. Itsa, for example, is presently being teased about being the father of one of Kaialu's daughters, but the matter is little more than a joke. Although he occasionally had sexual relations with her in exchange for beads or soap, she refuses to recognize him as the father and so the matter will stop there. Women simply refuse to acknowledge liaisons that they may come to regret, such as affairs with notorious witches, gossips, or other unpopular individuals.

The relationship of children produced by a man in his marriage and through his affairs is said to be of the "same foot" (*ikitsapa pinyerí*). The Mehinaku can not explain the exact significance of this image, but it means that the children are "real kin" who are prohibited from having sexual relations or marrying and who will one day have important in-law relationships with one another's spouses. Given the extensiveness of extramarital relations, it is surprising to learn that relationships of the "same foot" are not common. Only a handful are presently acknowledged in the village, for parents are anxious to leave their children some latitude in choosing marital partners. If the system were followed through to its logical conclusion, the incest taboo would prohibit virtually all sexual contact within the village. To avoid this dilemma, a mother in characteristic Mehinaku fashion will explain to her children that a certain man had sexual relations with her only a "few times"; he is therefore only a "little bit" their father and they may therefore marry his children.

A second important limitation on the recognition of relationships "of the same foot" is that some of the ties it engenders must be kept hidden. A mother carefully instructs her children to call a paramour *papá* only when her husband is out of earshot. A husband does not enjoy being reminded of his wife's indiscretion by his own children.

Other embarrassing relationships deriving from the extension of paternity are also concealed. Consider the accompanying diagram (fig. 24). Kama regards both villagers 1 and 2 as fathers-in-law, since villager 1 is his wife's father and villager 2 has had a long-standing affair with his wife's mother. Villager 2, however, is his clandestine father-in-law. Both he and Kama are careful not to refer to their relationship in the presence of villager 1, who is almost certainly aware of it but who does not want to have his wife's infidelity brought repeatedly to his attention.

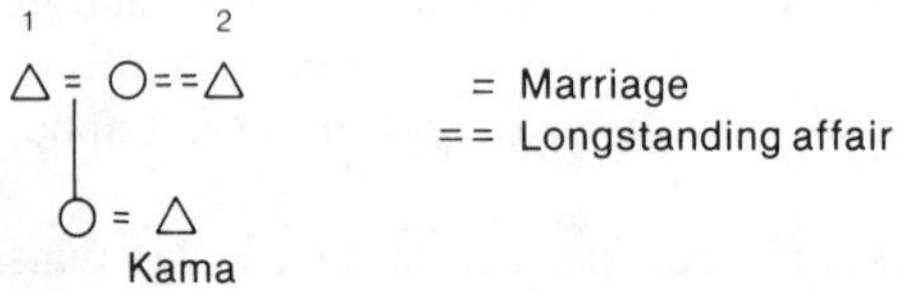

Fig. 24. Kinds of fathers-in-law.

Even though there are not many relationships of the "same foot," the choice of partners for extramarital affairs can become the basis for establishing new kinship relations. These choices not only establish the roles of lovers but also affect the kin ties of the next generation. Since the recognition of paternity depends on the interests of those affected, the Mehinaku are partially in control of the kinship system and their position within it.

Manipulating Affinal Kinship

A Mehinaku marriage presents an opportunity to radically change kinship relations; it is an occasion when some individuals can choose to become either the bride's or the groom's in-law. In 1972, for example, the marriage of Keie and Tana caused many changes in the network of kinship. Almost everyone in the wife's kindred and many of her classificatory relatives became the in-laws of the groom. The bride's parents and their brothers, sisters, and cousins became his parents-in-law, and the bride's brothers, sisters, and cousins became his siblings-in-law. Not all of these relationships inevitably followed from the marriage. The Mehinaku say that a person is necessarily an in-law only of his spouse's nuclear family. Whether he is the in-law of his spouse's more distant kinsmen depends on their willingness to assume the responsibilities of the relationship. The responsibilities of affinal kinship are assumed by persons who are well disposed to their kinsmen's spouse. In practice this includes all the members of a new husband's wife's kindred. It would be a serious breach of custom for any of them to refuse to become his in-law. The wife's more distant classificatory relatives, however, have an option. Generally, they will choose to become the husband's affinal relatives if they have a special relationship with his wife and her family. Thus the wife's mother's paramours usually become fathers-in-law because they are considered to have an important paternal tie to the wife. Similarly, a close friend of the wife's father is usually thought of as her father's brother. No matter how distant the actual relationship, he may be one of the new husband's important fathers-in-law.

A number of circumstances tend to inhibit the formation of affinal roles. A Mehinaku is unlikely to initiate an in-law relationship with one of his fellow tribesmen when he is having an affair with that person's wife, for it is wrong to have sexual relations with an in-law's spouse. The Mehinaku who has many affairs tends to have few affinal kinsmen. A person is also unlikely to establish an affinal relationship with someone he does not like, as the displays of respect expected between in-laws would be incompatible with his true feelings. Finally, there are some villagers who don't want any more in-laws because they already have too many. Keeping track of still more names that cannot be spoken and people who must be avoided is considered just too much effort. So widespread is this attitude that numerous in-law relationships are a sign of one's willingness to assume social burdens. Kuyaparei, a pillar of the community and one of its most sociable individuals, puts it like this: "Look around the village. In every house you will find my brothers-in-law. I go fishing with them, and they with me. I respect them and honor the naming taboos. I am not like that trash yard man, Teme, who has practically no in-laws at all."

Following each marriage there is a shakedown period in which the Mehinaku work out who will and who will not be their affinal relatives. A number of practices help to make the process orderly, the most important of which is that the spouse's

relatives must make the first move. Affinal relationships are unequal in that a person's spouse's kinsmen command more respect than they reciprocate. A new husband does not initiate
in-law relationships but waits for his wife's relatives to suggest
them. Some of his wife's distant kin, for example, may approach
him directly and say that they will be his brothers-in-law. There
is no possibility of rejection because an offer to become an
affinal kinsman is never turned down.

Occasionally the offer to form an affinal relationship is relayed through a third party, for it would be considered inappropriate for a man to approach his classificatory daughter's new
husband and suggest they be father- and son-in-law. Usually
he asks his "daughter" to establish the in-law relationship for
him. A third party can also be called in to help clarify ambiguous relationships when there is a marriage between two persons
who are on the periphery of a villager's kindred. If a second
cousin on his father's side marries a second cousin on his mother's side, he faces the dilemma of whether to consider both as
consanguineal kinsmen or whether one will become an in-law.
The Mehinaku sometimes respond to this kind of problem by
turning to an older member of the kindred who resolves it by
fiat, usually in favor of consanguineal relationships.

In-law relationships that can be created at a person's convenience can also be broken. This does not happen often and
when it does, it gives rise to scandal and excites a great deal of
gossip. Most frequently, affinal relationships are terminated between brothers-in-law when one has been having sexual relations with the other's wife. Brothers-in-law are honor bound to
avoid such indiscretions because, even when not prohibited by
the incest taboo, affairs are regarded as disruptive and antithetical to the generalized respect in-laws owe one another. So
widespread is the network of extramarital affairs, however, that
it is a rare villager who is not conducting a clandestine affair
with at least one of his bothers-in-laws' wives. The situation is
usually tolerated until the adulterous couple become so indiscreet that the cuckolded husband must take notice, as when he
enters the house unexpectedly and finds his wife and brother-
in-law together in her hammock. He may then terminate the
brother-in-law relationship with a public announcement that his

wife's lover is no longer his in-law and that from then on he will feel free to speak his name. A more common alternative is to retain the relationship while privately violating the name taboo.

Some Conclusions About Kinship

Two noteworthy characteristics of Mehinaku kinship are its ambiguity and its flexibility. The ambiguity of Mehinaku kinship seems to derive from the small size of the social unit, the bilateral system of reckoning kinship, and the practice of endogamy. In this setting it is often possible to trace a number of relationships to any single person, each of these representing a potentially different social tie. By manipulating the system a villager can choose the role most congenial to him, such as in-law, lover, or consanguineal kinsman. The result of these choices is that relationships become highly adaptable to events and personal desires. I recall, for example, that one of the women returned to the village with her husband after an absence of many years in a neighboring tribe. Keje explained to me that he could make a reasonable case for being either a cross or a parallel cousin. After looking her over, however, he decided that she was so unattractive that he had no interest in having sexual relations with her. On the other hand, her husband was strong, tough, and a good worker. The two men became brothers-in-law, and in a short time the husband was helping Keje in his garden. Keje had chosen between the girl and the garden and settled for the latter. Admittedly not every role bargain is guided by such carefully weighted self-interest, but it is often an element in the process. The flexibility of the system thereby gives the Mehinaku an opportunity to maximize their emotional needs and their material resources.

A third characteristic of Mehinaku kinship relations is that they are a matter of degree. Thus, cross-cousins can be "very much" cross-cousins or only a "little bit" cross-cousins. The notion of relatedness itself is subject to the same modifications. Villagers can be "true" relatives, "distant" relatives, or not relatives at all.

Sometimes these relationships are elaborately scaled. Kuya-parei has many fathers-in-law. These include his "true" father-in-law, Huyukai (his wife's father); a somewhat "lesser" father-in-law (Huyukai's brother); and a "little" father-in-law, his wife's mother's former paramour. He does not ride in the same canoe with his true father-in-law and avoids him on paths and in doorways. He will ride in the same canoe with his somewhat lesser father-in-law (though at the opposite end) but still avoids confronting him on trails and at house entrances. Everything is permissible with the "littlest" father-in-law, with whom he also recognizes a classificatory consanguineal relationship, except the mentioning of personal names.

The scaling of affinal roles is purely personal, the result of tacit role bargains, worked out as in this case by Kuyaparei and his fathers-in-law. It is typical, however, of the continuum of social relationships that exist between villagers. Each role partner in effect writes his own ticket within the framework of rules that state what such relationships are supposed to be like. Departures from the rules and amendments to them are regarded as matters of degree, so that social relationships are "little," "true," "distant," "close" and so forth.

The quantification of relationships affects other roles in Mehinaku society as well. There are big and little chiefs, shamans, musicians, friends, lovers, fishermen, story tellers, farmers, and even witches. Such measurement of relationships is not entirely foreign to us, although in general we allocate roles on an all or nothing basis. We have no "little bit" presidents, garbage collectors, fathers, or sons; neither do we have a set of affixes that we can tack onto status terms to measure the size and fit of the incumbent and his social position.

It is well to note, however, that the Mehinaku are not unique or even extreme in their pattern of flexible, scaled kinship relations. Robert Murphy in a study of Tuareg kinship tells us that, as among the Mehinaku, ". . . the ethnographer soon discovers that a Tuareg has more cross-cousins, especially female ones, than any other type of kin. . . . There is a remarkable flexibility in such a system, for terms may be adapted to conduct rather than conduct to terms (1967: 167)." Similarly, Eva Hunt (1969), in a detailed examination of the kinship system of a Mestizo community in Mexico, finds much of the same flexibility in allocating kinship roles that we do among the Mehinaku: biological kinsmen are occasionally said to be unrelated; unrelated individuals are often incorporated into the kindred; and kinship terms are used asymmetrically and applied without respect to the genealogical network of relatedness. Hunt suggests that the flexibility of the system is based on the inherently bimodal nature of kinship: biological connectedness and social relationship. These two models are noncongruent among Hunt's Mestizo informants because differences of class and political factions divide and separate members of the same kindred.

Among the Mehinaku, kinship is also a matter of "deed as well as blood." It is a matter of blood because the fundamental notion of relatedness is derived from the act of procreation, the "planting" of the "seed" in the body of its mother. It is a matter of deed because social relationships are conducted in the idiom of kinship, whether or not a biological tie can be demonstrated. Kinship by blood and deed are noncongruent among the egalatarian Mehinaku because of the small size of the community and the tendency for social relationships to overlap. Thus the Mehinaku are related in a variety of ways, simultaneously kinsmen by blood and marriage through the paternal and maternal lines. In this setting we could imagine institutional devices that would segregate these relationships in ways that would minimize overlap or deny it when it occurs. Exogamy and unilineal kinship are two such devices. If the Mehinaku married nonrelatives and traced kinship through one parental line, there would be neither "double relationships" between blood kinsmen nor in-laws who also recognized consanguineal roles. Given the bilaterality and endogamy of the small Mehinaku community, however, multiple relationships are inevitable. The measurement of these relationships as "real," "distant," "little," and so forth is the villagers' way of recognizing the ambiguity of the system and their rationale for playing upon it. Occasionally the system is an embarrassment, as when a young man must sort out exactly who is to be a cross-cousin and who is not, but more often it is an opportunity to emphasize those portions of the total relationship that are most congenial to the role players.

18

Being a Mehinaku: Tribal Identity in the Xingu System

This half is Mehinaku and that half is Waura.
Kuyaparei, drawing an imaginary line down his body

The task of the actor is to identify himself to his audience, to let them know who he is within the drama. The "portraits of self" described in chapter 12 and the roles I have analysed in this part of the book are some of the social identities of the Mehinaku villagers. The previous chapter, however, suggests that even when dealing with fundamental kinship roles, our real-life cast is not easily pinned down. Unlike stage actors who obligingly wear the mask assigned by the playwright, the Mehinaku may slip from one part to another. Only slightly less fluid than kinship, tribal identity among the Mehinaku provides the villagers with a sense of esprit and yet permits them to reach out to others well beyond the limits of their community. In this chapter I describe the cultural boundaries, exchanges, and oppositions between the Mehinaku and the peoples surrounding them.

Humans and Nonhumans

Members of groups define who they are with respect to other groups. For "us" to feel together, there must be a "they" that is separate and apart from us. Even an all-inclusive group, such as mankind, is only socially meaningful when it is contrasted with nonmen like animals or Martians. For these reasons, a good way to understand the basis of a social group is to look at the attitudes and interaction between it and its environment and not simply its internal structure. We begin with an examination of two myths that comment upon the social and natural boundaries between the Mehinaku and the world around them.

Among the most thought-provoking of all Mehinaku myths are the legends of metamorphosis (*iyákene*). Reflecting concern about the relationship of men to the nonhuman world, these tales are informally regarded as forming a group of stories to be told in succession. In each myth a plant, an object, or a force of nature turns into a Mehinaku, but as the story of Fire (*itsei*) shows, it can never remain an ordinary villager for long:

> A beautiful fire burned in the hearth. A woman looked at it, admiring the height and color of the flames. Later that day, a handsome man (really the fire turned into a man) came to the woman and took her to wife. For a while they lived well together, but he would never accompany her to bathe as a good husband should. At last, teased by his sisters-in-law, he went to the river—but he refused to go in. Laughingly, the women splashed him with water; tsssss! He disappeared in a puff of steam.

In other stories we meet Pequi Woman, Fish Poison Man, Salt Woman, Frog Child, and others, all of whom enjoy brief sojourns as Mehinaku villagers only to be rejected because of their nonhuman status—the myths of metamorphosis thus draw the line between men and the world of nature.

Let us now look at a legend that describes the origin of men and delineates the frontiers of the Xingu tribal system:

> In ancient times the Sun shot three arrows into the ground. Two of these arrows were feathered and became the Xingu tribes (*putaka*) and the wild Indians (*wajaiyu*). The third arrow, an unfeathered fishing arrow, became the Brazilians and the other white men who are sometimes bald.
> The chiefs of the three peoples sat in the center of the Sun's village and smoked. The Sun then passed gifts around the circle. He offered the chiefs milk, which was accepted by

the Brazilians but turned down by the Indians. He offered the Indians machines and guns and cars and planes, which they foolishly refused and the Brazilian chief cleverly accepted. He gave the wild Indians clubs, mantraps, and filthy food, while he gave the Xingu Indians shell necklaces, belts, earrings, and other beautiful things. Then the Sun told the wild Indians to live far away where they could not hurt the Xingu peoples, and he gave to each tribe its own village.

The Mehinaku reserve their strongest feelings for non-Xingu Indians. The term *wajaiyu*, which I roughly gloss "wild Indian," not only labels Indians who are unlike the Mehinaku and their neighbors but evokes extreme contempt. A mother whose child wriggles while she delouses him may say "Stop moving or you'll crawl with lice like a *wajaiyu*." The *wajaiyu*, however, are worse than simply unclean. As one villager said:

They kill you in the forest. They steal children and attack the villages at night. They never bathe; Orlando (the administrator of the reservation) had to order the Txicão (*wajaiyu*) to take baths. They sit on the prows of their canoes and defecate into the water. They eat frogs and snakes and mice. They rub their bodies with pig fat and sleep on the ground. They don't have a men's house; they don't wear shell belts and necklaces and arm bands and proper earrings. Their skin is very black. They don't wrestle each other in the afternoon; they just kill each other.

What these comments add up to is a powerfully negative stereotype of the non-Xingu Indian that is shared by all the Mehinaku. A *wajaiyu* is unpredictably violent and ugly; his speech is laughable; his food habits are repulsive; he is not quite a human being. The term for human (*neunéi*) is regularly applied to Xinguanos (*putaka*), Brazilians and other Westerners (*kajaiba*), and to monkeys (*pahï*; *Cebus, Latin*), who are considered to be of human origin in Xingu mythology. As proof for their allegation that the *wajaiyu* are not human, some of the villagers cite both the *wajaiyus*' supposedly revolting habits and a series of myths in which they are said to hatch from snake eggs and spring from a bestial union of a man with a Capybara (a one-hundred pound semiaquatic rodent resembling a giant guinea pig). Mythology is generally on the side of these villagers, since the principal creation myths (in contrast to the story of the Sun's Arrows) assign a unique origin to the Xingu peoples. Nevertheless, the term *neunéi*, much like the English "human," has a biological as well as social meaning. When pressed, the Mehinaku will reluctantly admit that in the biological sense the *wajaiyu* qualifies as a human: "They have skin, teeth, lips, tongues and eyes. They are people."

A graphic presentation of the prevailing attitude toward the "wild Indians" is presented in the pictures drawn by the talented and self-taught artists Amitiwana (a Trumaí) and Kuyaparei. The monkey is most probably a capuchin, a prehensile-tailed, tree-dwelling member of the genus *Cebus*. His grey-black fur stands on end; his eyes are widened; his mouth is opened in an "O" as he faces the reader in a posture of threat. The animal is accurately drawn except that the limbs are far too heavy, resembling the arms and legs of men—a regular feature of Mehinaku drawings of monkeys (see fig. 25).

Consider the picture of the "wild Indian," a member of the Carib-speaking Txicão. In common with all Mehinaku drawings of *wajaiyu* the picture badly distorts the subject who, except for his adornment, looks like a slightly-built Xinguano. In the picture, however, he appears as a hulking blackened golem. While the monkey has been humanized, the "wild Indian" has been turned into a monster, providing a powerful visual expression of the low esteem in which the Xinguano holds the *wajaiyu* (see fig. 26).

Contact and Interaction with the Wajaiyu

The Mehinaku and the other Xingu peoples hate and fear the *wajaiyu* primarily because they have been frequent victims of unprovoked attacks. The Xinguanos form a self-contained system; all their economic and social needs are satisfied within each village or by neighboring villages. Some of the wild Indians, however, have needs that can only be satisfied by raiding the more peaceful Xinguanos. The Mehinaku vividly remember their nightmarish experience with the Carib-speaking Txicão.

In the mid-1950s some of the Mehinaku were walking along one of their trails near the port on the Culiseu River when they

Fig. 25. A monkey. "Lets go hunt people," a villager may say to his friends, meaning that he wants to go on a monkey hunt. Citing a number of myths as proof, the Mehinaku claim that the capuchin monkey is of human origin—either the issue of a brother-sister marriage, or the descendent of a group of men gone feral. Almost human, the monkey is only reluctantly a part of the villagers' diet, and is considered far inferior to fish—the best food above all others.

Fig. 26. A wild Indian. Violent, unpredictable, repulsively adorned, the wild Indian is the antithesis of the peaceful, cultured, and esthetic Xinguano. In Kuyaparei's portrait, a club-carrying Txicão stands ready to split the head of anyone unfortunate enough to get in his way. Although the blackened skin, oversized genitals, and monster hands (notice the sixth finger added to the right hand as a sly afterthought) correspond to no actual individual, the picture tells an emotional truth about the artist's view of the wild Indian.

came upon three arrows of an unknown make pushed into the ground to form a tripod. It could only mean that there were wild Indians nearby who knew the location of their village and wished to terrorize them. Everyone was very frightened and there was talk of abandoning the community but for a while nothing happened. Then suddenly one morning while the villagers were on their way to their gardens, arrows began to fly. The Mehinaku ran home, cowered in their houses, and randomly fired the one gun in the village until the Txicão had left. The raiders came back frequently, and at night arrows would come whistling through the thatch while everyone hid behind the housepoles. Once when the Mehinaku had left the village to make salt, they returned to discover that their ceramic pots and other valuables had been stolen, their manioc silos thrown over, and their nonportable possessions destroyed. The terrorism continued until the Mehinaku chief was shot in the back with an arrow while hunting some distance from the village. The wound was serious and his life was saved only through the medical intervention of the Indian Post. In fear of their lives, the villagers decided that they could no longer put up with Txicão terror and moved north along the Tuatuari River to their present location.

Today (1976) all of the wild Indians in the immediate vicinity of the Xingu reservation have been pacified. The Txicão live within three hundred yards of the Indian Post, and, encouraged by the administrators of the reservation, occasionally visit the Mehinaku. I had an opportunity to see an intertribal trade session that occurred in November 1971.

Before the Txicão arrival, the Mehinaku began to express their contempt for the *wajaiyu*, assuring me they would never put up with the visit were it not that the Txicão possessed some valuable trade goods. The chief made a speech reminding everyone to trade only his cheapest and most shoddily-made possessions, while the men on the bench in front of the men's house accompanied the address with laughter and occasional grotesque imitations of the Txicão language.

When the Txicão arrived, with their children and wives in tow, I was astonished to see them all walk directly into the men's house. If a Xinguano woman had entered the men's house, she would have been gang raped. A Txicão woman, however, is so far outside the Mehinaku social world that she is primarily a foreigner and only secondarily a woman; the invasion was therefore tolerable.

As the trading began, the Mehinaku heaped verbal abuse on their guests while the children pelted them with hard lumps of dried-up manioc flour and other small missiles. One Txicão with a badly splayed big toe was the subject of special ridicule, some of the villagers even trying to borrow my movie camera to provide me with a record of the poor fellow's foot. During the trade session the Mehinaku made every effort to intimidate the visitors by laughing derisively at their requests and ridiculing their offers.

The bad manners of the Mehinaku, who ordinarily receive their guests with hospitality and decorum, was an unmistakable expression of the difference between themselves and the outsiders. The reception was also a dramatization of the Mehinaku's feelings, and like many dramatizations, it tended to oversimplify and exaggerate the message. As a group the villagers were at pains to differentiate themselves from the hated Txicão. As individuals, however, they are quite capable of interacting courteously.

Many of the Mehinaku have trading partners among the Txicão and other wild Indian tribes they meet at the Indian Post. The Mehinaku like to trade, because these tribes have access to certain kinds of bright feathers for headdresses. In addition, the villagers enjoy getting a close look at their things, much as we collect souvenirs from foreign lands that have no value other than their strangeness. Individual trade contacts are conducted on a congenial and even friendly basis, for the relationship is valued as well as the trade goods. The amiability of dyadic interaction indicates that the Mehinaku can look past the stereotypes incorporated in social roles and see the man behind the mask. On one level they see wild Indians so far outside the social universe that their very humanity is in question; and yet on an interpersonal level they are capable of dealing with them in a courteous fashion.

The basis of interaction between individual Mehinaku and wild Indians is primarily self-interest and personal conviviality rather than mutual expectations of proper conduct. In contrast, within the Xingu community the Mehinaku and their neighbors form a society within which interaction is predictable, guided by social rules, and enforced by informal sanctions. Let us now examine how the Mehinaku define their tribal identity and their position within the intertribal system.

Tribal Identity Within the Xingu System

Kuyaparei puzzled over my question for a few moments and finally drew an imaginary line down the center of his body with his index finger. "This half," he explained, "is Mehinaku, and that half is Waura." For the better part of an hour Kuyaparei had been trying to tell me who was a Mehinaku and why. The question turned out to be a difficult one since the rules assigning tribal membership are not spelled out. Instead, they are a composite of attributes consisting of language, parentage, public opinion, and residence.

To be a "true" Mehinaku one must speak the language fluently and without accent. The Mehinaku value their speech as an aesthetic accomplishment. Other languages (including, alas, English) are derided as the speech of animals and imitated with malicious humor in the presence of the speakers. If members of other tribes speak Mehinaku badly, the villagers' reaction combines amusement, scorn, and a measure of pain at seeing something beautiful badly treated. Accordingly, the Mehinaku do not encourage foreigners to speak their language. If outsiders try, they may be sure their errors will be imitated and laughed at by the villagers. Expatriate Xinguanos living among the Mehinaku often understand the language long before they dare to speak it. After four years of residence in the village, one Matipú woman knows Arawakan perfectly but speaks her native language to her husband and children. She uses Mehinaku only when obliged to speak it. As the villagers say, "You should not speak your in-laws' language if it is different from your own."

A second criterion of being a Mehinaku is parentage. There is a vague notion that all Mehinaku have some ultimate kin relationship, members of the tribe referring to themselves as "all of us" (*natu-não*) as opposed to members of other tribes who are labeled "all others" (*patóawa-não*). Mehinaku who think of each other as "all of us" almost invariably refer to each other by kin terms regardless of how remote their actual relationship. Kinship and parentage, then, form an important part of tribal identity. Given that marriage and sexual affairs across tribal lines are common, an individual may theoretically belong to several tribes at once. Hence, Kuyaparei is both Waura and Mehinaku. In practice, however, he makes a choice between them on the basis of where he lives and the language he uses most fluently. I know of no Mehinaku who is equally at home in more than one Xingu village.

A final and more subtle measure of being a Mehinaku is the opinion of the tribe. Antagonism is occasionally expressed by insinuating that a certain person is not really Mehinaku. This allegation is only made against persons whose tribal affiliation is ambiguous, but it suggests that membership is not fixed by rules or contract. As measured by the fickle climate of public opinion, tribal identity can vary from day to day.

Becoming a Mehinaku

Under certain conditions there is a possibility that tribal membership can be changed. If, for example, a Kamaiurá wanted to become a Mehinaku, he could move in with a distant kinsman and after a period of time inform him that he wanted to take up permanent residence in the Mehinaku village. In the evening the chiefs of the tribe and the older men would call him out to the plaza and ask if he intended to make a garden or "just hunt and fish." The question is important, since making a garden is proof of a permanent investment in the community. Then the chiefs would say, "You are a Mehinaku; your mother's relatives are Mehinaku. You are only a little bit Kamaiurá. The Kamaiurá are not good; they gossip and practice witchcraft; you will stay with us and be a Mehinaku." Then the chiefs, as an act of hospitality, would call a collective labor party (*wanaki*) to cut a garden for the new villager.

In reality the new tribesman's status is fictive, and it is never forgotten that he is "really" a Kamaiurá. If he stays many years in the village, however, he will begin to address all the Mehinaku by kin terms and build his own house in the village circle. His children and their children will be considered "true" Mehinaku.

Being a Mehinaku is no simple matter, then, but a complex of attributes consisting of speaking the language, maintaining good social relationships with one's fellows, being of the right parentage, and being considered a fellow tribesman by the rest of the community. Membership in more than one tribe, disagreements about who is a Mehinaku and to what extent, and the ability to change groups suggests that the boundary between tribes is far less formidable than the vast gulf separating the wild Indians and the Xinguanos. The boundaries among Xingu tribes are nonetheless important because they define participation in the intertribal rituals, economic exchanges, and attitudes which are a prominent part of everyday life.

Interaction and Opposition Among the Xingu Tribes

Levi-Strauss, writing in a review article in the *Handbook of South American Indians* (1948), wisely suggested that learning about intertribal relations in the Xingu culture area was as important as knowing about any one of the Xingu tribes. Intertribal life is so rich that it approximates an independent culture. The Mehinaku provide an especially good vantage point from which to document this culture, since much of it seems to have been Arawakan (and often specifically Mehinaku) in origin. In this sketch of intertribal life I plan to describe the exchanges and patterns of interaction that occur across the boundaries of tribal groups.

Monopolies and Trade

Virtually all observers of the Xinguanos have noted that most of the tribes manufacture a trade specialty such as shell belts, necklaces, hardwood bows, and ceramic pots. Used as gifts to affinal relatives and payments for ceremonial services, these valuables play a key role in the economic system of each village. There is also a large set of trade goods of lesser value made especially well by certain tribes and in large quantities for export. A partial list of the monopolies and trade specialties appears in table 24.

Most of the important monopolies seem to have some basis in ecological variation. The shells used to make belts and necklaces, for example, are available only near the traditional villages of the Carib-speaking tribes and the hardwood for bows is most accessible in the forest near the Kamaiurá. Although the bow wood monopoly is no longer enforced, the Mehinaku believe that for them to gather shells would risk retaliation by Carib witches, who are reputed to be the most dangerous in the area.

The tribal specialties unsupported by variations in natural resources are difficult to explain. Deposits of reasonably good clay, for example, exist in a number of areas outside the Waura's

Table 24	Xingu Trade Specialties and Monopolies
Arawakan tribes:	Mehinaku Salt (KC1) and cotton (not ceramics as erroneously reported in the literature)
	Yawalapití Cotton; well-made fish spears
	Waura Ceramic pots; cotton
Carib tribes	Kuikuru Belts manufactured from the shell of a land snail; wood for ceremonial flutes
	Matipú Necklaces made from the shell of a fresh water mollusk
Tupian tribes	Kamaiurá Bows made from a hardwood, genus *Tecoma* (monopoly partially defunct); medicines for ceremonial and ritual use
	Auití No specialties of importance from Mehinaku point of view
Trumaí tribe	Trumaí Formerly stone axes imported from outside the Xingu region

normal territory, and yet only Waura women make ceramic pots. Since these pots are important in subsistence as well as in measuring wealth, it would be very much to the advantage of the Mehinaku women if they were ceramicists. The villagers offer several explanations of why they do not make clay pots. The most significant is that making pots is "properly" an activity of Waura women; if a Mehinaku woman tried to make pots, everyone would ridicule her bad workmanship. In addition, if the village women were to make pots it would break the Waura monopoly; and maintaining the tribal interdependence is in itself perceived a virtue. As Kuyaparei puts it: "They have things that are really beautiful, and we have things that they like. And so we trade, and that is good."

Trade is one of the principal bases of intertribal contact. During the rainy season, friendly tribes spend several days trading, visiting, wrestling, dancing, and playing their hosts' sacred flutes (see Basso 1973, for a description of a Kalapalo trade session). Even on more casual visits, however, hosts and guests feel obliged to trade. So strong is this obligation that many of the Mehinaku are careful when visiting neighboring tribes to take only goods they can easily replace; otherwise they might find themselves in a situation where they would be required to give up prized personal possessions.

Rituals

Mehinaku ceremonial life is built around two types of rituals. The first of these, "Giving Food and Gifts to the Spirits," (*kulekẽipei, iyejútapai apapainyei*) is concerned with the world of spirits and their relationship to men. Usually observed only by the Mehinaku, these rituals cure disease and propitiate potentially malevolent spirits with food and presents. The second set of rituals, *kaiyumãi*, include major festivals, most of which are of a semisecular character. The "Piercing Festival" (*pihiká kaiyumãi*), "Bark Festival" (*akajatapá kaiyumãi*) and "Wood Festival" (*áta kaiyumãi*) celebrate the initiation of the male and female chiefs and the mourning of the dead. These ceremonies are necessarily intertribal, for without the participation of their neighbors the souls of the Mehinaku dead could not ascend from the burial ground in the plaza to the village in the sky, nor could the village chiefs acquire the full credentials for their office. In short, internal social needs compel the villagers to ask other tribes to their ceremonies and to reciprocate by honoring their guests' invitations.

Stereotypes and Antagonism

Perhaps nothing expresses more clearly the social boundaries separating the Mehinaku from their neighbors than the stereotypes they employ to characterize other tribes. Among the most striking of the prejudices are the Mehinaku's attitudes towards the Carib-speaking groups of whom the Kuikuru are regarded as the most ill-mannered and grossly unrefined. According to the Mehinaku, they respect no man's privacy, freely enter his house, lie down in his hammock, insist on seeing his possessions, demand presents, and dare to offer poorly crafted trade goods in exchange for irreplaceable Brazilian manufactures. The Kuikuru, like the wild Indians, have violent tempers. They wrestle brutally, openly accuse each other of misbehavior, abuse their children, and murder their fellows over false allegations of witchcraft. Most of the Kuikuru are dangerous witches, one Mehinaku informant being able to name only three who are not. One of their sorcerors, unlike any other, has the power to blast apart entire villages with house-demolishing winds and lightning bolts. Together with several of his comrades, he has been responsible for ant invasions, crop failures, and other natural disasters in the Mehinaku community.

Whenever a large group of Kuikuru enter the village, they receive a standard reception that reflects the Mehinaku's fear and distaste. Deliberately staged by the villagers, the reception is a performance for which they make careful preparations. It begins when the Kuikuru are spotted a long way off on the trail leading into the village. The first Mehinaku to detect the visitors lets out a distinctive high-pitched whoop (see table 1) that alerts the community. Immediately the women rush to the doorways of the houses to watch the approach, talking in hushed and excited voices about who the visitors might be and how many of them there are. When they are positively identified as Kuikuru, the women's comments are filled with expressions of distaste and anxiety. Quickly rounding up their children, mothers herd them into the darker recesses of the houses. It is dangerous to leave the little ones unwatched since a Kuikuru sorcerer could steal a lock of their hair, take it back to his village, and cast a spell upon it at his leisure.

The men are also reacting to the impending visit. They carefully store valuable possessions out of sight while the elders gather near the house adjoining the main trail, muttering among themselves about the meaning of the visit. At the last minute before the Kuikuru arrive, the women retreat into their houses and join their children. The men then greet the visitors with great false smiles of welcome. The Mehinaku chief invites his guests inside where they are seated near the doorways on wooden benches and offered bowls of manioc porridge.

Conversation is rudimentary because of the language barrier, but it almost always turns to possessions the Kuikuru would like to beg or trade. The Mehinaku at first maintain that they do not have the items requested, treat the request as a joke, or make an unacceptable demand in return. More often than not, however, they eventually produce the wanted item, usually gaining in exchange only a promise of some future gift. Despite the smiles, laughter, and clasps over the shoulder that usually accompany this interaction, the atmosphere is tense and the villagers are visibly intimidated. After approximately a half-hour, the visitors leave, and the women and children return to their doorways to watch them depart.

The Mehinaku's low opinion of the Carib tribes is also shared by the other Arawakan-speaking tribes in the region, by the Trumaí, and by at least one of the Tupian groups, the Auití. At a loss to explain the Carib's misbehavior and lack of refinement, the Mehinaku simply say, "It has always been that way." My speculative explanation is that the Carib-speakers may be relatively late arrivals in the Xingu basin and have not as yet fully adapted to the expectations of the other tribes. Certainly they seem to have less influence on intertribal culture than the Arawakans, whose language forms the basis for most of the songs sung at intertribal rituals. The American anthropologist Ellen Basso, who has studied the Carib-speaking Kalapalo, informs me that even in the course of local rituals the Kalapalo sing Mehinaku songs, quite unconcerned that they cannot understand a word.

The stereotypes labeling other Xingu tribes are more muted than those damning the Caribs. The Tupian-speaking Kamaiurá and Auití are said to be less violent and better-mannered than the Carib speakers, though still disputatious and lacking in refinement. The Kamaiurá especially are regarded as only recently civilized. In a malicious pun on their name, they are called *kamãi nula* (literally, corpse food or "corpse eaters") by the Mehinaku; the name refers to their alleged practice of mortuary cannibalism before becoming proper Xinguanos (*putaka*).

The Mehinaku also complain about the tribes who are speakers of Arawak like themselves. Significantly, the complaints resemble those that the Mehinaku make about each other. The Waura and the Yawalapití, for example, are never accused of being corpse eaters, but they are criticized for being gossipy and quarrelsome.

Avoidances

Although most interaction between the Mehinaku and their neighbors occurs on an interpersonal rather than group basis, the villagers have mixed feelings about visitors and visits. It is nice to go traveling and see relatives and friends in different tribes, but there are risks. Visitors to the Mehinaku, who are among the most decorous and nonviolent of the Xingu tribes, run the hazard of losing their possessions, being bewitched, or being assaulted. Any outsider who is foolish enough to enter the village when a men's house is under construction is severely beaten. Any Xingu woman, whatever her tribal affiliation, who appeared in the village when the sacred flutes were being played on the village plaza would be gang raped.

Casual intertribal visits are also discouraged for less dramatic reasons. A visitor to another tribe, for example, runs the risk of being shamed by his inability to speak the local language. The Mehinaku often avoid this kind of embarrassment in foreign villages by speaking their own language exclusively. Since their hosts may follow the same strategy, the result is a conversation that neither is wholly able to understand. I have seen such garbled interchanges endure for as long as thirty minutes at a stretch. Although some information manages to get by the language barrier, the Mehinaku are not comfortable in this kind of situation and understandably prefer to communicate with Xinguanos who speak their language.

Another impediment to casual intertribal visitation is the Mehinaku belief that it is not proper to spend too much time among foreign tribes. Like the man who moves from house to house, the inveterate traveler slights his fellows. The target of quiet resentment, rumors circulate insinuating that he will never return to the Mehinaku village again, or that he intends to trade stolen goods or recruit foreign sorcerers to bewitch his comrades back home.

Given the hazards of intertribal visits, it is understandable that they are sometimes avoided. At times the Xinguanos take pains to bypass their neighbors. The trail from the Kuikuru settlement to the Indian Post leads straight through the Mehinaku village. Nevertheless, many of the Kuikuru avoid the village by taking a longer rough trail that they have opened up through the forest. Only the more aggressive Kuikuru attempt the village route and then only in large groups. A Kuikuru will rarely enter the village by himself unless he is a kinsman of one of the Mehinaku or has a specific piece of business to transact, such as the purchase of a large quantity of cotton.

Intertribal Marriage

The best kinds of marriages, say the Mehinaku, are marriages within the village, for no one likes to live among strangers who speak a different language. Atala, who married a Kamaiurá woman, explains how hard it was to live in a different tribe:

> I couldn't speak the language and didn't know anyone there. During the first few days I just stayed around the house. I didn't go to the men's house and paint up or even go fishing with anyone. I was ashamed when people spoke to me and I didn't understand. I learned the language after two years, but I never spoke it. I never had girl friends because I was too ashamed to ask them.

Even worse, Atala was subject to the most humiliating teasing by his wife's lovers. This pattern of teasing in-married spouses (*inyerí,* masculine; *inswí,* feminine) from other tribes is typical of many of the upper Xingu tribes, although it is somewhat muted among the Mehinaku. Taking the form of nasty practical jokes, the hazing is justified on the grounds that the outsider has "stolen" a potential spouse. When the victim, for example, gets into his hammock after dark he finds it filled with ashes and earth. After he cleans away the dirt and lies down several men grab the sides of the hammock, dump him out, and run off into the night. When at last he falls asleep his hammock cords are twanged to wake him up. Daylight brings no respite. If he laughs, his laughter is imitated from behind one of the houses. If he whoops, a mocking echo of his voice returns from some unseen villager. If he trips or falls down, an outline of his body is made on the spot so that everyone can take pleasure in his discomfort. The tricks and practical jokes continue until the target's wife has had her first child, at which time she is no longer considered attractive enough to bother about.

Given all this unpleasantness, why should anyone marry outside his own village? The answer is that the small size of most of the tribes makes it difficult to find a spouse within the community. Although no one likes to leave home, approximately 35 percent of Mehinaku marriages involve a spouse from another tribe. Similar figures have been reported for the neighboring Kuikuru (Carneiro 1957: 296).

If one must find a wife in another tribe, he is in a particularly advantageous position if he already has a family contact. A young man with a parent from a neighboring village has a good chance of finding a bride in that village. Such a husband-to-be considers himself especially lucky if, instead of seeking a wife from another tribe, he can wait until an eligible girl and her family come to visit the Mehinaku. The advantage of this strategy is that the groom stands a good chance of evading bride service in his wife's village and runs less risk of incurring the enmity of her former lovers.

Blood Kinship Between the Tribes

One consequence of intertribal marriage is the extension of bonds of kinship among all the Xingu tribes. A child of an intertribal marriage has kinsmen in two villages, using his parents' place in the kinship system to trace relationships to everyone in the two tribes. If a Mehinaku has a Waura mother, for example, his kinship ties to the Waura will be reckoned exclusively through her line. As a result he will have many classificatory mother's brothers and mother's sisters in the Waura but no paternal relatives.

Bonds of kinship may also be created between unrelated members of neighboring tribes. Because intertribal trading relationships and friendships may be equated with "distant" siblingship, conscious agreements can be made to create bonds that reflect the interests of those who invoke them. I was once present when the Mehinaku chief arranged such a fictive tie with the daughter of a man with whom he was anxious to cement an enduring relationship. He said to this man's daughter, "I am your father's kinsman, my child. I say your father's name, therefore he is not my in-law. In the future, when your father dies I will come and cut your mother's hair (as would a relative of the girl's father). I will call you daughter."

Initially these "negotiated" relations do not carry the legitimacy of true kinship. Nevertheless, such "relatives" will offer the chief hospitality when he visits and in the future will help his son to find a spouse.

Hospitality and Visiting

The Mehinaku visit other tribes to look for a wife, to trade for shell belts, hardwood bows, or ceramic pots, to visit close kin, or to avoid intolerable social pressures at home. In theory, the villagers expect hospitality from all the Xingu tribes. A visitor is supposed to be able to walk into any house in any Xingu community and be offered a place to tie his hammock, wood for his fire, and fish and manioc for his dinner. Normally, however, the Mehinaku expect hospitality only from those who have received it from them; namely, friends and kinsmen.

A visitor to the Mehinaku village arrives with little warning. Instead of passing directly across the plaza he takes one of the smaller paths and enters his host's house through the back door. The visit is a matter of contact between individuals, not tribes, so the traveler does not want the attention of the entire community focused upon him.

As soon as he arrives he is greeted by everyone in the house. If he is a "true" kinsman of one of the residents, he ties up his own hammock and receives no more special hospitality than any Mehinaku who enters his own house. If the visitor is a somewhat distant kinsman or friend, however, he is regarded as a "guest" (*nuputakalā*, literally, "my Xinguano"). A well-mannered guest arrives with fish or monkey and perhaps more substantial gifts. The host takes his visitor's hammock and suspends it near his own, the act symbolizing the guest's welcome and the host's acceptance of his role as a provider of hospitality. After the guest has been given food, firewood, and water, the host takes him out to the central plaza where he will wrestle and later smoke with the other men of the tribe, conversing with them as best he can across the language barrier. The host has provided shelter and food, and acted as his guest's social sponsor as well.

Intertribal Relations

Interaction between individuals from different Xingu groups is different from the interaction of tribes. Between tribes, interaction is colored by hostile stereotypes and regulated by the rules of ceremonies and formal trade sessions. Between individuals, relationships progress on the basis of a flexible system of intermarriage, kinship, and hospitality. The boundaries between the tribes are never impermeable and always seem to make allowances for individual needs. In this sense the relationship between foreigners resembles the relationships among the Mehinaku themselves. Roles are not rigidly defined but are subject to manipulation and new agreements, interaction depending less upon the fact of group membership than upon the ability of individuals to make role bargains with their fellow Xinguanos.

A consequence of this pattern is that the villagers do not regard themselves as members of rigidly defined social units. Being a Mehinaku is a matter of degree and depends upon a multiplicity of factors, including the network of involvements with other groups. Hence a villager can reasonably explain that he is a lot Mehinaku, a little Waura, and a tiny bit Kuikuru. From the point of view of the individual, the system is open-ended, flexible, and responsive to his own inclinations.

The trumpet knows its own song.

Kuyaparei

The concept of the social role has been the theoretical basis for organizing much of the material presented so far. From a dramaturgical point of view, a role is a complex of behavior given to an actor to perform in a larger drama. The role stands beyond the actor's reach. He is given it for a while, performs it, and then passes it along to someone else. Although he may perform the role in a unique and personal style, he does not write the lines; the script for social relationships is dictated by society as a whole.

Useful as this model of social life may be, it tends to leave too little room for the man behind the social mask. Roles are not rigid and unchanging. Even when the social mask appears fixed and immutable, the actor may alter it or design it anew, for roles are human inventions, cumulative products of numerous acts of personal creativity. Nevertheless, traditional social science finds the dynamics of conduct in the structure of the group or the dictates of culture. Occasionally in the anthropological literature, there is a bow in the direction of the individual (see Barnett 1953), but unless the perspective of the re-

search is explicitly psychological, the individual is seldom encountered. Erving Goffman, whose theoretical work informs
this book, is no exception to the pattern. In much of his work
the individual exists only in "fleeting moments" of interaction,
and even then the presented "self" is one that has been pre-
fabricated by his society. There is a man behind Goffman's
performer, but we must search hard for him, prying away many
layers of artifice and contrivance:

> . . . the individual who performs the character will be seen for
> what he largely is, a solitary player involved in a harried
> concern for his production. Behind many masks and many
> characters, each individual tends to wear a single look, a
> naked unsocialized look, a look of concentration, a look of
> one who is engaged in a difficult, treacherous task
> (1959: 235).

The man behind the performer seems a rather pathetic individual, cut off from his fellows by the social mask he wears and
driven by a consuming anxiety that his performance will not
measure up. Such a character has little chance of being more
than a bit player in the larger social drama, much less an author
of the lines. And yet there is good evidence from our own society (and in Goffman's descriptive sociology) that the actors
may have a vigorously creative role. Not only can individuals
redefine social situations to their own advantage, they can turn
established institutions to new and unanticipated purposes.

The sociologist Peter Berger takes note of these possibilities:

> There have been instructive cases in which motor-pool ser-
> geants successfully ran call-girl rings, and hospital patients
> used the official message center as a bookie joint, such op-
> erations going on in subterranean fashion for long periods
> of time. . . . The ingenuity human beings are capable of in
> circumventing and subverting even the most elaborate control
> system is a refreshing antidote to sociologistic depression.

After examining such cases and the effects of charismatic individuals on history and social movements, Berger concludes that
society is much more open to the contribution of the individual
than may have been apparent. In fact, such considerations
". . . may lead to a sudden reversal in one's view of society—

from an awe-inspiring vision of an edifice made of massive granite to the picture of a toy-house precariously put together with *papier mâché*." (1963: 131, 134)

In recent years sociology has begun to show greater awareness of the creative role of the individual in social relationships. According to the current terminology roles are not externally forced upon the actor, but are accepted "voluntaristically," and manipulated through "role bargains" and "transactions." A small but growing field of sociology (see Peterson 1975) focuses on the so-called "culture makers" who produce and market their personal creations for the greater society. Thus far investigators in this area have examined art, popular music, and scientific research, but I suspect their work could be successfully broadened to the area of ordinary social relationships as well.

Certainly Mehinaku relationships seem to require a sociology sensitive to the role of the individual villager. We have already noted in the case of Mehinaku kinship that the actors can radically modify the roles assigned to them. Even the stage for these roles may be manipulated and reshaped as the villagers shift from house to house or cut new paths through the woods. Although this creativity and flexibility in relationships is evident on every level of Mehinaku culture, its importance is probably greatest in the sphere of religious activities. Here we not only find the same openness to the contribution of the individual, but we can clearly see the hand of each author and watch the creative process as it occurs.

Religion and Spirits

The basis of most Mehinaku ceremonies and rituals is a belief in spirits (*apapãiyei*). A partial clue to the nature of spirits is that the large animals such as deer, pigs, and cayman are called by a similar term, *apapãiyei mune*. The meaning of *mune* is complex, but in this context translates as "substantial," suggesting "nonsubstantial being" as a literal gloss for *apapãiyei*. The Mehinaku point out that a spirit differs from ordinary creatures in that it is not tangible. Ordinarily invisible, the *apapãiyei* moves about "like the wind," creating effects such as whirlwinds, waterspouts, meteor showers, or eerie sounds. Shamans, however, as well as men who are sick, dying, or just dreaming may see spirits directly. They have reported that they are extremely frightening, being equipped with giant heads, long teeth, eyes that glow in the dark, and hideous deep voices. Just as there are many people and animals, however, so are there many spirits. The spirits are not classified in neat linguistic categories like humans and fauna, but several principal classes are distinguished. Among these are the *wekehe*, the spirit masters of important natural resources such as *pequi* fruit, corn, and manioc. Considered less dangerous than many others, these spirits are associated with calendrical harvest rituals, such as the *pequi* festivals held each fall. Quite different are the demons who stalk the forest and haunt the lakes surrounding the village, the "spirits that eat" (*apapãiyei aintyá*). An example of such a monster is Jalapakumá, the giant leafcutter ant who frequents the site of Jalapá, the present Mehinaku village. As big as a house, with huge mandibles and luminous eyes, Jalapakumá prowls outside the community in search of his prey. Any villager unfortunate enough to meet him is devoured on the spot and never heard from again.

The reality of Jalapakumá and the other malignant spirits comprising the Mehinaku pantheon is not doubted by the villagers. A strange sound from the forest, a sudden wind in the trees, an unexplained eddy in the waters may be cause for alarm. Mothers round up their children and men speak in subdued voices as everyone leaves the area as rapidly as possible. Certain regions are known to be the homes of particularly dangerous spirits, and these areas are avoided by the cautious. On occasion the villagers have cut new trails through the woods to avoid "spirits that eat" as well as the neighborhoods of ghosts (*ĩyeweku*, shadows) of recently executed witches.

The final class of spirits, the *apapãiyei*, may appear in as frightening and monstrous form as the *apapãiyei aintyá*, but this is an external appearance. Their skins are garments (*nãi*) that can open, as one informant explained it, "like a zippered duffle bag." Behind the frightening masks and beneath the ghastly costumes are the real spirits, very much like the Mehinaku in appearance but ageless and physically perfect. These spirits are nonetheless dangerous, for they can "take" (*etuka*) a man's soul (*iyeweku*, a homonym of "shadow," which refers to the intangible identity of each individual as seen, for example, in a dream).

A villager who is hungry or lonely, misses his girl friend, or just feels sorry for himself is especially vulnerable to soul loss. A spirit whose sympathies have been aroused by the plight of the villager's soul may take it away to live with him among the trees, under the water, or in the sky. The soul may be happy residing in the village of the spirit, which looks exactly like the Mehinaku settlement. Gradually, however, the villager himself languishes and sickens over his loss.

Fortunately there are certain techniques for restoring a snatched soul. One is to send all the village shamans out to the area where the soul was lost. The lead shaman makes a small doll, while the *yakapa* shamans (see chapter 20) try to find the soul. When they do, two of the shamans manually force the soul into the doll. The lead shaman carries the doll to the sick person's hammock as fast as he can run so that the spirit will not resteal the soul. He pushes the doll against his patient's chest, forces the soul back into his body, and thereby restores his health.

Early during the curing ceremony, a shaman diagnoses which spirit stole the soul. His diagnosis is of great consequence, for the patient may then become a sponsor (*wekehe*) of a ceremony designed to prevent the spirit from returning. He thereby obligates himself to participate in important ceremonies and provide food for the entire community.

On assuming the sponsorship the patient appoints "organizers" (*petewehehe*) who, provided the spirit is not especially formidable, sets up a modest ceremony during the dry season. The spirit, in the guise of grotesquely costumed dancers, is brought into the village, given food, and enjoined not to make anyone else ill. Although the dancers are considered something of a "joke" because they are not "really" the spirit, the spirit is nonetheless believed to be present and content with what the villagers have done. Once the ritual is over, the costumes are stored in the men's house in which the spirit himself then takes up residence. Six months later the costumes are carried to one of the main roads that lead to the spirit's forest or river abode; there they are burned and the spirit is urged not to return to the village again.

Spirits cannot always be dismissed so lightly, for some are particularly dangerous and persistent. They are responsible for more serious diseases and tend to strike the wealthy and the socially prominent, who are thereby motivated to provide the large quantities of work and food needed for the rituals. When, for example, Kauká, the demon of the sacred flutes and the "chief of the spirits" steals a soul, the patient selects several ritual organizers and purchases three flutes for them. Between himself (the sponsor) and the organizers, there is now a relationship which may endure the rest of their lives. Every few days the organizers and other villagers play the flutes while the spirit is "fed" large buckets of manioc porridge provided by the sponsor and actually consumed by the entire village. The garden from which the manioc comes is cleared, weeded, and harvested by all the men working collectively, and they are "paid" with gifts of fish by the sponsor.

In the course of many months, the sponsor and especially his wife will have invested a great deal of labor in preparing the manioc flour for the porridge. Eventually the organizers of the ritual become "ashamed that they have done so little," and put on an intertribal festival to "give gifts" (*iyejútapai*) to the spirit. The gifts, which consist of valuables such as shell belts and necklaces, are presented to the sponsor in the name of the spirit. Although they are said to be the spirit's property and may not be traded, still they are intended for the personal use of the sponsor and may be worn on secular occasions.

Other spirits do not demand quite such expensive gifts as does the flute demon, although their requirements are still impressive. Kuyaparei, for example, who is presently sponsor of the Takwara trumpet ritual, received an arrow from each man in the village so that he could shoot fish "for the spirit." Shumōı, sponsor of the Kaiyapa dancing ritual, was recently the recipient of a huge stack of firewood that his wife will use in baking manioc bread for the Kaiyapa demon. Gifts such as these can be put to personal use on a limited basis, but it is clear that the sponsor does not profit substantially from his position. His real dividends arise from his enhanced prestige within the community.

The Origins of the Spirits and
Their Rituals

The Mehinaku have no myth which accounts for the origin of the *apapãiyei* demons. Some villagers say that they just "came up like corn" out of the ground; others insist that they have always been around. Everyone agrees that the shamans have been discovering the demons since ancient times and organizing rituals to feed them and present them with gifts. No one knew about the spirits until the shamans saw them and told the Mehinaku how to conduct the appropriate ceremonies.

I had always believed that this account of the origins of Mehinaku religious knowledge was to be taken with a grain of salt. After all, rituals and myths usually have no single author. They are cultural products, influenced by history, changed by contact with other societies, and distorted by the process of transmission from one generation to another. Mehinaku religious beliefs are of course subject to the same influences, but I now have good reason to believe that the villagers' religious system is unusually open to individual contributions.

The pantheon of spirits is virtually without limit. Every animal species and many objects are potentially associated with a spirit. Some of these spirits are known to the Mehinaku and are identified by the animal or object name plus the affix *kuma* (or a morphophonemic variant *tyuma*) meaning big or monstrous. A similar pattern of naming demons exists among both the Tupi-speaking Kamaiurá, who use the affix -aruiap (Villas-Boas 1973: 252) and the Carib-speaking Kalapalo, who use the affix -kuegi (Basso 1973: 22), suggesting that a similar conception of spirits exists among most of the Xinguanos. Some examples of such spirits include Ant Demon (Meintyumá; the tocandira ant), Snake Demon (Uikumá), Wasp Demon (Atapujekumá), and Canoe Demon (Itsakumá). Other animals such as the armadillo and objects such as the house are also said to be associated with spirits, but they have not yet been seen and reported on by the shamans and their character is unknown. They supply a reservoir of new titles from which a

shaman can draw when he makes a diagnosis of an illness. Since
there are no ceremonies associated with unfamiliar spirits, the
shaman can make up his own. The Mehinaku spiritual world
is still only partly explored; the shaman may expand its frontiers through his own ingenuity.

The symbolic details of Mehinaku rituals suggest that this
process actually occurs. Some ceremonies seem to be relatively
slight variations on others, as if the creator of the ritual was
engaged in small-scale experimentation. The three sets of sacred
flutes currently in the men's house, for example, represent three
different forms of the spirit Kauká. Not only are there slightly
different songs for each set of flutes, but the Yukuku-Kauká
spirit requires the services of a fourth musician who sings the
name of the spirit ("Yu - ku - ku —") in a high falsetto voice
while the flutes are playing. The ceremonies for the Kaiyapa
demons show still greater variations in the dance steps and the
song lyrics (fig. 27). The Mehinaku say that the variations
reflect the actual conduct of the demons as perceived by the
shaman at the time of his diagnosis of his patient.

A final line of evidence suggesting that spirits, as well as the
attendant ceremonies, are personal discoveries is that many of
them have a faddish nature like popular songs and other ephem-
eral creations in our own society. Some spirits, for example,
seem to be on the verge of extinction. Yakwikató used to make
many Mehinaku ill. At present there are no ceremonial sponsors
associated with him in the village, nor has he taken anyone's
soul in a good many years. "Yakwikató used to be very dangerous," says one villager, "but ever since we started making
his mask to trade at the Indian Post he hasn't made anyone
sick." Other spirits seem to lose popularity with even less cause,
suggesting that there is constant turnover. As some drop out,
others are invented.

The Cult of the Deer Spirit

The openness of the Mehinaku religious system to individual
innovation would be a matter of conjecture had not an odd set
of circumstances occurred during my January 1972 field trip.
One morning Kuyaparei was walking through his garden when

he saw a deer. Ordinarily the villagers shoot deer, although their meat is taboo, because of the damage they do to their crops. Lacking a gun, Kuyaparei decided to wrestle the deer to the ground and tie it up. The animal struggled free, however, and Kuyaparei fell to the ground, severely straining his knee. Six days later he was still in pain and unable to understand why he had not recovered. He recalled that the day before his adventure with the deer he had walked through the forest on an empty

Fig. 27. The dance of the Kaiyapa demon. Kaiyapa is one of the major spirits in pantheon of the Upper Xingu tribes. Represented by sponsors (wekehe) and organizers (petewekehe) in each of the villages, the dance and song of Kaiyapa is a basis for intertribal ritual. In the photograph the singer (*apáiyekehe*) stands holding a rattle and leaning on a bow while the seated drummer keeps time to his song. The dancers in the picture represent the snake (*ui*) Kaiyapa, but there are other versions current in the Mehinaku community in which the dancers (wearing different costumes and following a different step) represent the *tocandira* ant (Mein) and a variety of species of birds.

stomach, a sure invitation to a spirit to take his soul. A full week after his experience with the deer, Kuyaparei had a dream that confirmed his suspicions:

> The spirit of the deer came to me. He looked like a wild Indian, entirely naked and frightening. He said: "My grandchild, why did you assault my wife? I am angry with you. I have taken your soul. It will wander with me through the forest, while you just stay in your hammock in pain.

The next morning Kuyaparei told his dream to his wife and his father's brother, a village shaman. The news immediately spread through the community. No one had previously considered that the Deer Spirit could be malevolent. In the evening the shamans gathered in the plaza to smoke and discuss the case. Normally when a spirit takes a man's soul, everyone knows what songs to sing and what dances to perform in order to attract the spirit, feed it, and induce it to give back the soul. But what could one do about the Deer Spirit? The shamans were concerned.

Again Kuyaparei had a dream. Once more the Deer appeared to him, this time accompanied by his deer kinsmen. Decorated with feathers, they were dancing and playing panpipes and trumpets. The spirit told Kuyaparei:

> My grandchild, these are my trumpets. I will give them to you and you will be their owner. You will feed me and give me gifts. I will stay with you until you die.

The dream marked the recognition of a new spirit and the beginning of a new cult. Hearing of the dream, an elderly shaman came to Kuyaparei's hammock and listened attentively to his account:

> The panpipes played by the Deer Spirit consist of four small flutes; their headdress is crested with four long hawk feathers; and they danced slowly in a line of four, stamping their feet and frequently reversing direction.

The shaman and Kuyaparei's family assembled the headdresses and other necessary paraphernalia to summon the Deer Spirit. With Kuyaparei still confined to his hammock, the shaman directed the entire performance, frequently returning to his patient's side for additional information. At such times Kuyaparei added dramatic embellishments that he had "not remembered" before, including the stance of the dancers and their prolonged falsetto whoops.

The shaman chose four villagers to represent the spirit and taught them the stamping dance and the tune to be played on the panpipes. After fifteen minutes of rehearsal they whooped and moved onto the village plaza, encouraged and guided by their director. As they entered Kuyaparei's house, they were greeted by one of his relatives: "Deer Spirit! You hurt us, you attack! Return the soul! Take out the arrow from your grandson's leg!" They came to Kuyaparei's hammock, sucked briefly at his knee to remove the spirit's arrow, and then left. Several months later, long after his knee was better, Kuyaparei selected organizers for his ritual and was planning to make long trumpets similar to those in his dream. These instruments were to be played every few days, quite like the sacred flutes in the men's house.

An interesting question arises concerning Kuyaparei's sincerity. The invention of the Deer Spirit, a newsworthy event, has not only enhanced his prestige within the village but has given him some prominence among all the Xingu tribes. My assessment is that Kuyaparei believes he saw the Deer Spirit. He had been confined to his hammock in semidarkness for six days before his first dream, during which time numerous curing rituals were taking place in his behalf. The prolonged period in semidarkness (a form of sensory deprivation perhaps conducive to hallucination), his anxiety about his knee, and the dramatic efforts of the village shamans placed him in a highly suggestible mood. Whatever the exact nature of his dream, he was psychologically prepared to have the Deer Spirit demand the organization of a ritual.

To some degree, however, the ritual is also a consciously creative act on Kuyaparei's part. The Deer Ceremony must not only be efficacious, it must be dramatically impressive and aesthetically attractive as well. The spirit must be frightening, yet his costumes and songs should be beautiful. Kuyaparei is still not certain how he is going to put the final production together to satisfy these criteria:

The Deer Spirit did not give me a complete picture of what the ritual ought to be. The dance step, costumes and song will work themselves out. The trumpet knows its own song. In short, he feels free to fill in the details. He will make a trumpet and play around with it for a while until he comes up with a melody and rhythm that seem right; this will be the song of the Deer Spirit. Kuyaparei is not wholly unaware of his role as author and producer of a new ritual.

Whether the Deer Spirit will catch on and join the other major demons in the Mehinaku pantheon remains to be seen. At present there are four spirits associated with regularly performed ceremonies among the Mehinaku. If the Deer Spirit is to survive he must be diagnosed as the cause of future illnesses. Even if he does not, however, his discovery by Kuyaparei strongly suggests that other Mehinaku spirits have also had their origin in the fantasies and dreams of creative individuals.

Creativity and Mehinaku Culture

Admittedly the Deer Spirit has not been made up of whole cloth. The general structure of Kuyaparei's ritual is just like every other: a spirit steals a man's soul and is induced to return it by means of a ritual; the sick man becomes the sponsor of a ceremony repeated at regular intervals long after his recovery. Further, even some of the Deer Spirit's costume, music, and dance are clearly borrowed from other ceremonies. The feather headdress used in the ritual, for example, is taken from the Kaiyapa ceremony. The panpipes and some of the dance steps are very much like those used in still other rituals. Kuyaparei's innovations fall within a set form, much like the classic drama that introduces some new ideas, recombines some old ones, and yet still follows an established dramatic line of unity of time, place, and action. What impresses us in the Mehinaku case is that although the "play" is open to variation and experimentation, it is nonetheless not a transient element of Mehinaku expressive culture. Indeed, it is an important element in the villagers' religion, perhaps destined to unite them in life-long social, economic, and ceremonial relationships.

The fact that Mehinaku religion institutionalizes creativity suggests to us a fundamental limitation of the dramaturgical approach to social life. We can no longer characterize a villager simply as a performer of a set of culturally given lines. We now recognize that he can be an author, director, and producer as well. We can never factor out the man behind the mask. He is continually present, not only manipulating his relationships with others, but also dreaming up altogether new lines for the script.

The rituals we have been examining appeal to the Mehinaku on several levels. They diagnose and treat all manner of illness, and they give aesthetic pleasure to both the spectators and the performers. Yet if we are to understand the inventiveness that is characteristic of these rituals, we must take a hard look at those persons who are most deeply involved in their production. In the next chapter we shall note that much of the creativity marking the shaman's behavior in the rituals is a self-interested response to the dilemmas of staging his role.

*There are only two real shamans. Myself and
my brother-in-law.*

Tama

Throughout much of aboriginal North and
South America, there are broad similarities
in the techniques used by shamans to cure
their patients. The shaman may remove an
intrusive object from the patient's body by
sleight of hand, he may go on a trip with
the aid of hallucinogenic drugs to retrieve
the victim's soul which has been stolen by
spirits, or he may do battle with spirits on
behalf of his client. Although the shaman
may sincerely believe he can cure disease,
he often resorts to tricks and other staged
effects to convince his patients. Among the
Mehinaku, where the theatrical side to the
shaman's role is unusually developed, and
where the successful shaman is above all a
good performer, the dramaturgical approach
to the art seems particularly appropriate.
Let us therefore turn to an examination of
the problems Mehinaku shamans face as
they struggle to cure their patients, manipulate illusion-producing apparatus, and at the
same time preserve their reputation before
very skeptical audiences.

Kinds of Shamans

Beliefs about the spirit world and illness are highly idiosyncratic in the Mehinaku community. As we have seen, the villagers are intellectually creative in their beliefs about the supernatural; methods of curing and the nature of spirits are subjects not fixed by any ultimate authority. The information presented below is, in broad outline, the thinking of the entire community and, in detail, the beliefs of several of the older shamans.

The Mehinaku recognize several kinds of shamans, some of whom have functions other than curing. The least prestigious is the "master of medicine" (*pyanalaiwekehe*), who is an herbalist skilled in treating fevers, infections, and other common disorders with roots and leaves. All the Mehinaku have some knowledge of this kind of medicine, although there are one or two villagers who exceed the others. Kuyaparei, for example, knows herbal cures that he willingly provides for his fellow villagers in exchange for gifts. He maintains his preeminence in this kind of curing by not sharing his knowledge with anyone else. On collecting trips to the forest and the brush around the gardens, he checks the paths and listens carefully to make sure no one is nearby to discover his secrets. No one ever questions him about how he makes his potions, any more than we would cross-examine a casual friend about the source of his income.

In addition to the "master of medicines," the Mehinaku shamans include the *yakapa*, a shaman who specializes in communicating with spirits, and shamans who have mastered a number of specific curing techniques, such as the "master of the breath" (*ejekekiwekehe*) who cures by blowing on his patients and the "master of the song" (*pukaiyekehe*) who cures by singing. These are more peripheral methods, however, and such shamans as the "master of the breath" and the "master of the song" are invariably also *yetamá*, the shaman par excellence.

Sickness and Smoke: The Yetamá

Disease has many sources. A man becomes ill when a spirit shoots him with an arrow or steals his soul, when he is bewitched, when he fails to honor seclusion taboos, when he is too close to menstrual blood, when he is refused food, or when he is struck by the white man's "witchcraft," that is, by diseases brought into the Xingu region by the Brazilians.

No matter what the cause, the initial response to illness is usually to call a *yetamá*, a shaman who cures with smoke. Smoking is essential in curing because tobacco and smoke are "the spirit's food" and have the special power to reach the source of illness, the tangible intrusive object called a *kaukí* that lodges inside the sick man's body. The smoke blown by the shaman slips under the patient's skin, destroys the *kaukí*, and thereby restores health. So close is the association of smoking and curing that the words for smoker and shaman (*yetamá*) are identical. The verb for shamanistic curing (*ayetamátapai*) is derived from the same word.

Smoking is a badge of social maturity. Smokers alone may take part in semisecret rituals and join the exclusive circle of shamans who assemble each evening on the plaza to discuss the day's events. Still, smoking is not without hazards because of its close association with potentially malevolent spirits. Children are routinely warned to steer clear of the smokers' circle because of the proximity of these spirits. But the prestige and the status of social maturity brought by smoking outweigh an aspiring shaman's fears. With the exception of the three "trash yard men," all mature men in the village are either *yetamá* or are hoping to be.

Becoming a *yetamá* brings rewards that go beyond getting into the smokers' club. A successful curer may look forward to valuable gifts of shell belts and feather headdresses. A prestigious member of the community, he arouses fear and respect even when he is not engaged in his healing duties.

Becoming a Shaman

"In former times," complains Yanapa, one of the older villagers, "only mature men were *yetamá*. Young men who presumed to try were laughed at and ridiculed by their elders. Nowadays it seems as if any ten-year-old can do it."

It appears that among the Mehinaku as among ourselves, the pretensions of the younger generation irk the older. Nevertheless, no ten-year-old can in fact become a *yetamá*. The apprenticeship is long, difficult, and open only to adults. Let us follow the initiation of Kupatekuma, the most recent enrollee in the ranks of Mehinaku shamans.

Kupatekuma, like all traditional Mehinaku shamans, did not consciously choose to become a *yetamá*. His career began with an encounter with a spirit. In the course of a dream the monkey demon (Pahɨkuma) came to him and said, "My grandson, I will stay with you; I will be your 'pet' (pʊpʊje)." The following day Kupatekuma became ill and he recounted his dream to one of the village *yetamá*, a shaman of great experience and reputation. He concluded that with the proper instruction Kupatekuma could become a shaman and smoker, retaining a relationship with the spirit (his "pet") that would enable him to be a curer. Two teachers now stepped forward, an established Mehinaku shaman and one of the better-known curers from the Arawaken Yawalapití tribe. After bathing Kupatekuma in a tea made of a small hard fruit (*akukute*), they led him by the hand to the village plaza where the village shamans were awaiting him. All the women and children had already left the area and were sequestered in their houses. Every smoker gave Kupatekuma a long thin cigar, each of which he smoked completely, often clearing his throat in the language of the spirits, calling, "He - he - he - he!" Faint from the smoke, he was half-carried back to his house, where he vomited and collapsed in his hammock.

Three months of seclusion now followed. During the first day, Kupatekuma abstained from all food except a little manioc porridge. As he lay in his hammock, a gourd rattle for his future use in curing rituals was placed on his chest while his body was rubbed with a latex material from the *mangaba* tree to make his hands sensitive to the intrusive *kaukí*. After the first day, the restrictions were slightly relaxed. Each day he sat on a bench behind a seclusion barrier eating foods that made his lips sensitive to disease-causing *kaukí*. Honey was the most effective, for it makes the lips and mouth supple and pliant. Painful foods, including pepper, salt, and tobacco were added to his diet to make him tough and put him in communication with the spirits. Kupatekuma tried hard to follow all the restrictions imposed upon him by his teachers, for he knew that if he ate forbidden foods, had sexual relations, walked in the sun, or permitted his family to speak loudly or unnecessarily in his presence, his medicines and tobacco would lose all their power and he would not become a skilled shaman.

After several months, when Kupatekuma's skin had become pale from staying indoors and he had become fat from inactivity, his mentors came to him and led him to a bench in the center of his house where they washed his body with water and *akukute* medicine, decorating his hair in the shaman's *bajua* design (see fig. 17a). Then, holding him by the arm on either side, they took him out to the center of the plaza where the other shamans were assembled. Addressing his as *"yetamá,"* each offered him a long cigar. Kupatekuma was now one of them, a smoker and curer.

Illness and Once Again, the Case of the Strained Knee

In all societies being considered sick is only partly a physical matter. Among the Mehinaku I have seen a woman in agony from chronic arthritis virtually ignored by her kinsmen, while a whole ceremonial complex may be built around a man with a minor ailment. A fever and headache, for example, symptomatic of chronic low-level malaria, is a fact of life among the Mehinaku and is ignored by everyone but the poor sufferer. An unusual symptom, such as bleeding gums, however, is more likely to awaken the interest of the shamans. Illnesses that keep a villager from his subsistence activities also gain attention. The woman who suffered from arthritis received care only after her condition had deteriorated to the point that she was no longer capable of carrying water from the river to her home, at which point she was said to be extremely sick, or "dying." In short, sickness is culturally defined and only some illnesses reach the attention of the village shamans and provoke a community reaction.

Since all cures, whatever the ailment, follow more or less the same course, we can make out the general pattern by examining a specific case, that of Kuyaparei's sprained knee. Kuyaparei, we recall, injured his knee while wrestling with a deer in his garden. After several days his wife approached Iyepana, one of the more powerful shamans, with the request that he "look at" her husband. In typical Mehinaku fashion, Iyepana replied that he was only a "little" shaman just learning how to cure, but eventually he allowed himself to be persuaded.

Iyepana then called all the shamans: "Shamans! Let us cure
our kinsman. He is as we may be in the future! Come, let us
cure him!" Quietly assembling in the men's house, the smokers
removed their belts and ornaments to express their sadness
about Kuyaparei's illness. They smoked to "fill their bellies"
and then urinated through the thatch of the men's house "so
that the spirits would accompany them." Finally Iyepana formally addressed each shaman in turn: "Are you ready, *yetamá*?"
After each assented, they left the men's house in order of their
seniority and prestige within the group. Iyepana was first, since
he was a singing shaman (*pukaiyekehe*) who had been hired
for the cure. He was followed in order of seniority in the ranks
of smokers by the other "true" shamans (*yetamawaja*), those
who knew how to sing, use a rattle and take out *kauki*. The remaining shamans including the beginners and "worthless shamans" (*yetamamalú*), those who did not sing or remove *kauki*,
brought up the rear of the line.

Before the shamans arrived at Kuyaparei's house, the children, the women, and nonsmokers had already left. The doors
were closed "to keep out dangerous spirits" and the house was
pitch black except for a few tiny fires. Kuyaparei's hammock
had been slung between the two center house poles, so that all
the shamans could sit comfortably nearby.

Iyepana went up to Kuyaparei and asked, "What is wrong?
What is hurting you?"

"My knee."

"You will get better."

This short interview was the shamans' only verbal exchange
with the patient; during the remainder of the treatment Kuyaparei was little more than a stage property for their performances.

After a few moments of silence, Iyepana, shaking his rattle
above Kuyaparei's body, repeatedly brushed him with the fronds
of a "life-giving plant" (*maipayana*) to the accompaniment of
a thunderous chorus of all the shamans shouting "*ha - fe*," an
onomatopoeic magic word deriving from the noise of sucking
the *kauki* from a sick person. Iyepana then began a crucial part
of the curative performance, the shaman's song.

Some of these songs are passed on from "Master of the Song" shamans (*pukaiyekehe*) to their novices, while others are only known to those curers who claim to have learned them directly from the spirits. On several occasions Iyepana has taken me aside to whisper that he had learned some new songs from *ahira*, the spirit of the hummingbird. We would slip out of the village together so that he could sing to me in privacy. For the most part, however, the songs were a bit of a disappointment, considering their origins. The verse below, chanted in a slow rhythm with a monotonous two-note melody, is typical of many others:

> I am the spirit of the hummingbird
> I am the spirit of the hummingbird
> My "pet" never dies.

All the shamanistic songs that I have recorded roughly follow this pattern. The shaman sings as if he were the spirit; then, changing persons, he sings that his "pet," meaning the spirit, cannot die. Hearing the songs, the spirit is pleased and may be inclined to help return the patient's lost soul or to destroy the *kaukí*.

Despite their prosaic lyrics, everyone treats the songs with the utmost gravity. When a shaman sings a new song of the spirits, everyone strains to listen. As he shakes his rattle over his patient and sings in the darkness, the other curers, "true" shamans and novices alike, join in with shouts of "*ha - fe*" so that the house fairly rocks with sound. On the far side of the village where the women and children are listening, the combined chorus of masculine voices has a strangely powerful and unsettling effect.

Extracting the Kaukí

After Iyepana had sung his songs and summoned the spirits, he began to remove the *kaukí*. The most difficult and prestigious technique employed by the village shamans is to withdraw the *kaukí* by hand. In the course of initiating a future *yetamá*, his teacher pretends to take a miniature arrow from beneath the skin of his own palm and to insert it inside his pupil's. Permanently lodged just under the skin of the new shaman, the arrow will seek out the intrusive *kaukí* in patients. As he glides his hands over the body of his client, he feels the arrow guiding him to the right spot, and at the same time he senses the *kauki* just under his patient's skin as it forces its way to the surface. Eventually the *kauki* works its way loose, the shaman grabs it with a sudden motion, and shows it in triumph to the sick man.

The second method of removing *kauki* is sucking. As the shaman sucks, he feels a heaviness in his hands and arms, then in his stomach and chest, and finally in his throat as the *kauki* moves from the patient's body to his own. This was the technique Iyepana used to cure Kuyaparei. Carefully inspecting the knee, he placed his mouth on the skin, drew in his breath with a loud rasping noise, and began to suck vigorously: *"Ha - fe, ha - fe, ha - fe, ha - fe!"* After several minutes of noisy sucking, spitting, and violent retching (the *kauki* is nauseating to the shaman's stomach), Iyepana produced the disease agent: a bit of grass, lying in a copious puddle of saliva. He showed it to Kuyaparei and said, "This is the deer's food; this is what has hurt you." There were immediate murmurs of assent from the seated shamans, for the nature of the *kauki* had confirmed their own diagnosis—Kuyaparei had been wrestling with no ordinary deer but with a spirit that had inserted a bit of its own food into his knee.

But when the turn of each of the other shamans came to suck at Kuyaparei's knee, all they could produce were bits of charred wood, ashes, wax, and other "all-purpose" *kauki* typical of no particular spirit. Iyepana had stolen the show and displayed considerable creativity and independence. Normally *kauki* are chosen from a limited set of objects related in some way to the spirit that caused the disability. The Monster Fish Spirit (Kupatekuma) slips miniature fish into his victims, while the Spirit of the Angry Woman (Japujaneju) inserts tiny balls of female body paint (*epitsiri*). The Deer Spirit, however, had just entered the Mehinaku pantheon and only the wily Iyepana had been prepared for him.

Once the shamans had performed their cures, Iyepana addressed each of them in turn: "Are you through, shaman?" After all had assented, they returned to the men's house where they smoked and "fed the spirits" by themselves consuming peppered fish stew and other spicy dishes that are the spirits' proper food. Some time later, the shamans were paid for their work, not so much to permit them to turn a profit as to compensate them symbolically for the discomfort of all the smoking, sucking, retching, and kneeling they had performed in Kuyaparei's behalf. The lesser shamans received small gifts such as cotton or arrows, and Iyepana, the main singer, was given a valuable feather headdress. These fees were not set in advance nor was there any bargaining or recrimination. A poor patient usually gives less than a wealthy one, but any gift is acceptable.

The following day Iyepana returned to call on his patient, who fortunately was feeling a little better. Iyepana completed the cure by extracting a bit of "deer's food" that he had missed on his first visit. He left assuring Kuyaparei that he would soon be better. As the days went by, however, the knee grew progressively worse. Finally Kuyaparei decided to call in a specialist, the most powerful and frightening of the shamans, the *yakapa*.

The Yakapa Witch Hunter

A *yakapa*, like other shamans, has an association with a spirit who is referred to as his "pet." Unlike other shamans, however, the association between the *yakapa* and his spirit is much more intimate. A *yetamá* smoker simply calls upon his spirit as a kind of familiar to assist him in cures. The *yakapa*, however, is literally possessed by his spirit. The term that describes the process of possession is "to metamorphize" (*iyákene*), the same word used in a number of myths to describe men who turn into animals. Once possessed by his spirit, a *yakapa* can perform extraordinary feats, such as locating lost and stolen objects and identifying the witches that cause windstorms, diseases, and plagues of mosquitoes.

Kuyaparei sent his wife to ask the *yakapa* Teme to come to "look at him." Teme accepted the shell belt she offered and showed up at Kuyaparei's hammock the same afternoon, accompanied by his father and mother. He sat down by the fire, lit a long cigar, and began to smoke furiously. After several long drags on his cigar, apparently swallowing the smoke in great gulps, he gasped and rolled his eyes so that only the whites were visible. He slowly leaned further and further forward until his head was on the ground while his father, blowing smoke over his body, summoned his son's "pet," Walama, the Anaconda spirit: "Speak, speak, speak Walama; it is good that you speak to us and tell who has hurt the sick one." For a while there was silence, and then suddenly, the uncanny clicking noise of the jaws of the Anaconda was heard. Walama had come "like an unseen wind" and lodged himself in the back of the *yakapa* between his shoulder blades. Teme, the Mehinaku, no longer existed. His eyes were eyes of the Anaconda and his body was the body of the Anaconda.

He began to move slowly, shouting in pain at his transformation into a spirit. He got onto his knees, grunting rhythmically: "Huh! huh! huh!" He stood in a half-crouching position for a time and then began to race erratically back and forth through the village, a gait so typical of *yakapas* that the word *yakapa* is a cognate of the verb *yákapai*, "to move about unpredictably."

Teme's grunting was loud enough to alert the entire community. Women and children deserted the village through the back doors of their houses. Men put their valuable possessions in high baskets suspended from the rafters and uneasily watched from their doorways—a sensible precaution, for a possessed *yakapa* can be dangerous. On one occasion in the past, Teme attacked his in-laws and raced through the houses snapping arrows and destroying personal possessions. He once entered the men's house and attempted to smash the sacred flutes and scatter the pieces before the women; when frustrated in this effort by several of the men, he seized a parrot kept as a pet and bit its head off.

This time Teme's performance was relatively tame, and I was able to follow it through to the end. After he had dashed about the village several times, he "found" the witchcraft causing Kuyaparei's disability: a bundle of cotton used for knee ligatures. Clutching his bundle in his hand and shouting from the pain of the witchcraft, he raced back to his father and collapsed at his feet. Once again his father blew smoke upon him: "Go away spirit, go away, go away; go away to your home in the waters; it's over, it's over, it's over; you have spoken to us; you are good to have told us where the witchcraft is."

Gradually Teme emerged from his stupor and described how he had been sent to the source of the witchcraft. Kuyaparei's wife took the bundle and placed it in a pot of water sweetened with sugar cane, and thereby broke the spell.

The Tricks of the Trade

Mehinaku shamans accomplish their spectacular effects by means of sleight of hand and clever staging. Like professional magicians in our society, they are not enthusiastic about revealing the tricks of their trade. Nevertheless, since they generally regard each other as competitors, they will sometimes gleefully give away the secrets of the "charlatans."

The illusion of removing intrusive *kauki* requires that the shaman manufacture the objects in advance, secrete them on his person, and slip them into his hand or mouth during his performance. All the Mehinaku are aware that some shamans are illusionists. On the other hand, they also believe that there are some shamans who can genuinely remove *kauki*. Consequently the villagers watch a curer very carefully until they are convinced he is a true shaman. To disarm the skeptics, a shaman is expected to rub his hands together and hold them up to the audience before treating his patient, much as our sleight-of-hand artist will roll up his sleeves to show that he has nothing to conceal.

Shamanistic tricks vary in ingeniousness and sophistication. At the most amateurish end of the scale, the "worthless" shaman (*yetamamalú*) pretends to find a *kauki* but shows it to no one. He noisily sucks out the disease object, spits it into his hands, exclaims about its size, and throws it quickly away where no one can examine it. Shamans who are unable to show their patients the "real" *kauki* stand little chance of getting out of the minor leagues.

True shamans are more skillful. When they enter a patient's house, they have already secreted the *kauki* on their person, frequently under their leg and arm bands. Once the performance has begun, it is shifted to a less obvious place such as behind the ears, in the mouth, under the arm, between the thumb and first finger, or, when squatting, between the upper thigh and the abdomen. My instructors have urged me to give special attention to the way a shaman holds his cigar, for if he handles it awkwardly the chances are that he is using it to conceal a *kaukí*.

Once a shaman slips a *kaukí* into his hand or mouth, the remainder of his performance is relatively simple. He need only pretend to remove the object from his patient to complete the illusion. His chances of success are greatly enhanced by darkness, for the *yetamá* performs at night, or, if during the day, only when the doors are closed and the house barely lit by small fires.

Fig. 28. Shamanism. In Akanai's watercolor a *yakapa* shaman rushes along the path followed cautiously by a *yetamá* "smoking shaman" carrying several cigars in his hand and behind his ear. Although neither of the men is adorned, the *yakapa* is drawn entirely in black, reflecting his close connection to the world of spirits. In contrast to the *yetamá*, who retains a somewhat more distant relationship with his spirits, the *yakapa* turns into (*iyákene*) a spirit the moment he is possessed.

Unlike the *yetamá* shaman, the *yakapa* creates his magical effects in the full light of day. On several occasions I have carefully watched Teme produce his unnerving sound of the anaconda spirit snapping his jaws, and despite good lighting I never saw him move a muscle. Yet according to his rivals, he makes the sound with his own teeth. When Teme found the cotton bundle near the men's house, I was close behind him and was convinced he had actually discovered it there. His critics, however, quickly assured me that he always plants his devices before a performance. I was urged to keep watch on where he went just after he was summoned to cure a villager and to notice if he returned to the same area during his search for evidence of witchcraft.

Skepticism and Credulity

An institution that flourishes on credulity, shamanism nevertheless is hemmed around by nonbelievers. Potentially the most skeptical Mehinaku is the shaman himself, for he knows that the reality behind his staged performance does not live up to its front-row appearance. The *yakapa* must be especially cynical about his role, given the elaborate tricks he regularly concocts. Teme, for example, "rids" the community of the mosquitoes and flies that plague the villagers during the early months of the wet season. These insects are believed to grow from wax pellets planted about the village by the local witches. In a great show Teme thwarts the witches by "finding" the pellets before they can mature, having himself salted the ground in advance of his performance.

Although Teme has never discussed his own activities with me, his quick condemnation of other shamans as charlatans may help us to understand why he behaves as he does. False shamans, he says, behave as they do simply for the gifts and attention they receive. He neglects to say that he himself has become one of the wealthiest men in the community because of his performances, the recipient of numerous shell belts, collars and feather headdresses from his patients. He is also politically powerful because he is able to denounce almost anyone as a witch. The luckless Ipyana (see chapter 5) was slain partly on evidence trumped up by a *yakapa* then visiting the Mehinaku. I must conclude that what drives Teme to put on his charades is at least in part what he gets out of them for himself.

Self-aggrandizement, however, does not entirely explain a *yakapa*'s conduct. The trances, spirit possession, and other bizarre behavior often seem too spontaneous to be explained solely by economic or political motives. I have seen one *yakapa* in search of a child's lost soul suddenly fall upon the ground and cry uncontrollably about having been deserted by his wife, an unguarded burst of emotion completely irrelevant to the performance. Further, the highly aggressive conduct characteristic of the possessed shaman, entailing the most outrageous violations of the basic rules of the culture, seems to spring not from a deliberate effort to stage a shocking performance but rather from deep-seated emotional needs of unstable individuals. Although I am chary of interpreting shamanism as mental illness (an hypothesis perhaps best stated by Silverman [1964]), a few of the Xingu *yakapa* seem to make persuasive cases for this view. These considerations suggest that, although some of the *yakapa* are motivated by self-interest, there may be others who are so unstable that they are at least partly taken in by their own performances.

There is a third possibility, however, typical of a number of the smoking shamans (*yetamá*), that is perhaps the most interesting resolution of the question of the shaman's self-doubt. When *yetamá* begin their course of training, they do so with the innocent expectation that they will eventually be able to cure by removing a true *kauki* from the bodies of their patients. The young shaman Kupatekuma, for example, was told by his instructor just what sensations to expect as the *kauki* emerged from the patient and entered his mouth. But once the official course was over, he was taken aside and presented with a *kauki* together with instructions on how to conceal it on his person and present it in triumph to the patient. The young shaman was terribly mortified, for he had always believed in his teacher and the genuineness of the shamanistic performance.

A novice like Kupatekuma presents a serious threat to the entire profession, for if the "mark" is not "cooled out," he might

denounce not only his teacher but other practitioners as well
(a course of events, as we shall see, that occasionally happens).
His teacher, however, managed to quiet him down by explaining
that as a beginner, just a "little shaman who had learned how
to smoke," he could not expect to remove *kauki* like the masters. But until that time came, there was no reason that he
should not practice his profession by pretending to take out
kauki. Not only would pride be preserved but he would assist
his patients, for his mentor's artificial *kauki* had a magical origin, having been made by a spirit in ancient times and passed
down from master shaman to pupil. As disappointed as Kupatekuma was, he faithfully adhered to his mentor's suggestion but
never seemed to draw any closer to a genuine performance. Finally, he gave up completely and accepted his position as one
of the "worthless" shamans who smoke but cannot cure illness.
Today he blames his failure not on the shamanistic system but
on himself or, more precisely, on his wife. While he was in
seclusion, he recalls, she began to menstruate and failed to leave
the house immediately so that her blood destroyed the medicines
and thereby ruined his chance to become a "true" shaman.

Kupatekuma's experience suggests a solution to the problem
of how stable and unaggressive individuals can nevertheless
take to the tricks and illusions of the successful shaman. Their
teachers offer them a rationalization for their initial disillusion-
ment (they are "just beginners") and a method for hiding their
failure while still helping their patients (instruction in sleight of
hand). Not many of the Mehinaku are as scrupulous as Kupatekuma, and instead of abandoning the whole show they go on to
develop more skillful techniques of deception.

Skepticism and the Shaman's Colleagues

If a shaman is doubtful about the reality of his own performance
then his colleagues are also likely to be skeptical, for no matter
how convincing the act, they better than all others know what
feats of illusion were employed to stage it. In public, however,
like professionals in our own society, they tend to support one
another. They address each other with grave formality as "*ye-*

tamá" and never fail to applaud a skillful performance by one of their number.

In private, however, they are highly derisive and skeptical about each other. I have yet to meet a shaman who says he believes in the performance of anyone but prestigious curers in other tribes, his own close kin, and himself. Shamans are aware of their colleagues' skepticism, so much that they bend every effort to disarm it, seeking at times to impress their fellows rather than assist their patients. During one cure I attended, the chief *yetamá* after extracting a *kaukí* made it disappear, spat it back into his hand, made it disappear once more, and finally made it reappear in the other hand. Everyone was fascinated except the patient, who lay in her hammock with a high fever, a forgotten prop in the show. The only act of medical significance in this legerdemain was the removal of the *kaukí*; all the other feats were intended to impress the assembled shamans with the genuine power of the *yetamá*.

On occasion a shaman may break the professional code and debunk his colleagues' pretensions. One of the so-called "worthless" shamans told me that he had discovered a medicine that, when poured in the eyes, allowed him to detect the tricks used by his fellows. He claims that the number of their sleight-of-hand acts fell considerably after the announcement of his discovery.

In 1972 the same skeptic concealed a borrowed tape recorder at a curing ceremony at which Kailu, a woman with shamanistic ambitions, demonstrated her command of a language taught her by a snake spirit. The reptilian language, a rapid-fire repetition of rhyming consonant-vowel patterns such as "tu - tu - bu - bu - tu - tu - tu," struck her critics as extremely funny. Two years later the cassette record of her demonstration still provoked hilarious laughter whenever the villagers could find someone at the Post willing to play it.

Given the widespread skepticism that often greets the shaman's performances and the relative simplicity of some of his illusions, why should anyone believe in shamanism at all? Part of the answer lies in professional competence. A mere novice who claims to be a powerful shaman is usually suspect, but an older man who has gone through the prerequisite training is more likely to be believed. Good technique is also important. A real *yetamá*, I am told, clearly shows that his hands are empty before he begins his performance. He carefully probes and explores for the *kaukí*, for it is hard to find in the patient's body. Finally, unlike the charlatan, he takes long drags on his cigar and inhales deeply during the entire cure.

Originality and skill in performing magic tricks are also crucial to success. Some *yakapa* and *yetamá* have so mismanaged their performances that they have been exposed as frauds. A Mehinaku *yakapa*, for example, was recently caught in the act of "seeding" wax pellets around the edge of the village in preparation for uncovering them as larval mosquitoes later that evening. His credibility is now very low and he has never attempted to repeat his aborted performance.

A shaman who is a flawless master of his craft and who can throw in some spectacular new tricks has little difficulty in gaining the confidence of the villagers. Such is the case of the most trusted and impressive shaman in the entire Xingu region today, Takama of the Kamaiurá. He does not have to resort to sucking to remove intrusive objects from the body of his patients. All he has to do is smoke! He may be several yards from the sick man's hammock and yet after a few vigorous drags the *kaukí* somehow finds its way into the tip of his cigar.

Added to professional competence is another factor that bolsters trust in a shaman: his presence. A subtle quality that is hard to define precisely in any culture, it means, so the Mehinaku say, that its possessor is worthy of fear and respect; he is *káukapapai*. The polysemic root of this word, *kau*, may mean either pain, a dangerous root medicine used in seclusion, or a class of "painful" foods, such as hot peppers. Cognates of *kau*, including Kauká (the most dangerous spirit in the Mehinaku pantheon), *káuʊpai* (thorny, splintery), *kaukí* (disease-causing objects), all convey the same idea of fear, pain, and danger. In explaining why Takama is *káukapapai*, the villagers point out that like a true shaman he dresses differently from ordinary men. He frequently blackens his body with ashes and assumes the *bajuá* hair design. He also acts differently from ordinary men. He neither laughs nor jokes, nor is he found fraternizing often in the clubby atmosphere of the men's house. Instead he is off in some unknown part of the forest, smoking and communicating with the spirits. He looks at others with an intimidating, unnerving stare. In a word, Takama has presence, so much of it that many of the villagers no longer address him by his name; instead they call him "spirit" (*apapãiyei*).

Why the Tricks?

Why does the Mehinaku shaman place so much reliance on sleight of hand and other forms of illusion in his curing performance? Herbs, spells, and charms can be just as effective as cures and certainly create far fewer problems in staging. Let us look for an answer in the area of the Mehinaku concept of the supernatural and the peculiar position of the shaman in the society.

The Mehinaku make no verbal distinction between the supernatural and the natural. The reality of spirits is as unquestioned as that of trees or rocks. Spirits, however, are perceived differently from ordinary creatures and only by those who are in exceptional states of consciousness—when they are dreaming, dying, or in a trance. Malevolent, dangerous, and horribly frightening, the spirits are different in kind from ordinary beings. They must be approached differently and they inspire a whole set of special attitudes. To bridge the wide gap between spirits and ordinary beings requires the aid of a very unique sort of person, the *yetamá* or *yakapa* shaman.

Shamans, however, are also very ordinary persons, since they have wide-ranging secular relationships with their patients that have nothing to do with their roles as curers. They may be coworkers, kinsmen of varying degrees, partners in extramarital affairs, and so on. In such a setting it is not easy to establish the distance, the awesomeness (*káukapapai*), that is expected of one who deals with the spirits.

Consider the dilemma confronting a Mehinaku who aspires to become a *yakapa* shaman. Looked upon by the other villagers as a member of the tribe, a kinsman by blood or marriage and a participant in the men's cult, he acts out his everyday roles as appropriate with no sense of discontinuity or of assuming a new identity. A man who becomes a *yakapa*, however, acquires a very different kind of status; at times he is regarded as a spirit, no longer responsible for his activities. Linguistically the distinction between everyday roles and the *yakapa*'s is very plain: a man *is* a brother-in-law, a husband, or a flute player, but he metamorphoses (*iyákene*) into a *yakapa*. The *yakapa* role is therefore highly differentiated from secular roles. Already bound by so many temporal ties to his fellow villagers, the *yakapa* finds that it is not easy to manage the differentiation. He must somehow convince them that he is quite capable of departing from this world and gaining admission to the world of the spirits. In part he persuades his audience by dramatizing his role. His long period of seclusion and training, the special terms used to address him during the curing session, and the secrecy associated with *yakapa* shamanism announce to the villagers that here is no ordinary man.

His bizarre activities in the midst of a curing ritual fulfill a similar purpose. They are "disidentifiers," serving to remind the audience of who the shaman is not. A wildman tearing through the village assaulting his close kin and destroying personal property cannot be mistaken for the commonsense everyday person he was a few minutes before the ritual. His gross violation of the rules of proper conduct attests that a villager has vanished and in his place a spirit rages through the community.

The tricks of the *yetamá* are susceptible to the same interpretation. His feats of legerdemain underscore the difference between the shaman who mediates with the spirits and the citizen who lives a mundane life as kinsman, coworker, and neighbor.

The Credulous and the Skeptical

Since the shaman's everyday relationships should tend to compromise his patients' belief in his powers, we may suspect that his credibility will vary according to his position in the social network of the village. Mehinaku women, for example, are more impressed by the shamanistic performance than are the men. The explanation would seem to be that while the men are in regular contact with the shamans in the men's house, on labor projects, and on ceremonial occasions in which all interact as equals, the women are usually found at a greater social distance. Having fewer secular contacts than the men, it is easier for them to believe in the supernatural abilities of the shamans.

Confidence apparently varies directly with social distance. When the Mehinaku require the services of a shaman, they normally avoid selecting a close relative. A *yetamá* shaman is never asked to be the lead singer (*pukaiyekehe*) at a kinsman's curing ceremony, although he may volunteer a diagnosis or remove a *kauki* or two. While professing trust, the Mehinaku say that between close kin payments for medical services are improper and, besides, the cure "will not work." I suspect that there may also be a lack of confidence in the shaman who is a close relative. Like patients in all cultures, they seek charisma in their curers and charisma seems to thrive best outside the circle of close kin.

If it is true that secular relationships tend to undermine confidence in shamanistic power, it follows that where there is no secular contact at all between shaman and patient trust will be greatest. This is precisely the pattern among the Mehinaku. They are convinced that although their shamans may be good, outsiders are better. Whenever a villager becomes extremely ill, therefore, he disregards the roster of curers at home and summons a shaman from another tribe. It is interesting to note that some Americans exhibit a roughly similar tendency, for when an ailment is especially grave or intractable they are likely to visit a medical practitioner who is of a different race or ethnic group than themselves (Hughes 1945: 354).

Shamanism and Social Drama

The dramaturgical approach to social relationships holds that identity rests on appearance as well as on substance. To let others know who we are in a given situation, we must overcommunicate certain information about ourselves. Many studies in the social psychology of American society tell us, for example, that to be taken as a good doctor or professor a person must act the part. Those who do not skillfully manage their demeanor, costume, and setting are downgraded, whatever their "real" qualities may be. When I came to study the Mehinaku, I assumed that members of a small-scale society would be freer of the need to overcommunicate social relationships than are North Americans who live so much of their lives among strangers. After all, every Mehinaku knows who his neighbors are almost from the day of his birth. What need is there to over-communicate when everyone already knows who one is and the role one acts? The answer, of course, is that this knowledge is in itself part of the need for overcommunication. Any villager who wishes to lay claim to a social position that is new, out of the ordinary, or unexpected must find a dramatic way of telling everyone else who he is not, namely the everyday character they know as a kinsman, comrade, or housemate.

The position of shaman makes a nice illustration of the problems faced by such a villager. To be successful, he must become a skilled and creative actor. He must learn not only to manage a treacherous performance before an audience ready to pounce on his first mistake but also to write his own lines and invent ever more clever and spectacular stage tricks. And once the performance is over, his day's work has not ended. While not engaged in his practice he must, like Takama, go right on engendering fear and respect. His dress and demeanor must continue to separate him from other men: he is quiet, moody, and has a hard look in his eyes. A physician in our society can close the office, go to the ball game, and stop being a doctor for a while, but a successful shaman is truly the full-time specialist. For him the job of careful impression management may have no end.

Shortly after completing much of the manu-
script for this book, I returned to the Mehinaku to make a film concerning the roles
of the sexes. Although the villagers had always cooperated with my amateurish photo-
graphic efforts in the past, I was concerned
that our three-man film crew and the bulky
sixteen-millimeter equipment would make
them camera shy. I need not have worried.

As soon as we arrived and I had explained
the purpose of the film, the Mehinaku enthusiastically began to participate as actors,
directors, authors, and stagehands. Maiu-
sheka rigged a platform in his half-com-
pleted house so we could get a better camera
angle for filming everyday life. Shumõɪ, on
his own initiative, organized the children in
a series of "spontaneous" games of role playing that he thought would be interesting to
the *kajaiba*. During the filming of a series
of rituals that formed the dramatic highlight
of the film, the chief insisted upon becoming
our director. He made sure everybody wore
the right paints and ornaments and exhorted
the villagers to give a spirited performance.
Whenever he was dissatisfied with the singing or felt that too much of a ceremony was
occurring off-camera, he halted the action
and demanded that everyone do the scene all
over.

Again and again the Mehinaku turned relatively simple scenes into major productions. I instructed Kuyaparei to walk into the village carrying some fish and hand them to his wife as she stood in the doorway of their house. I told him that the intent of the shot was to show the relationship of husband and wife within the Mehinaku society and the division of labor that united them. I then sent him a few hundred yards outside the village with his fish and, as soon as the cameras began to roll, he started to walk towards us. Instead of doing the scene straight, however, he decided that he had better make sure that we really understood what was happening. "My," he said as he walked along closely followed by camera and microphone, "I hope my wife has a fire lit to cook these fish and make manioc bread—they are delicious together."

Meanwhile, the villagers watching the filming from the plaza and the men's house began to participate: "Look at all those fish Kuyaparei is bringing home. Kaialuku can make lots of good stew with those fish. I wish I had those fish to bring home to my wife."

And, of course, Kuyaparei's wife couldn't resist getting into the act as well: "The fire is ready, my husband. You've caught the fish and I'll make manioc and distribute them."

After I had translated the byplay for our film director, he shook his head and said, "My god; they are a bunch of natural hams."

In one sense his judgment was quite perceptive. The Mehinaku were deliberately overacting in order to communicate the plot of a drama that was nothing more than an episode arising out of their everyday social relationships. In effect, they were looking at themselves from the same dramaturgical perspective that I have promoted throughout this book: ordinary activities were transformed into staged scenes. Costumes and props were supplied to bolster the authenticity of the performance. Scenes were intentionally overcommunicated so that the audience could make no mistake about the thrust of the drama and the position of the actors participating in it.

Filmmaking is admittedly a highly artificial activity and it is doubtful that the villagers display the level of self-awareness in day-to-day social life that they do when they perform before the cameras of the *kajaiba*. Nevertheless, the ease with which they began to view their own life as theater and the evidence provided by their culture and conduct strongly suggest that the dramaturgical attitude is not unfamiliar to the Mehinaku. In judging this point, recall that the villagers design their community around a central area used as a forum for public performances, reserving the trash yards and the men's house as a back region and green room. Remember that the stage for social relationships is not wholly fixed by custom but reshaped with an eye to the visibility of the action each time the villagers move their community or cut a new trail through the forest.

Consider too that like all good stage designers the Mehinaku exhibit in their attention to space and form a preoccupation with aesthetics and a pride in appearance. Whether decorating a bowl, a bench, or a body, their first concern is visual impact. Related to this interest in appearance is a demonstrated sense of the dramatic. The villagers' concern for effective public speaking, their admiration of a master story teller, and their nearly manneristic attention to dress—all bespeak a feeling for theatrical composition, an awareness of audience reaction, and an attitude of being on stage.

In evaluating the appropriateness of the dramaturgical metaphor, give full weight to the villagers' attitudes towards relationships. Recall especially the "portraits of self," those character masks the Mehinaku assume in order to project a positive image for their fellows. Consider also how a villager, like the director of a play, can take distance from the scripted roles, add up their utility, recast the actors, and alter the course of the drama. Give particular attention to Mehinaku religious life, for myths tell us that basic institutions such as sex roles are deliberately selected human creations. Rituals equally reflect the presence of the villager-dramatist as he devises, produces, directs, and choreographs new ceremonies. And the shaman, the most prominent performer in village religious life, is so skilled a master of stagecraft that he can convincingly present his magical art to the most critical audience of skeptical colleagues. Finally, recall that theater invades the world of the spirits, for the moment the demons' frightful costumes and make-up are stripped away, they are seen to be men and women: like the villagers who perform in masked ritual dramas, the spirits participate in their own theater of everyday life.

What these data suggest is that the dramaturgical perspective may be consistent with the villagers' own world view. It is not that they are full-time actors, for normally habit and custom inhibit the awareness of the stagecraft that goes into social action. Rather it is that everyday relationships demand of each individual participation in the production *as if* he were an author, an actor, a makeup man, or a stagehand. And unless, like the trash yard man, he chooses to mope backstage, he has little choice in the matter, since the script for social life is often ambiguous and demands innovation in performance and staging.

The Script

Consider the system of relationships that may leave the villagers uncertain about how they stand in relationship to one another. Kinsmen are at times not quite sure who will be their in-laws, their potential marriage partners, or their joking companions. Tribal identity is imprecise, since it is sometimes hard to establish who is a Mehinaku and who is not. Shamans are often hard pressed to confirm their statuses in the face of suspicion that they are pretenders and quacks. These facts are reflected in the way the villagers talk about the roles they perform. Relationships are a matter of degree and are regarded as "big, small, close, distant, true, or false." The distance between the man and the social slot is measurable and may be specified with a system of affixes tacked onto the names of the social positions. The choice of the affix depends not only on the objective qualifications of the actor for the role but also on the mood and opinion of the larger community. The imprecision in the definition and allocation of roles leaves the Mehinaku in the position of being authors and directors of everyday relationships. Somehow they must get along with their fellows, despite the ambiguity in the instructions provided by their society.

The villagers' response is to write their own script, playing upon the uncertainties of the system to maximize their position within it. Distant kinsmen, thanks to their susceptibility to "genealogical amnesia," can selectively extend paternity to their mother's paramours and thereby choose parallel-cousins and brothers-in-law. Kinship manipulation may terminate a confused or conflicting relationship and replace it with a clearly defined role more to the benefit of the actors. Members of different tribes may also make role bargains that submerge their differences and establish enduring relationships in their mutual interest. Shamans, by means of legerdemain and bizarre conduct during curing ceremonies, can establish a special position for themselves within their community.

In a perceptive article, "Les Rites de Passage," Max Gluckman argues that ambiguous relationships, like those characteristic of the Mehinaku, are part and parcel of the organization of every small society (1962). Roles in such societies are necessarily diffusely defined because the same small group of actors are called upon to perform many parts. Two Mehinaku, for example, may be blood relatives, kinsmen by marriage, work partners, members of the same ceremonial team, commoner, and chief. Roles are not neatly segregated among different sets of persons as they are in a large, complex community where kin are separate from colleagues and homes are distant from offices. Instead, the Mehinaku must somehow preserve distinctions in a setting that tends to obliterate them.

According to Gluckman, small societies make use of ceremonies, elaborate patterns of etiquette, and rites of passage to mark off and dramatize distinct social statuses. It is not enough to occupy a social status; it must be occupied conspicuously. Many Mehinaku institutions reflect this pattern. The long cycle of seclusion, for example, can be interpreted as a device for dramatizing new statuses in the community. Adolescents and novice healers slip behind the partition and reappear months and years later as adults and full-fledged shamans. The rituals surrounding the role of the chief and the ceremonies of the men's house seem to perform the same function, that of marking off important relationships within the community.

The reader will also recall the villagers' fondness for embellishing ordinary social intercourse with an elaborate system of salutations and adornment, accompanied by names that spell out the social positions of the actors. The puzzle is that this information is already known to everyone in the community;

why burden the business of everyday life with the freight of a system of redundant communication? Given the diffuseness of social relationships, however, we can understand the redundancy. The villagers must not only be kinsmen, comrades, shamans, and chiefs; they must communicate these facts to each other on several levels of discourse. Conduct, speech, and visual cues constantly remind the Mehinaku of who they are with respect to their fellows.

In our own mass society, we also overcommunicate social identity. The need for redundancy arises from our knowing so little about others; we must rely on appearances rather than unverifiable realities. Our doctor must manipulate his demeanor, his dress, and his props if we are to perceive him as a doctor. In effect, he overcommunicates to tell us who he is. In a small society such as the Mehinaku, however, the villagers face very different dramaturgical dilemmas. They already know a great deal about each other. Their problem is to distinguish statuses within a play which must be performed by a tiny cast. The players overact not only to tell the other performers who they are but also to remind them of who they are not.

The Stage

The Mehinaku villager must not only be an occasional author of the social script; he must also be skilled in performance and stagecraft. The basis of this requirement is that Mehinaku social life is highly observable, the gossip network extremely effective, and privacy very scarce. In such an environment a man's identity as a good citizen may be jeopardized by a reality that is difficult to conceal. His laziness, his unwillingness to share food, his failure as a hunter or fisherman, his activities as a thief or adulterer, his distrust of his fellows, or even his sexual inadequacy—all can quickly become public knowledge. Confronted with such information, his fellow tribesmen may be tempted to sever their relationships with him. The openness of the community to the flow of information may thereby endanger vital social relationships.

To secure privacy, the Mehinaku take advantage of a number of physical and symbolic barriers to communication and interaction, such as areas of low visibility, seclusion partitions, affinal avoidances, and the use of falsehood. Despite these barriers, the efficiency of Mehinaku communication is such that only careful manipulations of the opportunities for concealment can control the availability of socially damaging information. The only sure escape from surveillance and excessive interaction is behind seclusion barriers and outside the tribe. Access to seclusion is limited, however, and trips away from the tribe afford only temporary relief. Informational exposure constitutes a stress on social relationships with which the Mehinaku must come to terms.

Perhaps now we can appreciate why the villagers were such enthusiastic participants in our film. Problems of staging and script have made the life-as-theater analogy come alive for the Mehinaku. If they are to get along with each other, they must be skilled as authors, actors, stagehands, and makeup artists in the social drama of day-to-day life.

The Actor

We have argued that the Mehinaku villager must come to terms with roles that are sometimes ill-defined and miscast. To add to his problem, the performance of these roles is jeopardized by the exposure of information that would give the lie to the image of self that he is trying to convey. Given these difficulties, we would expect to find a threatened and harried performer behind each Mehinaku mask. Ever fearful of exposure, uncertain in dealings with others, painfully self-aware, manipulating and cynical, he would appear to be the Dramaturgical Man come to life.

What emerges from the data and what strikes us about the villagers, however, is their remarkable flare for turning apparent liabilities into decided assets. To be sure, they are embarrassed when caught in an extramarital intrigue or left uncertain about the conduct expected in an ill-defined relationship, but they have developed the dramaturgical skills that enable them to rise to the occasion. Whether striking role-bargains with their comrades, creating new rituals, reshaping local topography with newly cut trails, or dropping temporarily out of the system to go "wandering," the Mehinaku are in control of their lives. Far from being harried and fearful, each villager shapes his own and his society's destiny. It is he who authors the improvisational drama of Mehinaku daily life.

Can our conclusions about the Mehinaku be generalized to other societies? At the outset we must recognize that the pressures on role definition and performance among the Mehinaku are not found in all small technologically simple communities. Not only is the Mehinaku cast unusually small but endogamous marriage, bilateral kinship, and life in a nucleated village augment the dramaturgically significant factors of overlapping relationships and an exposed social setting. Nevertheless, what we have learned offers a useful framework for examining social conduct among other peoples.

In all small societies there will be at least a tendency for relationships to be diffusely defined, leaving open the same opportunities for role-bargaining found among the Mehinaku. Although not widely reported in the past, such flexibility of relationships is now receiving increasing attention. Lloyd Fallers, writing about the manipulation of kinship and genealogies, for example, notes that "phenomena of this kind are extremely common in recent (ethnographic) literature, and they pertain not to exceptional members of a society, but often to the average person" (1965: 77). My colleagues studying South American tribal peoples are also increasingly impressed by the optative, voluntary quality of social relationships. The peoples of the South American lowlands are not simply egalatarian (a point recognized for many years); their institutions and relationships are malleable and subject to the control of individuals. In a review of the ethnography of lowland South America, for example, Jean Jackson (1975: 317–318) takes note of the variability in patterns of marriage and residence, implying that the standard models of kinship behavior do not always fit the highly flexible systems actually found among the people we study. I would suggest that the dramaturgical perspective, focusing as it does on performance rather than structure, offers a particularly apt approach for the understanding of the fluid nature of native life.

The public character of Mehinaku society as well as the flexibility of the role system also appears to be generalizable to other peoples. In all small-scale societies, the diffuseness of relationships insures that actors are curious about one another as total social persons. A cross-cultural study of privacy patterns (partially reported in Roberts and Gregor 1971) shows that this curiosity is likely to be satisfied. Focusing on the domestic unit, a sample of forty-two societies drawn from the Human Relations Area Files "blue ribbon" sample were scaled into five privacy categories on the basis of the permeability of dwellings to sight and sound, the presence of internal partitions and closable windows and doors, the number of persons who lived together, and the openness of the settlement pattern. The majority of these societies were classified as providing "low," or "very low" overall privacy for their members. Of the peoples in the sample, 75 percent lived in nucleated settlements where social conduct was judged to be highly visible. More than 60 percent of the sample built their houses from materials permeable to sight and sound, such as grass, leaves, bark, thatch, or hides. In 90 percent of the societies, more than one family lived under the same roof and only in a third of the dwellings did permanent partitions provide a measure of privacy for the residents. These findings suggest that many small-scale communities, perhaps a majority of them, render the individual highly observable, making his whereabouts and activities a matter of common knowledge.

All this leads me to suggest that our approach to the Mehinaku is applicable to other small-scale societies. Diffuse relationships and visible settings are widespread: the Mehinaku are not likely to be alone in defining and performing their relationships against a *mise en scène* of abundant information. A complete ethnography of a small society therefore requires more than the standard description of the culture's role system. It should also account for the observability of the setting of social life, the limitations on the flow of information, the conventions that communicate identity, and the methods actors customarily employ to evade, manipulate, or rewrite their roles. This material may provide us with what was previously missing: the setting, staging, and script for the drama of ordinary community life.

Bibliography

Agostinho da Silva, Pedro
1972. Information Concerning the Territorial and Demographic Situation in the Alto Xingu. *In* The Situation of the Indian in South America. Pp. 252–83. Geneva: World Council of Churches.

Allport, Gordon W. and L. Postman
1947. The Psychology of Rumor. New York: Holt.

Arvelo-Jimenez, Nelly
1971. Political Relations in a Tribal Society: A Study of the Ye'cuana Indians of Venezuela. Ithaca, New York: Latin American Program Dissertation Series, Cornell University.

Banton, Michael
1965. Roles: An Introduction to the Study of Social Relations. New York: Basic Books, Tavistock Publications.

Barnett, Homer
1953. Innovation: The Basis of Culture Change. New York: McGraw-Hill.

Basso, Ellen B.
1973. The Kalapalo Indians of Central Brazil. New York: Holt, Rinehart and Winston.

Benedict, Ruth
1934. Patterns of Culture. New York: Houghton Mifflin.

363

Berger, Peter L.
1963. Invitation to Sociology: A Humanistic Perspective. Garden City: Anchor Books.

Blumer, Herbert
1967. Society as Symbolic Interaction. *In* Symbolic Interaction. J. G. Manis and B. N. Meltzer, eds. Pp. 139–48. Boston: Allyn.

Burke, Kenneth
1945. A Grammar of Motives. Englewood Cliffs, N.J.: Prentice Hall.

Burns, Elizabeth
1972. Theatricality: A Study of Convention in the Theater and in Social Life. New York: Harper and Row.

Carniero, Robert L.
1956. Slash and Burn Agriculture: A Closer Look at Its Implications for Settlement Patterns. *In* Men and Cultures. Anthony F. C. Wallace, ed. Pp. 228–34. Philadelphia: University of Pennsylvania Press.

1957. Subsistence and Social Structure: An Ecological Study of the Kuikuru Indians. Ph.D. dissertation. Ann Arbor, Michigan: University Microfilms Co.

1958. Extra-marital Sex Freedom among the Kuikuru Indians of Mato Grosso. Revista do Museu Paulista 10:135–42. São Paulo, Brasil.

1961. Slash and Burn Cultivation Among the Kuikuru and Its Implications for the Cultural Development in the Amazon Basin. *In* The Evolution of Horticultural Systems in Native South America. Pp. 47–67. Johannes Wilbert, ed. Caracas, Venezuela: Antropologica.

Dahrendorf, Ralf
1968. Homo Sociologicus. *In* Essays in the Theory of Society. Ralf Dahrendorf, ed. Pp. 19–87. Stanford, California: Stanford University Press.

Dole, Gertrude E.
1958. Ownership and Exchange among the Kuikuru Indians of Mato Grosso. Revista do Museu Paulista 10:125–33. São Paulo, Brazil.

1962. A Preliminary Consideration of the Prehistory of the Upper Xingu Basin. Revista do Museu Paulista 13:399–423. São Paulo, Brazil.

1964. Shamanism and Political Control among the Kuikuru. Beitrage zur Volkenkunde Sudamerikas, Hanover, Germany.
1966. Anarchy Without Chaos: Alternatives to Political Authority Among the Kuikuru. *In* Political Anthropology. Marc J. Swartz, Victor W. Turner, Arthur Tuden, eds. Pp. 73–88. Chicago: Aldine.

Dumont, L.
1953. The Dravidian Kinship Terminology as an Expression of Marriage. Man 53:34–39.

Fallers, Lloyd A.
1965. The Range of Variation in Actual Family Size: A Critique of Marion J. Levy Jr's Argument. *In* Aspects of the Analysis of Family Structure. Marion J. Levy Jr., Lloyd A. Fallers, Ansley J. Coale, Silvan S. Tompkins, authors. Pp. 70–82. Princeton, N.J.: Princeton University Press.

Fejos, Paul
1943. Ethnography of the Yagua. Viking Fund Publications in Anthropology. Vol. 3.

Feldman, Saul D.
1975. The Presentation of Shortness in Everyday Life—Height and Heightism in American Sociology: Toward A Sociology of Stature. *In* Life Styles: Diversity in American Society, second edition. Saul D. Feldman and Gerald W. Thielbar, eds. Boston: Little, Brown.

Fenelon, Costa M. H. and M. H. Dias Monteiro
1968. Dois Estilos Plumarios: "Barroco" e "Classico" no Xingu. Revista do Museu Paulista 18:127–43.

Galvão, Eduardo
1953. Cultura e Sistema de Parentesco das Tribos do Alto Rio Xingu. Boletim do Museu Nacional 10:1–56.

Galvão, Eduardo and Mario F. Simoes
1966. Mudança e Sobrevivência no Alto Xingu. Revista de Antropología, Univérsidade de São Paulo 14:37–52.

Garfinkel, Harold
1967. Studies in Ethnomethodology. Englewood Cliffs, N.J.: Prentice Hall.

Gearing, Fredrick
1970. The Face of the Fox. Chicago: Aldine.

Geertz, Clifford and Hildred Geertz
1964. Teknonymy in Bali: Parenthood, Age Grading and Genealogical Amnesia. Journal of the Royal Anthropological Institute 94:94–108.

Gluckman, Max
1962. Les Rites de Pasaage. *In* Essays on the Ritual of Social Relations. Max Gluckman, ed. Pp. 1–52. Manchester: Manchester University Press.
1963. Gossip and Scandal. Current Anthropology 4:307–16.

Goffman, Erving
1956. The Nature of Deference and Demeanor. American Anthropologist 58:473–502.
1959. The Presentation of Self in Everyday Life. Garden City: Anchor Books.
1974. Frame Analysis: An Essay on the Organization of Experience. New York: Harper and Row.

Gregor, Thomas A.
1970. Exposure and Seclusion. Ethnology 9:234–50.
1973. Privacy and Extramarital Affairs in a Tropical Forest Community. *In* Peoples and Cultures of Native South America. Daniel Gross, ed. Pp. 242–60. Garden City: Natural History Press.
1974. Publicity, Privacy and Mehinacu Marriage. Ethnology 13:333–49.

Hall, Edward T.
1968. The Hidden Dimension. Garden City: Anchor Books.

Hoebel, E. Adamson
1970. The Law of Primitive Man. New York: Atheneum.

Hughes, Everett Cherrington
1945. Dilemmas and Contradictions of Status. American Journal of Sociology 50:353–59.

Hunt, Eva
1969. The Meaning of Kinship in San Juan: Genealogical and Social Models. Ethnology 7:37–53.

Jackson, Evelyn M.
1971. Morphophonemics of Verb Suffixes in Waura. Ms. Brasília: Summer Institute of Linguistics.

Jackson, Jean E.
1975. Recent Ethnography of Indigenous Northern Lowland

South America. *In* Annual Review of Anthropology, Vol. 4. Bernard J. Siegal, ed. Pp. 307–340. Palo Alto: Annual Reviews, Inc.

Junqueira, Carmen
1973. The Brazilian Indigenous Problem and Policy: The Example of the Xingu National Park. International Work Group for Indigenous Affairs Document No. 13. Copenhagen: IWGIA.

Levi-Strauss, Claude
1948. Tribes of the Upper Xingu River. *In* Handbook of South American Indians, Vol. 3. Julian H. Steward, ed. Pp. 321–48. Washington: U. S. Government Printing Office.
1963. Do Dual Organizations Exist? *In* Structural Anthropology. Pp. 132–63. New York: Basic Books.
1972. Tristes Tropiques. New York: Atheneum.

Lienhardt, Godfrey
1961. Divinity and Experience. London: Oxford University Press.

Lima, Pedro E. de
1955. Distribuição dos Grupos Indigenas do Alto Xingu. Proceedings of the International Congress of Americanists 31, i: 159–170.

Linton, Ralph
1936. Status and Role. *In* The Study of Man. Pp. 113–119. New York: Appleton-Century-Crofts.

Maybury-Lewis, David
1960. The Analysis of Dual Organizations: A Methodological Critique. Bijdragen tot de Taal-, Land-, en Volkenkunde 116: 2–44.

Mead, George Herbert
1934. Mind, Self, and Society. Charles W. Morris, ed. Chicago: University of Chicago Press.

Messinger, Sheldon L., Harold Sampson, and Robert D. Towne
1962. Life as Theater: Some Notes on the Dramaturgic Approach to Social Reality. Sociometry 25:98–110.

Meyer, Hermann
1897. Uber Seine Expedition nach Central-Brasilien. Verhandl d. Gesell f. Erkunde zu Berlin.

Mors, Walter B. and Carlos T. Rizzini
1966. Useful Plants of Brazil. San Francisco: Holden-Day.

Murdock, George Peter
1945. The Common Denominator of Culture. *In* The Science of Man in World Crisis. Ralph Linton, ed. Pp. 123–42. New York: Columbia University Press.

Murphy, Robert F.
1960. Headhunter's Heritage: Social and Economic Change Among the Mundurucu Indians. Berkeley: University of California Press.
1967. Tuareg Kinship. American Anthropologist 69:163–70.
1971. The Dialectics of Social Life. New York: Basic Books.

Murphy, Robert F. and Buell Quain
1955. The Trumaí Indians of Central Brazil. Monographs of the American Ethnological Society, 24. Seattle: University of Washington Press.

Nadel, Sigfried F.
1957. The Theory of Social Structure. New York: Free Press.

Oberg, Kalervo
1953. Indian Tribes of the Northern Mato Grosso, Brazil. Smithsonian Institution. Institute of Social Anthropology. Publication No. 15. Washington: U. S. Government Printing Office.

Peterson, Richard A.
1975. The Production of Culture Perspective: Prolegomenon. Ms. Dept. Sociology, Vanderbilt University.

Petrullo, Vincent M.
1932. Primitive Peoples of Mato Grosso. Museum Journal 23: 84–173.

Rapaport, Amos
1969. House Form and Culture. Englewood Cliffs, N.J.: Prentice-Hall.

Reichel-Dolmatoff, Gerrardo
1970. Amazonian Cosmos. Chicago: University of Chicago Press.

Richards, Joan
1973. Dificuldades na Analise da Possessão Nominal na Lingua Waura. Serie Linguistica 1:11–29. Brasília: Summer Institute of Linguistics.

Roberts, John M., M. J. Arth, and R. R. Rush
1959. Games in Culture. American Anthropologist 61:597–605.

Roberts, John M. and Thomas A. Gregor
1971. Privacy: A Cultural View. *In* Privacy. J. Roland Pennock and John W. Chapman, eds. Pp. 199–225. New York: Atherton Press.

Rose, Frederick G.
1960. Classification of Kin, Age Structure and Marriage Amongst the Groote Eylandt Aborigines. A Study in Method and Theory of Australian Kinship. Berlin: Akademic Verlag.

Schmidt, Max
1942. Estudos de Etnologia Brasileira. Brasiliana, 2. São Paulo, Brasil.

Schultz, Harald
1965. Lendas Waurá. Revista do Museu Paulista 16:21–149.

Schwartz, Barry
1968. The Social Psychology of Privacy. American Journal of Sociology 73:741–52.

Silverman, Julian
1967. Shamans and Acute Schizophrenia. American Anthropologist 66:21–31.

Simmel, Georg
1950. The Stranger. *In* The Sociology of Georg Simmel. Kurt H. Wolf, ed. Pp. 402–8. New York: Free Press.

Sommer, Robert
1969. Personal Space. Englewood Cliffs, N.J.: Prentice-Hall.

Steinen, Karl Von den
1885. Exploracão do Rio Xingu. Boletim da Sociadade de Geografia do Rio de Janiero, vol. 1, no. 3.
1940. Entre of Aborigenes do Brasil Central. Separata da Revista do Arquivo, nos. 34–58. Departamento de Cultura. São Paulo, Brasil.
1942. O Brasil Central. Brasiliana, 3. São Paulo, Brasil.

Turner, Terrence
1969. Tchikrin: A Central Brazilian Tribe and Its Symbolic Language of Bodily Adornment. Natural History 78:50–59.

Villas Boas, Orlando and Claudio Villas Boas
1970. Xingu: os Indios, seus Mitos. Rio de Janeiro: Zahar Editores.

1973. Xingu: The Indians, Their Myths. Kenneth S. Brecher, ed. New York: Farrar, Straus and Giroux.

Zarur, George
1975. Parentesco, Ritual e Economia no Alto Xingu. Brasília: Fundação Nacional do Índio.

Index